Mark
mfryb♡g2@~~com eastroot~~
icloud.com

P9-DGL-799

PUNCHING OUT

PUNCHING OUT

STORIES OF
HIGH-SPEED EJECTIONS

EDITED BY
JAMES CROSS

ST. MARTIN'S GRIFFIN ✹ NEW YORK

PUNCHING OUT. Copyright © 2011 by James Cross. Foreword copyright © 2011 by Dick
Rutan. All rights reserved. Printed in the United States of America. For information,
address St. Martin's Press, 175 Fifth Avenue, New York, N.Y. 10010.

www.stmartins.com

Book design by Kelly S. Too

Library of Congress Cataloging-in-Publication Data

Cross, James, 1951–
    Punching out : stories of high-speed ejections / James Cross.—1st ed.
        p. cm.
    ISBN 978-0-312-38315-2
  1. Survival after airplane accidents, shipwrecks, etc.   2. Pilot ejection seats.
3. Air pilots—United States—Anecdotes.   I. Title.
    TL553.9.C76 2011
    358.40092'273—dc22   2010044075

First Edition: April 2011

10 9 8 7 6 5 4 3 2 1

For my dad,
an officer and a gentleman

CONTENTS

ACKNOWLEDGMENTS

Many thanks are due to the writers and researchers whose detailed accounts and chronologies included here have allowed this book to take an overview approach. Just as the aviators of today, according to author Phil Scott, stand "on the shoulders of giants," the author gratefully acknowledges the many contributions made by the writers, scholars, pilots, and engineers whose firsthand accounts are the foundation of this endeavor, including literary agent William E. Brown, who guided and propelled it forward; editors Taylor Jesson and Maryann Newfield; Dick Rutan for his kind foreword; and Tom Smith and Paula Smith for offering up the world of flight testing. A very special thanks is due the eminent Lockheed test pilot Bill Weaver, whose own story of emergency egress from a Mach 3 manned missile called the SR-71 led to the collection of stories the reader is about to encounter.

FOREWORD

Sometimes, gravity doesn't work. The lump in your throat just won't go south.

Trying to shake off the inevitable, you finally give in. You realize what's going to happen to the jet in just a handful of minutes. You know what to do. You've trained for this. You grab your visor and pull it down. You sit up high, back straight, with your head firmly planted against the headrest. You take a deep breath and in one smooth motion, you pull up the handles and firmly squeeze the ejection sequence triggers. In a heartbeat, the rocket fires and you are propelled up the seat rails and into Heaven's abyss. You glance over your shoulder and see a fireball devouring what used to be your jet, spewing ignited pieces that rain down on Earth. Looking upward, you see a beautiful, billowing parachute as you drift safely and slowly back to terra firma. Time stands still. It's a Sierra Hotel moment.

You exhale and you realize you've survived to fly again. And talk about an E-Ticket ride! It's one of the most horrific, wonderful rides you'll ever experience! Every ejection is the same and yet so different. As you immerse yourself in the following recalls of *Punching Out*, you'll ride the rails with the best. Up and away!

One never sets out in a sky ride—airplane, jet, or balloon—with the intention or desire to do an emergency egress, but for those unexplained, unimaginable circumstances, you have to be prepared for that literal last-ditch effort when everything else fails. In fact, the moment you realize what is going to happen to your jet in just a handful of minutes makes you realize instantly that you don't want to be anywhere near the scene of that accident.

And I've prepared myself for the worst-case scenario every time I've settled into the pilot's seat. Even during the *Voyager* flight in 1986, we were "chuting up" and were faced with having to bail out for survival.

When I recollect the balloon bailout, I think of how fortunate we were. After all, we were fully loaded and prepared for a nearly month-long circumnavigation of calmly and casually floating around the globe. When things started going wrong soon after liftoff, however, they went south fast. I took my brand-new, gleaming knife that was inscribed AROUND AND AROUND AND AROUND THE WORLD (this was to be my third trip), and used that souvenir to quickly cut off extra weight from both myself and my copilot before we leapt toward the safety of Earth.

Our emergency parachutes were not designed for a lot of weight or extras. Sadly, we lost a lot on that bail—a multimillion-dollar project, the contents of which included specialized navigation and communication equipment, a state-of-the-art oxygen system, my Rolex watch . . . and most of all, our pride. I certainly didn't plan to emerge with a bloody face full of cactus tines after landing—although looking back, it did make for great television.

This collection of stories will, no doubt, keep you on the edge of your seat and ready to pull the rip cord. Are you ready for some white-knuckle recalls? Holy sugar! Get ready to jump!

—DICK RUTAN
Voyager Commander, Aviation Lecturer

INTRODUCTION

Knowledge is the wing wherewith we fly to heaven.

—William Shakespeare

An Air Force F-16 is raging through the night sky at 500 mph on a low-altitude training mission just one thousand feet off the desert floor when a warning light suddenly declares an engine fire. Airspeed is fading fast, and the ground is rushing up to smash the impaired aircraft into a huge fireball. There is no time to think, no time for decisions.

Time compresses and goes into slow motion. The pilot's hand instinctively grabs and pulls the lever under his seat, causing an explosion that blasts him out of the disabled plane right behind the jettisoned canopy. A half second later a rocket engine fires underneath the planeless pilot and shoots him skyward to await the opening of the parachute that will return him safely to the earth.

Elapsed time: 3 seconds.

This book is a collection of stories of ejection survivors, based on actual experiences by pilots who have survived high-speed ejections and lived. Pushed beyond the edge of endurance to encounters with their own mortality, all of these are firsthand accounts, generally unedited and completely unembellished. Military aviators can suddenly become animated and eloquent once they have been to the edge and back. Others have a matter-of-fact calmness about their daunting high-speed ejections, which belies the extreme danger they faced. Virtually all of these emergency ejections were life-changing events. The decision to eject, the split-second decision to abandon a deadly airship, is often the difference between life and death. Only through constant training can the ability to make this decision become like second nature. Any hesitation is lethal, making all of the life-saving technology useless without the decision to deploy it, a decision which must be made in the worst possible circumstances with no room for error. The title is taken from a classic example of "pilot speak," their comically codified approach to understatement. A near-death experience is an "attention-getter," while a sky full of enemy planes is a "target-rich environment." Earthbound workers punch time clocks or leave their offices at the end of the day, but the pilot's office is a dangerous, high-performance aircraft, so their euphemism for the dreaded ejection from their aircraft is typically droll: they call it "punching out."

These stories are exhilarating for their pure adrenaline and excitement, yet tragic for the loss of life when systems and people fail, or when fate steals another aviator. But the risks and the sacrifices have led to tremendous advances and thousands of lives saved, giving a renewed and resounding sense of purpose to those whose courageous efforts paved the way.

THE STORIES

THE STORIES

1ST LT. **JOHN BAILEY—1957**

In 1957, I was a first lieutenant in the USAF going through Advanced Interceptor Training at Perrin AFB, Sherman, Texas, after earning my wings in September 1956. I had about nine hours in the F-86D at the time, and the curriculum called for one flight dedicated to aerial acrobatics—this flight was it. It was a clear March day, warm and blue.

It was my second flight that day and I was probably a little fatigued. Over the practice area, above Oklahoma, I got off a few rolls and then tried a loop. I dove into the loop at perhaps 400 mph, began pulling up but not aggressively enough. The plane stalled at the top of the loop—upside down! The plane began violently shaking and turning. I had incorrectly been using trim to keep my controls neutral, something my flight instructor in basic training should never have taught me.

The plane was totally out of control, shaking and spinning violently, and I was upside down. I realized that I could never recenter the controls using my trim tabs, and that I was falling faster than I had time to recover. So I decided to eject. I managed to pull myself up into the seat snugly enough that the explosive launch of the ejection seat did not ram into my spine. I left the plane, seat and all. Chute deployment was textbook, meaning I later had black bruises across the inside of my thighs; at the time, though, I didn't feel a thing. I even smoked a cigarette on the way down. Based on time of descent, I think I must have ejected at ten thousand feet. I later learned the plane crashed in a pasture, panicking a horse that had to be destroyed.

My parachute landing was uneventful. The slightly rolling terrain was covered with light scrub and thin saplings. I nervously kept my ankles overlapped to hopefully avoid straddling a limb. As it happened, it was a relatively gentle touchdown with a textbook roll to break the fall. After wading through a deep creek, I got to a road and hailed a passing school bus full of third- to sixth-graders who giggled and stared. The school bus took me to the first farm that had a telephone. The owners raised Pekingese dogs. I had never seen so many Pekingese. Calling from there, a rescue team picked me up and I returned to the base. There was a routine accident inquiry and after analysis of the wreckage, *Flight Safety Magazine* ran an article about the accident, with disguised participants to protect the innocent. The article warned against the habit of routinely using the trim tabs to keep flight control pressures neutral, especially during violent maneuvers.

Except for a bitter complaint from one of the flight instructors who claimed I destroyed his favorite airplane—the one with the best radar set—I had almost no comment about losing a Sabre Jet. I got more grief because of my erratic formation flying.

LT. GARY L. BAIN (1)—1969

There I was, a long time ago, in a land far away, and it *was* a dark and stormy night! The date was January 12, 1969 and I was just off the coast of South Vietnam, over the South China Sea. I was level at four thousand feet and securely strapped in my Marine Corps F-4 Phantom, as was my RIO (Radar Intercept Officer), Lt. William C. Ryan. I had flown well over a hundred combat missions with VMFA-323 (Marine Fighter Attack Squadron 323) and on this particular night we were attempting to get rid of our ten 500-pound bombs that had malfunctioned and wouldn't come off while conducting a Steel Tiger mission in Laos. Those missions were secret at the time and were designed to interdict and destroy men and equipment transporting weapons of war along the Ho Chi Minh Trail.

After diverting to the jettison area out over the water I hit the "pickle" button to drop the bombs, and when I did the instrument panel started lighting up like a Christmas tree. It is theorized that one of the bombs got hung up on the aft lug and drove the fins through the underbelly of the aircraft and into the fuel lines, causing an immediate and catastrophic fire. First the starboard engine overheat light came on, then a fire light. Almost immediately the port overheat light and fire light came on. I stated rather emphatically, "Bill, we're going to have to get out of here!" I then started to make my "Mayday" call, but only got one Mayday uttered when an explosion rocked the ill-fated Phantom. I hardly got the word

"Eject!" out of my mouth before Bill was gone in a flurry of noise and smoke as the canopy was blown off and his ejection-seat rockets fired. I followed shortly thereafter and we both found ourselves floating slowly down into a dark void, punctuated only by the violent impact the pilotless Phantom made as the sea swallowed its flaming mass.

The sudden departure from the sanctity of the cockpit to hanging in a parachute, especially at night, is, to say the least, a humiliating as well as a frightening experience. That feeling was short-lived, though, as I soon splashed down and survival became the motivating factor. I had never been in an ocean at night and as I popped back to the surface, bioluminescence engulfed me and that was something I had never seen or even heard of! In my imagination, the harmless plankton that was causing the phenomenon was some alien creature attempting to devour me. That caused me to try even harder to gain the security of the life raft I had deployed on the way down, yet the harder I tried the more I churned the water and the brighter the plankton glowed. I probably set a record getting into the life raft because as I pulled myself up, the seat pan, which was still attached to me, started hitting me in the leg and all I could think of was, "Sharks!" Gaining the security of the raft, I soon got my composure back. Somehow, Bill and I found each other in that great expanse of water and rejoiced at our reunion and well being. We started laughing, blowing our whistles, and even discussed doing a little night fishing!

A really heads-up air traffic controller out of Da Nang heard my one Mayday and alerted the Jolly Greens stationed there—the 37th ARRS (Aerospace Rescue and Recovery Squadron). The Jolly Greens are an Air Force rescue team whose primary mission is rescuing downed pilots; at the time, the 37th was flying HH-3Es. The rescue is best told by Lieutenant Colonel Gerald W. Moore (a captain at the time). The following is an excerpt from a recent e-mail I received from him:

My playmate that evening (Jolly 28) aborted his first helicopter due to an APU [auxiliary power unit] problem; he changed aircraft and therefore was delayed in arrival in your area. He was supposed to make your pickup (he was "Primary"), but since he was delayed in takeoff, I made your pickup. It was a little sporty that evening in the rescue area, with about a nine-thousand-foot overcast, four-thousand-foot undercast (we came out to your pickup area between layers at around six thousand feet), and when we got to your location and let down we hit broken clouds between six hundred and nine hundred feet . . . Thank God and Sikorski Helicopters for the radar altimeter on the H-3s. Basketball was lighting up the area pretty good with flares, but until we got below the six-hundred-foot mark, the flares did not help much. Basketball said he would give more flares when I called for them and as soon as I saw your strobe, I asked for more flares and the sky really lit up. My concern then was for one of the flares (they were all over the sky) coming down through the rotor blade system and causing problems, but that did not happen. We made your pickup with a water landing (the H-3 is also a boat, as you know) and I steered the refueling probe right into your raft. Maybe you remember me telling you on your survival radio to "Stay in Your Raft"—which is not what they taught you at the Clark survival school. On water pickups with the helicopter in a hover, you should get out of your raft, as taught at Clark, but at Da Nang we considered it safer on water-landing pickups for the survivor to remain in the raft, which you and your GIB (Guy In Backseat) did. I put the air refueling probe right into your raft, as I recall, and you hand-walked down the refueling probe to the door of the helo, then the PJ [pararescue jumper] and FE [flight engineer] pulled both of you into the cabin. We had less than a minute on the water. At least that is the way I remember it.

On our trip back to Chu Lai after the pickup we had electrical fumes in the cabin. The smoke/fumes were reported to me by the flight engineer and so we shut off both generators and the battery to stop the electrical smoke problem. After popping some select circuit breakers, I turned on the battery and told my playmate—who by this time had joined up somewhere on my right side—that we had an electrical problem and that I would

join on him; that he was to make all radio calls to Chu Lai and
I would follow him in for landing with all my electrical systems
off, which we did. He mentioned later that as he was flying
formation with me on my right on the return to Chu Lai, all of
a sudden I was no longer there—all exterior lights went out when
I turned the generators and the battery off to stop the electrical
smoke problem. It was very dark with the overcast, and he did a
wild peel off to the right to get away from me since he lost visual
contact and did not know where I was. After I came back on the
radio with battery power only, and told him what had happened
with the fumes, I joined on him and we continued on to Chu Lai
with no more problems.

After landing, and dropping you and your GIB off, I pulled
more select circuit breakers and turned the generators and
battery back on and had no more fumes, so we returned to
Da Nang with me tied on to Jolly 28. Maintenance told me the
next day that the electrical smoke problem was the result of a
blower motor shorting out due to salt water getting into the
motor—salt water from *your flight suit,* I might add (just kidding).
The blower motor is directly below the cabin floor where you
and your GIB were sitting after the pickup. That blower motor
shorting was a new problem, but to my knowledge, it never
happened again on water pickups. Maybe maintenance sealed
the floorboards a little better.

3

LT. GARY L. BAIN (2)—1969

Bill and I were back in the air again in a couple of days and we continued flying as a team until I went on R&R (rest and relaxation) a few months later in May of 1969. My R&R destination was Hong Kong and I took a shuttle flight from Chu Lai to Da Nang to await further routing. I had to spend two days in Da Nang waiting for my flight so I decided to look up my Jolly Green rescuers, as they were stationed there. It just so happened they were in a festive mood, so for two days we consumed massive amounts of booze, told war stories, and I reveled in the camaraderie of my heroes. I made the acquaintance of Pete, one of the pilots. Little did I know the importance of our meeting, for we were to meet again in a few short days, but in much different circumstances.

Arriving back in Chu Lai a week later I once again set about winning the war. By this time I had well over two hundred missions under my belt and Bill and I had flown almost a hundred of those together as a team. Our personal call sign was "Boomslang," and when we checked in with the FAC (forward air controller) he knew the job was going to get done! We had both been recently transferred to VMFA-115, but were still flying out of Chu Lai. Bill was scheduled to go on R&R to meet his wife in Hawaii in a couple of days, so when I found out he was scheduled to fly with me twice the next day I insisted he cancel the flights.

He wouldn't hear of it, but after a lot of discussion, we compromised. He would fly the first mission in the morning and cancel the evening mission. This was, most unfortunately, a truly bad decision on both our parts. Bill, or "Rhino," as we fondly called him, would not return from the mission.

We launched early in the morning on May 11 as a flight of two, call sign Manual 42, our destination Laos, another Steel Tiger mission. This was my 213th combat mission. The target was in the area of Tchepone, a heavily defended part of the Ho Chi Minh Trail. I was carrying a load of Zunis—five-inch rockets used for antiaircraft fire suppression. As we reached the target area the FAC, call sign Nail 16—Major John Johnston, USAF—designated the enemy position and I rolled in "hot" (ordnance armed and ready to fire).

The delivery method I was using was a 500-knot, 60-degree dive angle run. Bill was calling me fast all the way down, as he read off the altitude, airspeed, and dive angle. Just as the piper in the gunsight arrived at the target I let loose the full complement of rockets. Following what I had been trained to do and had done hundreds of times before, I repeated the mantra: pickle, pause, pull. Just as I was getting a heavy load of G's on the airplane in the pull-up phase and starting the jinking turn (a high-speed turn to avoid antiaircraft fire) a tremendous explosion rocked the big Phantom. The aircraft rolled over to the inverted position and was heading for the ground, all controls lost. At 500-plus knots, impact was imminent and I told Bill three times to eject. Hearing no response I braced myself and reached for the alternate ejection handle nestled between my legs. With a sharp tug the ejection sequence started and the next few seconds of my life became a blur as my stationary body met with the ferocity of a wind twice that of a force-5 tornado.

This was about as traumatic as anything you could imagine. I'll try to slow it down for you. The canopy came off first, then the rockets fired that propelled me and the seat out of the aircraft at an instantaneous 18 G's (one G being the force of gravity). As I left the cockpit the horrendous wind blast ripped off my helmet and oxygen mask and inflated my MK-3C life vest. My left arm got thrown behind my back and snapped in half between the shoulder and elbow, the pistol that I wore on my right hip was ripped off, and the pockets on my G-suit were torn off. Then from bad to worse—the seat, which is supposed to separate from the pilot as the parachute deploys, malfunctioned. The restraint lanyards tangled on my left leg, breaking it, and the seat stayed with me all the way down. The parachute deployed and as I hung there—and I remember this just as vividly as if it were yesterday—I heard a loud whooshing noise. I said to myself, "They are shooting at me already."

Then a string of bombs went off underneath me. My wingman had seen the fire from my aircraft impacting the ground, thought it was the target, and dropped his bombs. I descended through all the debris and after just a few seconds in the parachute hit the ground like a ton of bricks. The most amazing part of this is that I never felt any pain. I didn't even know my arm was broken until I tried using it and just the stump would move, not the rest of my arm. I remember every detail of the ejection and events leading up to my rescue. To this day, I don't know how my thinking process remained intact, but it did, and my ability to communicate with the rescuers is what saved me. As OIC (officer in charge) of the Safety and Survival shop in my squadron I always made it a point to carry two survival radios, which if I remember correctly were the newer PRC-90s. It was a good thing I did because the first one I tried wouldn't work! I immediately got in contact with the FAC—call sign Nail 16 (OV-10)—on my emergency radio to let him know I had survived.

No one ever saw a second chute and most opinions concur that I must have taken a 37mm AAA shell in the area of the rear cockpit. I had landed very close to a huge North Vietnamese bunker complex and within fifty meters of some buildings; word was, they didn't take prisoners in that area.

For the next three hours, I would call on everything I had ever learned about survival to make it through the ordeal. In fact, what contributed most to my rescue was Nail 16 insisting that I stay with the parachute, drink water, stay calm, and that I was going to get out of there. The FAC witnessed my low-level ejection and immediately transmitted a Mayday call. The A-1s and Jolly Greens were alerted. They were launched from a base north of Da Nang, Quang Tri.

The Jolly Green choppers are escorted by the famous A-1 Skyraider, a big recip with over fifteen wing stations that carry an assortment of ordnance including cannons, bombs, rockets, gas and other goodies. The Hobo and Sandy A-1s were alerted and the Hobos commenced loading CBU-19s. My wingman, Jim Redmond, was out of ordnance but made dummy passes to keep the bad guys' heads down. Playboy 13—Captain Roy Moore, USMC—flying a TA-4F, responded to the Mayday and arrived on station. Nail 16 had him make some low passes, then over the course of the next forty-five minutes he expended all his rockets and two hundred rounds of 20mm ammunition. In the meantime I had gotten myself oriented, established a clock code for the FAC to reference the drops to, and had made a sling for my arm out of parachute cord. I always carried a snub-nosed .38 inside my flight vest and I took it out and laid it on my chest. I seriously doubt that it would have done much good, but it sure made me feel better. I could hear hollering, whistling, and shooting but never did see any enemy personnel.

Then the A-1s arrived on station. At this point Spad 11—Captain Clayton Hotchkiss, USAF—assumed OSC (on-scene commander) of the rescue and asked me for my son's nickname—a question related to personal authenticator codes. This was a system devised to prevent the bad guys from luring in our aircraft on a phony rescue. All pilots had to fill out cards with answers to questions like, what is your favorite drink, your favorite football team, etc., and then the cards went to a central location for use by the rescuing entities to verify it was actually the pilot talking. When Spad 11 asked my son's nickname, I answered correctly, but am reluctant to say that the nickname was "Pooter"! The Jolly's 03 and 07 out of Quang Tri had to divert because of fuel problems. Jolly Green 15 and 28, from the 37th ARRS out of Da Nang, were then alerted and they promptly headed my way escorted by the Da Nang A-1s, the Spads. While flying cover for the chopper during the extraction Spad 01—Captain Rufus Harris, USAF—took a 37mm hit in the tail. He was so close to the shooter that the ordnance didn't have time to arm, else he would have probably joined me on the ground. As it was, the round took out about a square-foot area of his horizontal stabilator.

What a sight those A-1s were! They would fly so low I could see the pilots smile when they went by. Every time I heard a noise I would call out the clock code and the Skyraider would devastate the area with deadly accuracy. On one run they didn't notify me prior to the drop and it happened to be one of those bombs that opens and drops a bunch of small bomblets, a CBU. I must have jumped ten feet high when those things started going off, thinking, of course, I was taking fire. I thought my number was up for certain. Some of them had to be within twenty to thirty feet of me because debris from the explosions rained down like a hailstorm. I very politely asked them to notify me before they dropped any more unannounced ordnance. I think they must have gotten a chuckle out of that, but I did get a big "Roger that" from them.

At other times the situation would become very quiet and I created things to do to stay busy and alert as I was feeling very faint. I even noticed that my beloved Seiko watch was still intact, although it seemed to have lost about four hours on the ejection! I also started gathering every different kind of leaf that was in reach of me and storing them in my survival vest to keep as mementos of my "vacation" in Laos. Also, I had started pulling the parachute and the ejection seat close in toward me so I could analyze why the seat lanyards had tangled on my leg. I reconsidered, though, and asked the rescue commander if I should pull the chute in or leave it out as a marker for visual contact with me. I was advised to leave it in place for easier eye contact with my position.

Sweat was pouring from every pore in my body and I was thirsty, real thirsty. I pulled the seat pan close to me and removed the contents of the survival pack, looking for water. I found the water in a gray can, but alas, no pull tabs back then. I took out my bright orange survival knife and decided to punch a hole in the top of the can so I could drink. Opening the knife one-handed presented a problem, though, and I tried everything—snagging it on my flight suit, with my teeth—and was about to give up when I realized, hey, this is a switchblade. With a quick flick of the button the knife was open. I then propped the can between my legs and, with a quick stab, smartly planted the blade squarely in my leg instead of the can. I actually laughed at myself—oh no, I wasn't shook up!

In December of 2008, through sheer luck, I acquired a complete audiotape of the rescue, from Mayday to pickup. After listening to it I have a fairly clear picture now of how the A-1s work an area. It is a well-coordinated attack, a daisy chain of death and destruction. There were twelve of the A-1s working the area and escorting the Jolly chopper. I can assure you I am more than glad that Nail 16 and the OSC encouraged me to stay with my chute. It seems that throughout the rescue my chute was what everybody referenced to locate me.

I would hate to be on the receiving end of the ordnance that was laid down because I had a front-row seat of the damage it could inflict. Those A-1s were a thing of beauty! The weather was deteriorating and the Jolly Green 15 chopper was starting to get low on fuel, so the RCC (rescue crew commander) of Jolly Green 15—Captain Joseph Hall, USAF—knew that it was then or never. Capt. Hall also knew he had to depend on the OSC, Spad 11, to make the ultimate decision for him to come on in. Jolly Green 15 had been holding in a designated area waiting for the OSC to give the all clear and that enemy fire had been suppressed. Spad 11 called him in and it was at this time I told the OSC that I was the Marine that spent two days with the Jollies last week. He laughed as he asked the Jollies if they had heard that. The Jolly said no and asked what I said, then he laughingly relayed the information to them. I was glad that in my hysteria I had found something they could laugh about! The Hobo A-1s then gassed the area, I popped a smoke flare, and with machine guns blazing the Jolly Green HH-3E chopper came in and hovered close to my position. What an incredible sight, forever etched in my memory: the chopper swooping in; the PJ coming down the hoist with a gas mask on; the copilot—Captain Martin Richert, USAF—laying down suppressing fire from his window with an automatic rifle while the flight mechanic—A1C (airman first class) James Thibodeau, USAF—hosed the area with machine gun fire. They took small arms' fire throughout the approach and hover. Capt. Richert said that during the final approach he could hear the slap of bullets above the noise of the rotor. Two rounds went through the cockpit and nose area while I was being picked up, which is something I didn't know until much later. As the chopper stabilized near me I attempted to hobble over to the hoist but the PJ—A1C Dennis Palmer, USAF—picked me up and carried me to the hoist and away we went. He told me later that it felt like I weighed a thousand pounds!

As we departed the area the crew pulled me inside and promptly started attending to my needs. They administered morphine, put an air cast on my arm, and checked all my vital signs. From that point on my memory becomes a little fuzzy, probably from the morphine, but it seems one of them traded me a cigarette lighter for my pistol. That was simply a diplomatic way of taking a weapon from someone whose state of mind was in question. I still have that lighter and will always treasure it. Dennis Palmer told me much later that he carried my pistol on every mission following my rescue, but when it was time for him to rotate home it was taken from him.

About halfway back to Da Nang the pilot got up out of his seat and came back to where I was. I looked up and there, standing before me, was "Pete"—which is Captain Joseph Hall's nickname!

4

LT. GARY L. BAIN (3)—1977

In 1971 the Marine Corps selected ten pilots to pioneer the AV-8A Harrier, the VSTOL (vertical short takeoff and landing) aircraft. I was honored to be one of those pilots. We made our first flights in May of 1971 and there were no two-seaters. The group of ten pilots flew the CH-46 for a few hours prior to the first Harrier flights, to learn the visual cues for the hover, accelerating, and decelerating transitions. In the Harrier we made one conventional takeoff and landing and then very apprehensively started flying in the hover. There were certainly some tense moments, but all went well and we all continued with the program. One of the most interesting things I participated in was flying simulated combat missions against the MiG-21. Another captain and myself went to St. Louis and flew 105 sorties in the domed simulator. This was a very realistic scenario and afterward paid great dividends when flying actual air-to-air simulated combat missions.

I flew the Harrier for the next six years and during that time, in 1974, I deployed on the first Harrier six-month Mediterranean cruise aboard the helicopter landing ship, the USS *Guam*. After completing that tour I was assigned to the 2nd Battalion, 4th Marine regiment as ALO (air liaison officer) for six months. My next duty station was MCAS (Marine Corps Air Station) Cherry Point, North Carolina, where I continued to pilot the AV-8A.

On February 11, 1977, I launched from Patrick AFB on the return leg of a solo cross-country flight. It was a perfectly clear day and I asked for and received a VFR (visual flight rules) clearance to Cherry Point. Almost immediately after takeoff I had a full electrical failure, although the Harrier is quite happy without electrics if properly managed. When I departed on the cross-country from Cherry Point I was under pressure to make sure I brought the aircraft back on time, which is what prompted me to continue the flight rather than divert back to Patrick AFB and land. I was cruising at fifteen thousand feet and it could not have been a prettier day. The flight, other than the electrical failure, was going as planned and I was over Wilmington, N.C. and just starting to commence my descent to Cherry Point when the engine flamed out. I immediately made a Mayday call, set up my recommended 250-knot glide speed, and pointed the aircraft out to sea.

The flameout procedures were so well embedded in my mind from our emergency drills in the flight simulator that the airstart routine was executed in a strict sequence of actions. Two minutes later—and having tried and failed three times to get the engine started—I was approaching seven thousand feet and it was time once again to make that fateful decision. (Seven thousand feet is the recommended minimum ejection altitude on a flameout.) I contacted Wilmington Air Traffic Control, told them to send the choppers and that I was ejecting, and I did.

I reached up, grabbed the handle of the face curtain, and pulled it smartly down across my head and chest. Even though I had ejected twice before, nothing can prepare you for the shock and uncertainty of an ejection. The Harrier was, at that time, outfitted with a Stencel ejection system, so that the canopy, rather than being blown off the airframe and into the wind stream, was imploded by plastic explosives. To this day I can still see a few remnants of the explosive material on my neck and shoulders. The seat performed as advertised and I was soon under a full and blossoming parachute. After checking that the chute was okay I looked down just in time to see the aircraft impacting with the ocean. All was eerily quiet as I descended and soon I splashed into the water.

After jumping into the life raft I started attempting to pull the chute in with me, but soon figured out that that wasn't such a good idea and just disconnected it and let the sea devour it. I watched it slowly disappear into the depths. The water was a chilly forty-two degrees and I wasn't wearing a poopy suit, which is a cold-water survival suit—I hadn't planned on flying over the water so I opted out of suiting up in that cumbersome piece of gear. After about forty-five minutes a Marine Corps CH-46 came out and hovered over me for the pickup. The pilots had no experience in plucking someone out of the water. They blew me and the raft all over the ocean trying to get over me, so I decided to get out of the raft. Even then they had problems getting into the right position for me to get in the chopper. The wind blast from the helicopter put a chill factor on my head and neck that was unbearable and I soon became hypothermic. I was lucky they were able to finally get me in the aircraft.

The crew chief showed me a heater and I hovered over it, shaking uncontrollably during the forty-five minute ride to Cherry Point. Even as I was taken to the dispensary and examined I continued to shake. I had never been so cold so long in my life. Then to make matters worse the scoundrels at the hospital, where I had been admitted for observation for twenty-four hours, wouldn't even offer me a drink! No problem, I just had a bottle of wine snuck into my room and got good and drunk anyway.

I'm sure not proud of having to dump three of the corp's finest jets during my career, but on the other hand, when it was me or the aircraft, I selfishly chose me every time!

In all three cases I was the OIC of the Seat and Safety Survival shop of the respective squadrons I was in, and the men who were working directly under me packed my parachute. I'm certainly glad I always took care of my troops because they always took care of me. At the same time the Safety Office was investigating my accident the powers that be at Stencel invited me to Asheville, N.C. to their main office. They wined and dined me for three days because I was the first Marine to use their seat, which totally aggravated the hierarchy at the Marine Wing level as, unknown to me at the time, they were plotting to make an example of me because of the rash of Harrier accidents that had recently occurred.

But that's a story for another time and another day. Suffice to say, I escaped with my wings intact, and flew until I retired on the first day of October 1979.

5

CAPT. **MICHAEL R. BRUNNSCHWEILER– 2001**

The six-week spring WTI (Weapons and Tactics Instructions) course was drawing to an end and, as one of the AV-8B students, I was looking forward to graduating on Monday. Saturday afternoon was devoted for planning; the last event, FINEX II, was scheduled for Sunday.

Since my Maverick shoot had been cancelled early in the syllabus, I was to fly it on Saturday afternoon while everyone else was planning. That suited me just fine. Why would I pass up the opportunity to shoot a Maverick, drop a couple of 1,000-pounders and then fire off 300 rounds of 25mm HEI (high explosive incendiary) ammunition? The flight lead for this sortie was the MAWTS-1 (Marine Aviation Weapons and Tactics Squadron) Ops O, and Dash 2 was another IP. The brief went as smoothly as a well-oiled machine; everyone knew their jobs and capabilities. Lead and Dash 2 were carrying 10 MK82 500-pound HE bombs, and an additional 300 rounds of 25mm HEI. The laser spot was going to be provided courtesy of a section of FA-18s. By all accounts, this was going to be a good deal!

After briefing all emergencies and contingencies, Dash 2 reminded me that, should I have to jettison my bombs, I needed to selectively jettison them to retain the LAU-117 launch rail of the Maverick. Little did I know that I would do this in an hour.

The preflight, takeoff, and transit to the training area were uneventful, and we contacted the FA-18s for a laser spot. I was detached from my flight, proceeded inbound to the target area, and began my profile. The target lock and target verification went as planned, and I rifled just outside of three nm, leveled my wings, and came off toward the south, watching for the impact.

On my way back to altitude to join my flight, I felt a slight thud with no secondaries. I double-checked my stores page to make sure I still had all my ordnance because it felt like an ordnance release. Since I was beginning my rendezvous with my division and had no other indications, I chalked it up to jet wash. Back in formation on the port side, I felt another thud. This time I double-checked all my pages and still saw nothing wrong. A few seconds later I got a caution light with audio tone. Hydraulic 1 failure! Checking the gauges, I saw HYD 1 counting down through 1,500. I notified lead of my problem.

"Knock it off," called Dash 3.

I proceeded to evaluate the situation. Having had a HYD 1 failure before, I started turning toward home, not being too worried. Then more caution lights illuminated that had no association with a HYD 1 failure. Something made the hair stand up on the back of my neck. I turned right again to position for jettisoning the stores. I remembered to selectively jettison my MK-83s in order to bring back my LAU-117, since I didn't want to do any paperwork later on.

Shortly after jettison, my situation got worse. I got an unsafe-gear indication and double-checked to make sure my gear was up. At the same time, I got a fire warning. I kept relaying what I saw to my wingmen. They confirmed that smoke was coming out of the bottom of the fuselage. I initiated emergency procedures for an in-flight fire as my stick started programming back and to the right. To counter it, I pushed the stick forward and to the left. The aircraft initially responded to my input. Seconds later, the aircraft started moving up and right again with my stick fully deflected.

Realizing that things were about to get uglier, I relayed I was ejecting, stepping on a simultaneous call from my wingmen to eject. As I let go of both stick and throttle and reached for the ejection handle, I felt the aircraft squat and pitch up violently. Data showed that in one second, I had gone from 280 knots to 70 knots.

WAKING up in my parachute, years of procedures seemed to come automatically. Step 1: make sure I had a good parachute. Steps 2 and 3 aren't recommended over land. Step 4: options. Visor. What visor? Mask and gloves were off. Now, what just happened and why is everything so blurry? I looked around and saw my wreckage off to the left. As I turned in my parachute, I saw the impact of bombs, dropped by my wingmen, in the vicinity of Blue Mountain.

Why is my vest all red? As I looked down, a steady stream of blood came from around my left eye. I touched the area, realized it was all puffy, but had no feeling. Add to that, my right shoulder was dislocated. Well, this was going to be an interesting landing.

After an eternity in the parachute (I ejected from eleven thousand feet), the ride came to an end in the desert. On touchdown, I released my Koch fittings and turned off my ELT (Emergency Location Transmitter). While waiting for SAR (Search and Rescue) to come pick me up, I had time to reflect on what just happened. I started feeling the pain from my injuries. Thirty minutes later, SAR, out of Yuma, arrived and transported me to Yuma Regional.

I had a dislocated shoulder, orbital skull fracture, and a traumatic injury to the left eye, which was the big problem. It was cut open through the cornea, and I had lost my lens, iris and eye fluid. They extracted several visor pieces. I have undergone four surgeries for the eye, and the end result is still up in the air. But that's where I intend to be again: in the air.

Several good things came out of this mishap. One, we are not flying with the old harnesses anymore, which were prone to riser slap. Second, my belief in Aircrew Coordination Training has been reaffirmed, especially for single-seat aircraft.

I never got a chance to thank the SAR crew that day, but I am eternally grateful for their quick response. I later found out that a KC-130 was diverted to the scene to provide fuel. The FA-18s that had given me a laser spot came back on scene, and my wingmen were able to remain throughout the recovery effort.

6

LT. COL. JOHN W. CAPITO—1985

The parachute canopy looked normal as I glanced at my Vietnam-era Rolex "fighter pilot" watch and noted the time to be one P.M. This was important because about forty-five minutes earlier an eight-year-old kid asked me, "Mister, have you ever jumped out of one of those airplanes?" I replied, "No. That does not happen very often and I have been flying for almost twenty years." Now here I was, hanging in a parachute somewhere south of Boston, Mass. I was in the goo, no helmet, cold and lonely after leaving my jet plane.

This story begins in Scituate, Massachusetts, at the home of my best friend from U.S. Navy flight school. We were Marine Corps second lieutenants then and maintained our friendship through the years. As the executive officer of the Harrier Training Squadron, I was on a cross-country flight with a lieutenant undergoing transition to the Harrier. We left our home base in North Carolina and ninety-degree weather to fly up north for some training in a couple warning areas. I had thrown on my old nylon flight jacket for good measure and forgot about the weather.

The morning of March 29, 1985, found us at South Weymouth Naval Air Station on our way back to North Carolina. We were flying brand-new AV-8B aircraft, a significant improvement over the AV-8A. My friend brought his family and their neighbor's son along to see the planes, help us preflight, and watch us depart. The weather at the field was overcast and the temperature was in the thirties. We were on our way to warm weather and home. Life was good.

Departure was normal and I was flying lead. We were in the weather early on and stayed in clouds from that time onward climbing to an intermediate altitude of FL 240. The AV-8B has a much longer range than the AV-8A and at the time, a significant improvement in cockpit accessories to include an autopilot and an INS. Center changed our route of flight and I began to program the INS with the new waypoints after engaging the autopilot.

I was busy punching the numbers into the system when all of a sudden there was a massive jolt, instant deceleration, loss of all electrical power—and a colorful comment from me to no one in particular. There was no doubt in my mind what happened. The engine had a catastrophic shutdown. I had experienced a couple turbine problems before and the result was a high-speed vibration that you could feel in the throttle. This was more like the feeling of a twenty-five-cent vibrating bed in a cheap hotel room. The entire airplane was shaking. I thought about a relight; looked for the standby gyro; saw my wingman pass me by and then took stock of my situation. I had no idea what was below the overcast, so I headed south hoping to find a break in the overcast, and water underneath the jet. I tried to hold my heading, maintain 200–250 knot airspeed, and set up a moderate rate of descent. I was counting on my wingman and emergency locator beacon to pinpoint my location.

That scenario was working well until smoke started coming into the cockpit and flames were visible in the mirror. After a quick attempt to relight was unsuccessful it was time to eject. An ejection is the ultimate divorce—there is no chance for reconciliation. As I was pulling the handle, my mind was on *What did I miss on preflight, where is the plane going to land, and am I still going to get command of the squadron?* This was, after all, the first AV-8B to crash and it was a much improved aircraft with the promise of a good safety record.

I was expecting the worst on ejection because I always flew with my harness very loose, but the sensation was of someone hitting you in the face with a Nerf baseball bat. It was, in fact, a fun experience.

I cleared the plane, still in the seat, and noticed my helmet was gone. That seemed to be unusual but I found out later it is not uncommon during ejection. Eventually I found myself with a good chute, in the goo, without a clue where I was relative to the ground. I was worried I would land in a populated area, concerned about how low the cloud deck was, and wondered where the Coast Guard helos would be when I broke out.

Not being one to pay attention in class, I started looking at all the gear I was carrying and thinking about which lanyard to pull to get what results. As I remembered, one would deploy the raft and one would jettison it. One-thousand-feet-per-minute sink rate in the chute seemed to stick in my head, so I was expecting a long parachute ride. That allowed me way too much time to think about what I may have done to cause the engine to fail, focusing primarily on Foreign Object Damage. I was in this state of mind until I began to get pelted by hailstones. I was in a thunderstorm, and—as I figured out later—was going up and down in my parachute excursion. At about one fifteen, I was still in the goo without a clue to my location. After a few more minutes, I broke out around five thousand feet over the eastern end of Long Island Sound. There were no Coast Guard helicopters waiting for my arrival, there were no boats, there was nothing moving either on the Sound or on the land. This was as rural an environment as the Kentucky farmland of my youth.

I was getting cold and it struck me I had to decide at that moment to live or die during these next few minutes. Wondering about the cause of the plane's demise, my command of the squadron and anything else paled in comparison to my situation. Cold temperatures, cold water, and a moderate sea state with no sign of a rescue effort were the facts at hand with which I had to deal. I was a good distance from land. I was going to find the shroud cutter, cut some lines, and steer toward land—but I did not feel like cutting lines was the appropriate maneuver at the time. Do I cut the right four lines, the left four lines? The chute was OK and I decided to concentrate on the landing and raft entry.

Following procedures, I removed my gloves, a decision I later regretted, deployed the raft after some serious review of which lanyard did what, watched it inflate, looked straight ahead, released the Koch fittings, and entered the water just like I had done it many times before. Entry into the raft was a challenge and I went in and out. Was able to get in on the second try, started to bail the water, but my hands were becoming numb. The water and air temps were thirty-eight degrees.

Handling my radio was difficult. Then I saw an airplane taking off from a local airport. That gave me some hope that I could be spotted from the air. The raft was black and very difficult to see from shore. It turns out the maps and pubs I brought down in my G-suit, and which were scattered everywhere, helped the pilots locate me. I brought out a smoke flare but could not get my fingers to work. I put the lanyard in my teeth to pull it open, but hesitated. One side was smoke; the other white phosphorous. If I pulled the wrong end, life would not be fun. After confirming the proper end and banging the flare on the raft's inflation bottle I expected to be quickly engulfed in a cloud of smoke, as I had been in training situations. Nothing happened. However, a Cessna was flying in my general direction. I then used the pencil flare, putting a cartridge in my teeth and screwing the flare gun onto it. That did not do much for locating me, but it helped my morale quite a bit. The Cessna spotted me, called a Coast Guard cutter, and I was picked up and taken to the Greenport hospital.

The Cessna pilot's son came to the hospital as the nurse began cutting my flight suit off and treating me for hypothermia. He inquired as to what he could do to help me out and I asked if he would take my wallet to go buy me some jeans, a shirt, and tennis shoes. He said, "Everything's closed out here, but you and my dad are the same size," and he left. I did not believe anyone was my same size. Well, I was wrong as he returned with a full set of clothes, including the size-thirteen shoes.

His mom and dad arrived at the hospital emergency room with a couple martinis, I toasted my good fortune, downed these, and headed to their house for the night. My squadron was sending a plane to pick me up the next day, so I was able to attend the weekly family dinner at a local restaurant.

It was quite a day in my life. The airplane fell harmlessly into Long Island Sound. My close Marine Corps friend was able to spend a month or so looking for the engine and found it. The engine had a fan blade sheared at the root, which punctured the fuel tank, and cut all electrical cables, both AC and DC. My helmet was later returned to me from Plum Island where it had washed ashore. And I became the commanding officer of the Harrier Training Squadron.

7

GEN. JAMES H. DOOLITTLE—1929

During the Cleveland Air Races in late August 1929, a Mr. Logan of the National Air Races committee asked me if I would come to the races on September 1, 1929, and put on a stunting exhibition. He said a new Curtiss Hawk would be available for me and that Lieutenant Al Williams, my old racing competitor, would be exhibiting his wares. I refused . . . but Major General James E. Fechet, then the chief of the Air Corps, issued the travel orders.

I wanted to get the feel of the plane and practice my act at a safe altitude, so I took off and flew to a spot about seven miles from the field to practice a few stunts without being observed, and where I would not interfere with the flying around the field.

Remembering that General Patrick had ordained that we were not to perform outside loops, I decided that I would do the first half of one at the show. I climbed to 4,000 feet and, with the throttle set about three-quarters advanced, slowly pushed into a dive. When I was about 30 degrees past vertical at about 2,000 feet, there was a sharp pop and the wings broke but did not separate completely from the fuselage. The airplane slowed down and began to tumble. I throttled back, unbuckled my safety belt and was literally thrown out of the cockpit.

When I was clear of the plane, I pulled the parachute rip cord but the 'chute did not open immediately. That gave me something to think about. I jerked the rip cord again and the 'chute came open at about one thousand feet.

I came down in a field about twenty feet off a road near Olmsted Falls, west of Cleveland. I gathered up the parachute and was soon picked up and driven back to the field. When I arrived at the Air Corps headquarters, a friend of mine looked up, startled, saw my parachute, and asked what happened. I said, "The airplane broke up."

He said, "Did you get out all right?"

It wasn't an intelligent question, but I assured him I had and asked for another Hawk. . . .

Since the Irvin Parachute Company had come up with the idea of the Caterpillar Club, I thought it appropriate to drop the company a brief note of thanks, saying: "Airplane failed. Parachute worked." I didn't think I had to say anything more.

DOOLITTLE would qualify for the Caterpillar Club three times during his illustrious career by bailing out of aircraft in distress, and using a parachute successfully. Eventually leaving the military was a hard decision for Doolittle, but allowed him the freedom to take his skills and knowledge to another level, and areas of inquiry beyond the Air Corps. By 1931, while working in sales, research, and performing exhibition and goodwill flights for Shell Oil Company, Doolittle saw an opportunity.

A Beech Travel Air owned by the company had been damaged during a crash landing, and was considered a total loss. Doolittle bought, redesigned, engineered, and rebuilt the plane using the family savings. The beautiful Travel Air "Mystery Ship" was ready for flight in June 1931, and several friends and colleagues and ten-year-old Jimmy Jr. all came out to watch the advent of the new speed ship. Doolittle took off and climbed to test the plane with some aerobatic maneuvers, then dived toward the field and leveled out, as his speed reach 300 mph. There was no time for jubilation, for in an instant he heard a metallic cracking noise above the roar of the engine. Doolittle wrote in his autobiography:

I heard the ominous sound of cracking metal. The wings had begun to break; the ailerons snapped off and my control was gone.

The sequence of events was so sudden that I'm not sure what I
did, but a motion picture crew photographed the disintegration of
the plane and my departure from it. The pictures show that I pulled
the rip cord immediately, the 'chute opened, and I hit the ground
almost as quickly as I can describe the incident. The plane hit the
ground simultaneously a half mile or so away. No need to say that
it was demolished beyond repair. I wrote in my logbook: "Lost ailerons, ship crashed. God passenger."

For the second time, I had joined the Caterpillar Club, that
group of pilots who had saved their lives thanks to a group of silk-
worms who had spun the silk for their parachutes.

MIRACULOUSLY, Doolittle was not injured, but the plane destroyed
itself. Among the first to arrive at the crash site was little Jimmy,
who saw his father standing apparently unhurt. He inquired, with
little-boy directness, "Dad, how much money did we have in that
airplane?"

"All of it," Doolittle replied.

8

LCDR. KEVIN L. DUGGAN—1997

Three and a half years have passed, but it seems like yesterday: briefing an SFARP (Strike Fighter Advanced Readiness Program) division self-escort hop into B-17, then walking out of the hangar. Minimal bogeys, TACTS control, pinkie launch. A beautiful Nevada day had given way to one of those crisp, high-desert evenings in January. The temperature drops fast in the desert and I remember thinking, "I should have on a dry-suit liner," as I watched the sunset.

An hour later and less than three minutes into our run, I pulled the handle. It didn't take a lot of thought, and it felt like a car wreck. Dash 2 and Dash 4 pulled away, temporarily blinded by the fireball from my midair. Plane captains on the ramp, sixty miles away, said they saw an orange glow on the horizon. Dash 3 died in the blink of an eye. I survived.

Survivor's guilt is real, even when everybody tells you it isn't your fault. I could have done a thousand things differently, and I don't have the time or space here to explain all the factors leading to the midair. But I can pass on some do-as-I-say-not-as-I-did thoughts on survival.

All I knew after pulling the handle was that I was alive. I saw wreckage falling away. Things seemed surreal: the seat and I stabilized, descended and separated. The opening shock was intense. Some long-ago training took over as I looked up at the canopy, and I pulled the beaded handles inflating my LPU (life preserver unit).

I pulled off my oxygen mask and raised the clear visor, which had snapped down with the opening shock of the parachute.

Then I panicked. I wasn't prepared for the anxiety associated with a sudden, unexpected ejection. At twelve thousand feet, the most important thing in the world to me was to talk to somebody, to tell anybody that I was alive. The feeling was overpowering. I wrestled my PRC-90 from its pocket and fumbled with it in the dark. Then I unsnapped the flashlight that, amazingly, was still with me. With the light I could see my breath and the radio. I realized I should get ready for landing. Looking down at the darkness, I suddenly became terrified that I was going to lose the flashlight, even though I had another in my vest.

As I tried to secure the flashlight in my G-suit pocket with my numb hands, I fumbled the radio. As it fell, I remember not being too concerned because I figured it was tied to my vest. It wasn't. In the Gulf, we had to switch between PRC-90s and PRC-112s, depending on our mission. I'd never secured it since I'd gotten back home.

I slammed into the desert floor but quickly hopped up and determined I wasn't seriously injured. (Adrenaline is a wonderful thing—I could barely move the next day.) After several minutes, I got the strobe light going. Dash 2 said it seemed like an eternity before he saw the strobe but that it was easily visible from fifteen thousand feet. I soon saw and heard him flying overhead. I secured the strobe because the combination of it and the snow was disorienting. I fired off a number of pencil flares for good measure.

A T-34 showed up several minutes later, and I fired off more pencil flares. I started to calm down, and with the decrease of adrenaline, I realized how cold I was. I inflated my raft and tried to sit on it to stay out of the snow. I lit a fire and sat by it until the helicopter arrived. Our CAG flight surgeon was a welcome sight.

I didn't do a great job surviving the mishap. I did a number of things wrong and a few things right. I had pulled the handle quickly; the first rule of being a survivor is "Know when to go." Here are the things that I could have done better:

First of all, dress correctly, and know your gear. I left a jet at

18,000 feet and 380 knots in January over Dixie Valley, wearing a flight suit, gloves, T-shirt, briefs, cotton socks and summer boots. Besides leaving my liner in the PR shop, I also left a watch cap and some chemical hand-warmers there as well. Why? I had been both lazy and rushed. Our squadron had just returned from deployment in early October. In the Gulf, I had taken out the watch cap and the hand-warmers, and I hadn't bothered to put them back into my survival vest. I had simply forgotten the liner. I had worn it on my previous night hop and on at least one day hop, but this time we'd had a long and involved brief, and I had walked in late. Plain socks and summer boots—chalk them up to laziness and the supply system.

The result was that I spent an hour and forty-five minutes on the ground, waiting for the helicopter, in two to three inches of snow, with the temperature in the teens, in the same outfit I wear flying in the summer.

I arrived on the ground without a scratch and was able to start a fire. I had matches in my vest but couldn't use them because my fingers were too numb. Instead, I got a fire going, using a night flare and sagebrush. If I hadn't been able to start that fire because I'd been injured, or if the helicopter rescue had been delayed, I could have suffered a bad case of hypothermia or frozen to death.

Dash 2 and the T-34 spotter found me because of my flares and strobe. They were trying to talk to me. Had the weather been worse, the poor preflight of my gear could have put my survival at risk. Later that night, a storm blew in and dropped a couple more inches of snow. A low under cast would have obscured my flares, causing the rescue effort to take hours longer, or even days.

You have to be mentally prepared. I had often played little survival scenarios in my head. My wife long ago got sick of hearing me say, "Wow, can you imagine coming down here in a parachute?" when we were on the ski slopes or driving past fields covered with grapevine stakes. But in hindsight, even these few thoughts of survival were too little, and I was ill-prepared for an actual survival situation. I was particularly unprepared for the anxiety associated with disaster and immediately after ejection. I had memorized

IROK (Inflate, Release, Options, Koch Fittings), but I hadn't thought about how clearly I'd be thinking when I needed it.

The next several weeks were among the toughest of my life. Before this accident, I had never been anywhere near a Class A mishap, much less one involving a fatality. Surviving a mishap makes you acutely aware of the human aspect, both in the cause of mishaps and their cost.

Now and then, I stand in front of a ready room and discuss my midair. Even though some of my mistakes can seem comical, the mood is always somber at the end. In a way, I'm marked for life as a guy who survived a midair that should have killed him. Pilots looking at a survivor are forced to consider the possibility of being one themselves. I hope I help them be prepared, because when it happens, it's too late to prepare.

[Midair collisions are the second leading cause of fatal mishaps, right behind CFIT/Controlled Flight into Terrain. Both are overwhelmingly caused by human factors—Ed.]

LCDR. STEVEN R. EASTBURG/LT. SEAN BRENNAN—1989

LCdr. Steve Eastburg of TPS Class 100 and Lt. Sean Brennan of Class 99, both thirty-three years old, were preparing to take the S-3 Viking antisubmarine aircraft up over the Chesapeake Bay to fly a "vomit comet" mission. The idea was to do the aerial equivalent of reverse engineering. First, they would fly the S-3 through a series of precise maneuvers while an elaborate network of instruments monitored and recorded what happened to the plane. Next, engineers and technicians on the ground would study the information gained and use it to fine tune the simulator. The payoff would be a more realistic simulator for pilots trying to master the S-3 under various flying conditions, including adverse ones.

The flight plan had been studiously developed before Eastburg and Brennan were assigned to execute it. They discussed what they were going to do, step by step, with other aviators and engineers before climbing into the S-3 designated Waterbug 736. Nothing looked particularly risky. Engineers at the Chesapeake Test Range at Pax (Patuxent) River would be watching for trouble the whole time they were airborne.

Eastburg, a naval flight officer, would be in the right seat of the S-3, working the radios, studying several of the key instruments in the cockpit, and taking down data. Brennan, the pilot, would be flying from the left seat and taking the plane from one point in the sky to another to complete a long list of maneuvers.

The rough part of their ride—the part that inspired the name "vomit comet"—would come when Brennan pitched the S-3 up and down, rolled it from wingtip to wingtip, and swerved it from left to right in a series of skids called yaws. The first set of these stomach-jolting maneuvers would be done at an altitude of 10,000 feet at a speed of 305 knots. The second set would be down in the rougher air at 5,000 feet at an even faster speed, 365 knots.

The S-3 is a twin-engine jet with thick wings and a tail so tall that it has to be folded over from the top to fit in carrier hangar bays. Pilots regard it as a solid aircraft that flies smoothly. Eastburg and Brennan felt safe in it. They had no fears the airplane would break during the maneuvers that lay ahead of them this sunny afternoon of 29 April 1989.

After a quick lunch and an extensive preflight briefing, the aviators took off without incident and steadied the S-3 at 10,000 feet in clear air over the Chesapeake a few miles east of Pax River. Brennan worked the throttles and trim until he had the plane straight and level at 305 knots. Eastburg watched the gauges and answered such standard radio calls from the ground as "Waterbug 736, you're five miles from the boundary." Sean Brennan pushed the stick forward and backward in ever-decreasing intervals. The plane pitched up and down like a bucking bronco. He swung the stick left and right in the same quickening sequence. The plane rolled like a canoe being smacked on its sides by higher and higher waves. Sean went into rudder sweeps to generate the yawing, pushing the left rudder pedal, then the right, then the left, then the right. The motion causes queasiness in the guts for even veteran pilots.

All that done, with lunch swirling uneasily in their stomachs, Steve and Sean descended to 5,000 feet. Sean put the plane through the same set of punishing maneuvers at 365 knots. The ride became rougher at this faster speed in the thicker air. He was in the middle of the same sickening rudder sweeps when Steve heard the noise of catastrophe coming from somewhere in the aft fuselage.

Craaack!

Steve had never heard such a chilling sound in an airplane. It sounded like a tree snapping in half during a windstorm. They knew the plane had broken, but not where. Telemetry would show that the top of the giant tail had broken off—meaning that Sean could no longer make the plane move left or right with the rudder pedals. At about the same instant one of the elevators needed to make the plane go up or down snapped off. The plane went out of control. It rolled, pitched, and yawed violently. Each new gravitational force pushed or pulled the aviators in a different direction as they sat in their seats, their shoulder and lap harness straining to hold them down. Steve glanced over at Sean and saw he was still fighting the airplane. His body was so twisted by the pileup of gravitational forces that Steve doubted he could reach the ejection handle even though it was now obvious that they had to leave the wrecked plane or die. Steve managed to get his hand around the ejection handle under his seat as Sean started the "Eject, eject, eject" command.

It was less than two seconds between when they were confronted with the emergency and when Steve pulled the ejection handle. They would learn later that waiting another split second would have killed them both. The rockets under the seats of Steve and Sean ignited, blasting them through the plastic roof of the cockpit just before it became a death trap. The S-3 skidded around until it was hurtling through the air tail first, and the right wing broke off at its root in the fuselage, pouring fuel into the onrushing air. The atomized fuel exploded into a fireball, probably from the engine exhaust.

Steve and Sean did not know what was happening to the airplane at the time. Only later would telemetry tell the story: so much force slapped into the sides of the rudder that it could not take it and snapped.

Everybody on the ground who was plugged into Pax River would learn what happened almost as soon as it happened. They knew the plane had broken up near Bloodsworth Island, but not what had happened to the crew. Friends called friends and asked. I received one of those calls but would only learn much later what happened to Steve and Sean once they left their flying fireball.

For Steve there were sounds of *Whap! Whomp!* and then nothing but an eerie silence. For Sean, memory was mercifully blocked out by the ejection Steve initiated.

The *whap* was probably the noise of banging out of the cockpit at 3:18 P.M.; the *whomp*, the opening of the parachute; and the silence, the slow fall through the sky toward the surface of the bay.

"Am I still alive?" Steve asked himself as he experienced a sense of otherworldliness in his drift down through the sky. He saw plane wreckage floating through the sky with him. They were flotsam together. He struggled for a sense of reality. He looked all about him for assurance that he was still part of earthly existence.

Above his head, he saw the white blossom of his parachute canopy. Below dangled his feet, shod in his flight boots.

Beside him, off in the distance, was a limp body hanging from another parachute.

And far below, on the surface of the water, were white boats.

He put it together.

They had ejected from the airplane. They were alive and of this life.

He gave Sean a thumbs-up. No response.

His next thought was of his wife, Cathy. He told himself: "Boy! I've got to call her! She's going to be worried."

Navy survival training then asserted itself. IROK—the lifesaving acronym for his predicament: *I* for inflate your life preserver. He did by pulling the beads at his waist outward. *R* for raft. He pulled the handle alongside the metal cushion stuck to his rump, the seat pan, so that the raft and other survival gear could fall freely ahead of him, stopped by a tether whose yank inflated the raft. *O* for optional equipment. He checked those things: face visor, gloves, front snaps on his life preserver, oxygen mask. *K* for Koch fittings, which he must remember to unsnap when his boots touched the water, but not before. The Koch fittings kept him hooked into his parachute. Aviators worship their parachute while it is holding them in the air but curse it when they are in the water. Too many aviators have drowned when their still-attached parachutes filled up with water and pulled them under.

IROK completed, Steve was composed enough during this fall toward earth to fish the emergency radio out of the tight pocket of his survival vest and start talking over it.

"Mayday! Mayday! Mayday!" Steve radioed. "This is one of the S-3 crew members. Just had mishap one mile east of Bloodsworth Island. I'm OK. Condition of other aircrew unknown."

He then remembered that the automatic emergency radio beacon in the seat pan that was floating down with him would drown out his calls if he stayed on the 243.0-megahertz frequency. He dialed 282.8 megahertz and repeated his Mayday calls.

He wondered if any of the boats and ships he saw below had heard his calls or could see him in the sky above them. He need not have worried about being seen. Cpl. Thomas Shores and Officer Victor Kulyncz of Maryland's Department of Natural Resources had been horrified by the sight of a fireball in the sky above, followed by two parachutes dropping out of it. They had radioed the Maryland State Police in Salisbury to send out a rescue helicopter.

Steve saw the water rushing up at him. "Man, I don't want to get wet!" Executing his survival training, Steve unsnapped his Koch fittings connecting him to the parachute as soon as his boots hit the water. The parachute floated away from him, just as the survival instructors had promised. He climbed into the raft, which had hit the water ahead of him already inflated. He was safe if somebody saw him before he froze to death. He was shivering. Shock had drawn his blood into his vitals, leaving his body feeling cold.

Steve saw the Boston Whaler crewed by Shores and Kulyncz bearing down on him. While waiting for it, he looked around for Sean but could not see him for the two-foot waves. It was sunny and fairly warm, but the water—52.3 degrees Fahrenheit—had further chilled him. He discovered he was bleeding from gashes in his right knee, nose, and chin.

The men in the Whaler were like those crews in the landing barges that braved artillery fire from shore as they rushed toward Normandy beach during World War II. Shores and Kulyncz did not let the plane wreckage falling from the sky slow them up. They were soon alongside Steve's raft. With help from Shores and Kulyncz, he climbed over the port side of the boat and then asked the question that had moved to the top of his mind: "Did you see the other man?"

Shores and Kulyncz assured him they had. The Whaler raced off to rescue Sean and was soon beside him. Steve was not prepared for the sight.

Sean's face had been burned black when he shot through the plume from the rocket that had propelled Steve out of the cockpit just ahead of him. He had no eyebrows; the hair protruding from his helmet was frizzled; the front of his flight suit had been burned off, leaving much of him bare. He was lying unconscious in the water with his head tilted back. The life preserver, which had inflated automatically when it sensed salt water, was holding Sean up. But it was not snapped across the front. If Sean's head had fallen forward rather than backward after he was in the water, the pilot almost certainly would have drowned. Even if his head had stayed tilted back and no boat had reached him quickly, Sean—who had not been conscious to unsnap the Koch fittings attaching him to the parachute—would have been pulled under the water once the canopy filled up. Steve saw the parachute was already filling.

A Navy rescue H-3 helicopter arrived overhead and dropped a swimmer into the water. Steve signaled the helicopter to back away because its rotor wash was kicking up hurtful spray and complicating Sean's rescue. Steve saw that Sean, besides his ugly burns, had smashed his right shoulder as it caught on something in the cockpit while he was being rocketed out. Steve figured Sean would not survive being hauled out of the water on a helicopter hoist. The helicopter backed away from the Whaler. The helicopter swimmer was retrieved.

Steve, Shores, and Kulyncz unsnapped Sean from his parachute and life raft—no easy task while leaning out of the boat—and gingerly pulled the burned pilot out of the bay. They laid him as gently as they could on the flat spot in the bow of the Whaler.

Steve knelt over Sean, studied his breathing, and held him in his arms as the boat bounced eastward toward Deal Island. Steve was ready to administer CPR (cardiopulmonary resuscitation) if Sean's breathing staggered.

"You're going to be OK; you're going to be OK," Steve kept telling Sean. "We'll be there in just a few minutes."

Steve thought he heard Sean mumble, "Steve, are you OK?" in a brief break out of his unconscious state.

The two-foot waves were bouncing the speeding Whaler up and down. Steve worried what this was doing to Sean's smashed-up shoulder. He asked Shores and Kulyncz to slow the Whaler. They did. Steve asked for their coats to pile on the shivering Sean. They quickly handed them over. It took a seemingly endless eight minutes to reach Deal Island.

Steve saw islanders crowded on the Deal pier to gawk at the arriving aviators. He protested, "Vultures!" to himself. He would have been less angry if he had known an ambulance, a Maryland State Police Dauphine rescue helicopter, a Coast Guard helicopter, and the Navy H-3 chopper from Pax River were all on the ground behind the crowd.

Maryland Trooper First Class James C. "J. C." Collins Jr., a flight paramedic with ten years' experience, pushed his way to the dock. He saw old friends from the Princess Anne Volunteer Fire Company who had rushed to Deal by ambulance. Lorenzo Cropper, ambulance captain; Jim Foote, duty medic; and Steve Willin, a cardio-rescue technician, deferred to J.C. and asked him what he needed.

"I need a KED board and a stiff collar." A KED board has flexible sides so that it can be slid under an unconscious person easily but is stiff along its centerline in case the patient's back is broken. Collins also asked for and got from the ambulance crew the devices he might need to slide down Sean's throat to keep his breathing passages open. The medic, who had tended to many burn victims, was most worried that the pilot's singed breathing passages would swell to the point they would close. This would suffocate him. Sean was foaming at the corners of his mouth, a sign of "nose singeing." He had evidently burned his breathing passages when inhaling the ejection-rocket fumes. Collins also worried about Sean's severe burns, which had robbed him of vital insulation, and which may already have been infected with germs from the bay water. Collins knew infection often killed burn victims too.

With help from several others, Collins got Sean out of the Whaler and onto the KED board. Once they had Sean on the dock, they laid him in the Maryland police helicopter's stretcher. Collins inserted an intravenous tube into Sean's left arm and prepared to carry him to his elaborately equipped helicopter—virtually a flying intensive-care unit.

A Navy crewman from the Pax River helicopter said he was under orders to get Sean Brennan into the Navy helicopter. "Are you geared up for this?" Collins asked dubiously. Seeing the squeeze the sailor was in, Collins said he would tell the officer in the helicopter that the Maryland State Police should care for the critically injured pilot, not the Navy.

Collins, a former Marine, ran up to the Navy chopper, saw that it had little if any of the survival equipment Sean would need to stay alive, and told RADM Barton D. Strong, the top officer at Pax River: "Captain, my name is Trooper Collins. I have your pilot. He's got first- , second- , and third-degree burns over 50 percent of his body. He's got to go to the East Coast Regional Burn Center. This man has got to get there."

Strong agreed.

Collins took the Navy crewman along with him in the police helicopter with Sean. The Dauphine's rotors had been turning the whole half hour they had been on the ground.

"Where we going, buddy?" Joe McNair, the civilian pilot of the police helicopter, asked Collins.

"Straight to FSK," shorthand for the Francis Scott Key Medical Center in Baltimore. The Baltimore Regional Burn Center is part of FSK.

"No problem," replied McNair as he swung off the road where he had landed and headed north for Baltimore.

All this while, Steve Eastburg was watching over Sean Brennan like a soldier whose foxhole companion had been shot. Steve's bleeding had stopped to the point that the ambulance crew did not right away realize he was the second man in the plane and might be hurt. Ambulance Captain Cropper, fearing Steve might be more seriously injured than he looked, insisted he lie down on a stretcher board to keep his head immobilized. Cropper and his crew lifted Steve into the ambulance, intending to take him to Peninsula Regional Medical Center in Salisbury. Steve strenuously argued that it made more sense for him to fly in the Navy rescue helicopter to the hospital at Pax River, that he was not hurt. Duty medic Foote radioed headquarters for instructions and was warned that he should not turn Steve over to a lesser-skilled medic. The ambulance crew and Steve reached a compromise under which Willin of the Princess Anne fire company would fly with Steve in the Navy chopper back to Patuxent.

"You know," Willin confided to Steve after the Navy helicopter had lifted off Deal Island at 4 P.M. and began *thwack-thwacking* its way across the bay, "this is only the second time I've flown."

"You ought to be the one on this board," Steve quipped.

The first thing about his rescue that Sean remembered after ejecting from the S-3 "was the drone of a helicopter. But I didn't know I was flying in it. I must have asked where I was because I heard the medic say, 'You've been in an aircraft accident.'

"I kept coming in and out of consciousness. I realized I had to have had a plane crash. I kept asking these questions: 'Where's Steve? Is he all right? What happened to the plane? Did I kill anybody? Did it land on a house?'

"I remember the medic answering: 'He's OK. You didn't kill anybody. The plane landed in the water.' "

Collins said of Sean's conversation on their way from Deal Island to Baltimore in the police helicopter: "It was his training talking. When he got to asking about what happened to the airplane, I told him, 'Pal, don't worry about it. Your airplane is gone. They make them every fucking day.'

"I asked him how he was feeling," Collins recalled. "He said, 'I feel I've got a case of really bad sunburn all over.' "

Collins monitored Sean's blood pressure with mounting concern. The pilot's heart was having a hard time pushing blood through the vessels constricted by shock. The systolic blood-pressure reading had risen to 172, up from the normal 120. Collins gave Sean five grams of morphine to relax him. The systolic pressure plunged to 90. The medic put him on a respirator.

"Hey!" Collins yelled at Sean to keep him from passing out. "Don't you do that to me again." The systolic pressure rose and steadied at the desired 120.

The medic also worried about the pilot's heavy loss of fluids. He tossed tubing to the Navy crewman and asked him to prepare another intravenous tube. "Hey, Doc!" the crewman replied. "I'm not a medical person." Collins removed Sean's boot to find an unburned place to insert the tube. He found a full vein on the pilot's left ankle and started feeding in more fluids there.

The police helicopter landed on the pad beside the hospital. A six-person crew, alerted by radio, was waiting and whisked Sean inside. A former Army nurse, with a reputation for talking tough, saw that Sean was a Navy flier and asked, "What's he doing here? Isn't this guy military? He should go to Bethesda."

Collins, with little attempt to control his anger, lashed out: "Ma'am! You take a person who needs definitive care to a definitive facility!"

"Calm down," the nurse relented. "Go wash your hands."

Dr. William P. Fabbri, who was overseeing the team, winked approvingly at Collins and raced on with the job of saving Sean Brennan.

WITH Eastburg safely inside the hospital at Pax River and Brennan at Francis Scott Key in Baltimore, Navy leaders turned their attention to the delicate obligation of informing the wives of the aviators about the "mishap."

The Navy way is to send at least one officer, often with the chaplain, to the door of the aviator's home and inform the wife face-to-face. Aviators' wives dread an unexpected ring of the doorbell and feel stricken when they see an officer standing at their door.

Cathy Eastburg, Steve's wife, is a nurse. They met in the College Avenue Baptist Church in San Diego in 1985 and married in 1987.

This late afternoon of 29 April 1992 she was chatting happily with Gayle and Gregory Crabtree, old Navy friends from California, in the living room when her doorbell rang. Gregory Crabtree answered the door while Cathy rose and held her two-and-a-half-year-old son, Greg, in her arms. CDR Julian Hart, a friend from Force Warfare, was standing in the kitchen just beyond the back door by the time she reached him.

"I had a big smile on my face," Cathy recalled. "I figured Steve had asked Julian over for dinner. But then I saw how solemn he looked."

"We lost an airplane," Hart began. "Steve's OK."

Images of Steve's broken body flooded Cathy's mind.

"Do you want to make a phone call?" Hart asked gently. Chief Bob Croker, also from Force, who had been waiting outside, joined Hart in the kitchen.

Cathy had seen all kinds of horrors as a nurse. But this was different. This was her husband, Greg's father. Her knees began to buckle. She told herself that if this was a minor thing there would not be two Navy men come to the house. Why not just a phone call from the hospital? Her fears escalated.

"You know," resumed Hart, "we just wanted to give you a ride to the hospital. Do you want to call somebody?"

Cathy called her mother and told her what little she knew. That Steve's airplane had crashed; that he had ejected; that he was in the hospital; that she was going to see him; that the Crabtrees were visiting and would look after Greg.

During the drive to the hospital Hart and Croker were politely evasive about what had happened to Steve's airplane. She had been a Navy wife long enough to know the system: Don't tell the family anything until we're sure. But it was still maddening.

An old hand at end-running hospital bureaucracies, Nurse Cathy Eastburg strode right into the emergency room, found Steve's bed, and leaned over him.

"Hi, babe!" he greeted. "I'm doing just fine."

Cathy mechanically responded with something bland while her eyes and mind concentrated on their medical survey of Steve's body. "I knew it was a miracle he was alive." The gashes that Drs. Timothy Hannon and Gregory Johnson were sewing up while she stood beside Steve's bed did not bother her. It was the likelihood that he had broken his spine, or neck, or arms, or legs or suffered internal injuries. None of this had occurred from what she could see and what the doctors told her. "I was very thankful to God that He had spared Steve."

The official part of the Navy family started coming into the hospital to show Steve they cared: Rear Admiral Strong; Capt. Robert Parkinson, director of the flight test center; and Capt. Jim Keen, director of the Force Warfare Aircraft Test Directorate.

At 8:30 P.M., after what felt like hundreds of X-rays had confirmed Steve was still whole all the way through, the doctors released him from the hospital. A Navy driver on duty drove Steve and Cathy to their home in a blue Navy van. Steve put his arm around Cathy and tried to sort out the events of his traumatic day. He tasted the salt of the bay and wondered how so much could have happened to him in so little time.

At 9:30 that same night, after taking a hot shower that finally warmed him, Steve Eastburg was sitting on the floor of Greg's upstairs bedroom, reading him stories from Dr. Seuss and Sesame Street.

"It was incomprehensible to me, surrealistic," Steve said later.

"Here I was, five hours after almost losing my life, reading stories to my son. I had gone from something incredibly violent to a world of peacefulness with my little son and his innocent mind. I thank God every morning for sparing me."

Sandi Brennan, Sean's wife, was even more surprised than Cathy when she opened the door of her home in California, Maryland, and found an unexpected visitor, Lt. Dean Sawyer of Force, standing outside. Sandi had just come home from her job as an executive assistant to a defense contractor in Lexington Park and had relieved the sitter taking care of Megan, the Brennans' eighteen-month-old daughter. She did not know Sean was flying that day and was totally unprepared for the conversation that followed.

"Sandi," said Dean Sawyer, "we lost an airplane."

"Oh my God! Who was it?"

"It was Sean's airplane."

Sandi felt sick. Her mind spun. But she still managed to keep standing at the door, asking more questions.

"He's burned, and he's in Baltimore. And that's all I know. We've got a ride for you to Baltimore. Melinda and I are going to take Megan home with us."

Sandi packed a bag, made a few telephone calls, grabbed a picture of Megan to show Sean, and was inside the waiting room outside the Francis Scott Key emergency room by 8 P.M.

Sandi recollected that Sean had said his biggest fear was being burned in an aircraft accident. "I didn't know what to expect. I had never seen anybody burned."

She waited and waited. Dr. Fabbri was still working on Sean and came out of the emergency room long enough to describe the flier's condition. "He was just wonderful," Sandi said of Fabbri. "He didn't paint a rosy picture, but I could tell he was doing everything he could for Sean."

Captain Parkinson and Captain Keen, having already visited Steve Eastburg, joined Sandi and Julian Hart at Francis Scott Key. The three waited into the night. At 10:30 P.M. the emergency room door opened, and a stretcher with a man bandaged until he looked like a mummy with tubes plugged in whipped by on a gurney.

"That wasn't Sean, was it?" she asked the captains. "Oh my God, that couldn't be him. I don't believe it."

It was. A nurse came to her shortly afterward and asked if she would like to see him before his eyes swelled shut. She brought Megan's picture to show him. She was shocked, sickened to the point of feeling faint when she looked at Sean.

"It blew me away. I was so choked up, I could say only a few words. I had to run out of the room."

The thirty-three-year-old aviator who had looked so strong when she last saw him had lost his eyebrows; tubes and wires crisscrossed his body; an oxygen mask was clamped over his nose; what skin that showed was greased over and black; his head looked like "a giant Brillo pad" of singed hair; there was a big gash above his right eye; he was shaking and trying to talk.

Parkinson and Keen stayed in the room. Sean kept asking them how Steve was. Parkinson put Megan's picture on the bulletin board in front of Sean's bed and said, "We want you to be able to sit up and look at her."

"That's my goal," Sean replied weakly.

Dr. Andrew Munster, head of the hospital's burn center, kept Sandi apprised of Sean's progress. His first week was extremely painful, consisting mainly of taking baths during which his burned skin was scraped off so that new skin could grow and infection could be deterred.

Sandi stayed in a motel near the hospital the first night. After that, she drove from her home to the hospital and back every day for five days. The second week she stayed in Baltimore. Navy friends mobilized. Sue Ehlers, wife of Lt. Mark Ehlers, called to say she was flying in from California to help out.

"You don't have to do that," Sandi said over the phone. "That's too much money."

"I know you'd be there for us. I've already got my reservations."

After two weeks at Francis Scott Key, during which his burns healed miraculously without grafting, he went to the Naval Medical Center in Bethesda, Maryland, for treatment of his shoulder and other bodily injuries. Then it was home and daily therapy at the Pax River hospital to get in shape to go back to testing airplanes.

I asked both wives after their husbands had healed whether they wished their husbands would give up test piloting. Their answers typified those of fliers' wives the world over.

"There's nothing you can do to prevent anything like this," Cathy Eastburg said. "It's part of life. Something like this could happen on the road.

"The best response is to see what you can learn from it. Life is extremely fragile no matter how invincible you think you are. Test pilots think they're invincible. They're not."

10

DONALD D. ENGEN—1949

I flew my first flight in the F9F-3 in mid-June, 1949, and two weeks later several lieutenants JG and I were ordered to Bethpage, New York, to pick up four brand-new F9F-3s. The airplanes we had flown to date did not have ejection seats, and as a result pilot casualty rates were climbing. So we first went to the Naval Aircraft Factory in Philadelphia to be guinea pigs for the new and still untried (in the United States) British Martin-Baker ejection seat, now being installed in the F9F. There we found a 96-foot training tower that stood like a giant guillotine outside several workshops.

The Martin-Baker seat was essentially a seat sitting on a 40mm shell filled with slower burning propellant and fitted with racks to guide the seat upward and clear of the airplane. The 40mm shell fired when the pilot pulled a face curtain to its full length down over his head and face to protect himself against severe wind blast injury at high speeds. Before the shell fired, the cockpit canopy jettisoned aft. Then the force of the powder charge propelled the pilot clear of the airplane. The pilot then undid his seat belt and shoulder straps to kick himself clear of the seat and manually pulled his parachute rip cord. The Martin-Baker seat was an ingenious development and improved over time to ultimately save over six thousand pilots' lives during some forty-two years. Our view in 1949 was that this seat was to be used in an emergency. Not one of us looked forward to the honor of firing the seat on the ground.

Being the senior officer, I approached the tower first. The grains of powder propellant were carefully measured out and weighted according to our body weight to give each of us one-half to three-quarters of a full shot. I sat in the seat while my compatriots and passersby gathered to watch the show. Some of them opened lunch sacks to sit in the shade and munch while watching. Having been briefed and fully strapped in, I positioned myself and on signal pulled the face curtain over my helmet in one stroke. Nothing happened. I was sitting on a seat whose cartridge had supposedly been fired, and no one wanted to come near me. A loud voice said, "Do not move!" That was irrelevant—I was not about to move. I still firmly clasped the face curtain over my head and face to keep my arms from being broken should the seat accidentally fire. After some consultation, one person with a very long pole approached me cautiously. Using a metal hook on the end of the pole, he fished around behind the seat until he could manually insert the safety pin into the cartridge on the seat. Then everyone, especially me, relaxed enough to get me out of the hot seat.

Hours later the problem was determined to be a bad firing squib, and we set about to duplicate the morning exercise. This time I firmly grasped the face curtain and pulled as hard as I could to make sure that the thing fired. It did, and in a fraction of a second the seat compressed my spine, now elongated from the pull, and propelled me up the tower to stop some 48 feet above with a great display of smoke and noise.

After being let down by some ratchet-and-pulley arrangement, I told my friends not to pull so hard, and they fared much better than I. Still later, I found that I had compressed a disc in my spine, but I never doubted that I would use the ejection seat. Weeks later squadron executive officer Lieutenant Commander Bill Sisley also injured himself on the same tower, and Lieutenant Commander Dave Pollack said that he would never use the seat, but would choose to bail out. Dave was killed four years later when he did just that from an F9F-6 he was flight testing at Patuxent River. He chose not to use the ejection seat and hit his head on the leading edge of the stabilator; he never opened his parachute.

FINKLEMAN—1959

The night was extremely and unusually dark, without a horizon and cumulus clouds which could not be seen were present. These conditions make visual flying treacherous. The majority of flying was done under instruments; however, visual attitude was used frequently. The pilot was relatively inexperienced in actual flying.

The pilot experienced a form of fascination which was followed by true vertigo at low altitude. During this period he was incapable of controlling his aircraft. He attempted to bail out while highly excited. He held the parachute D-ring in his hand, crouched in the seat, and then attempted to exit from the cockpit. When he entered the windblast, his right arm was violently jerked back and the D-ring was pulled. The pilot chute streamed along the canopy. Fearing that the chute was entangled, the pilot sat back down and regained control of the aircraft. With the plane under control, he gathered in his chute, sat on it, and closed the canopy. He experienced vertigo a second time. He promptly went on instruments and was able to control the airplane satisfactorily.

CDR. WYNN F. FOSTER—1966

As commanding officer of an attack squadron, I led a routine mission against a suspected target in North Vietnam. My wingman and I launched about 0750 and rendezvoused overhead of the carrier. We departed on top at 0810 and headed for our planned coast-in point. We began our descent from altitude. Shortly after the coast-in point, we began picking up flak bursts to our starboard side, just north of our track. I called the flak to my wingman's attention and told him to keep jinking. A few seconds later I heard a loud "bang" followed by a "whoosh" and I felt a stinging sensation in my right elbow. I realized I had been hit and looked down at my right arm.

The arm was missing from the elbow down and half of my right forearm was lying on the starboard console. During the first few seconds I had a hard time convincing myself that most of my right arm was missing, but when I tried to move the stick, I was convinced. I took the stick with my left hand and started to head the aircraft back out to sea. I radioed my wingman that I had been hit, then broadcast "Mayday," giving my side number and general position. I told my wingman to keep jinking and to get clear of the area. My airspeed was dropping so I eased the nose down and tried to hold about 220 knots. The shell frag (I estimate it was at least a 57mm because of my altitude at the time I was hit) had blown out most of the canopy and it was very noisy in the cockpit. The cockpit was quite a mess with flesh and blood splattered over the windscreen and instrument panel. I made a couple of radio transmissions to my wingman to see if he was OK but the wind noise was such that all I could hear was garble.

Shortly thereafter I looked in my mirror and saw my wingman was still with me. My arm didn't hurt but I was bleeding quite badly. I momentarily considered trying to make it back to the ship but realized I would probably pass out before I got there. The nearest "friendly" was the SAR (Sea-Air Rescue) DD (destroyer) stationed about thirty miles to seaward of the coast-in point. I thought I had been hit in the engine as well as the cockpit since I was still descending while holding 220 knots. I thrashed around the cockpit, making radio transmissions, flying the bird, changing TACAN channels, and trying to arrest the bleeding by squeezing my right upper arm. About the time I descended through two thousand five hundred feet, I looked at my RPM and realized I had only 70 percent power. Things had been pretty confusing, and it was the first time I had looked at the RPM since getting hit. I advanced the throttle and the RPM began to build up. The engine seemed to be working properly, and I climbed back to four thousand feet. I heard a garbled radio transmission and recognized the words "your position." I replied that I was 240/15 from the SAR DD, that I had been hit in the cockpit, that I was bleeding badly and intended to eject as close to the SAR DD as possible. I then called my wingman and told him to tell the SAR DD that I would need medical attention immediately.

There were several subsequent radio transmissions by other stations, but they were all too garbled for me to understand. I was beginning to feel weak and decided I'd have to eject and get my flotation gear inflated before I passed out. As I neared the SAR DD, there was a broken under cast. For some reason, I decided I wanted to see the SAR DD before I ejected. The under cast wasn't very thick and I descended through it, leveling about three thousand feet. As I broke out, I saw the SAR DD below, churning white water and heading directly for me. I glanced at the DME (Distance Measuring Equipment), which read three miles. Since I was feeling quite woozy, and beginning to experience tunnel vision, I decided to eject. I made sure my heels were on the deck, sat up straight, and pulled the curtain with my left hand. The next thing I knew I was tumbling or spinning. I heard a sequence of several snaps and pops, then felt the bladders toss me out of the seat. Shortly thereafter the chute opened and I seemingly was suspended in midair.

My oxygen mask was still on, and my visor was down. I removed the oxygen mask and dropped it. I looked around. The view was beautiful—blue ocean, white clouds above, and the DD steaming down below. The war seemed a million miles away. I was feeling pretty woozy and couldn't concentrate on any one thing for very long. I held tight on the stump for a few seconds and then remembered to inflate my C-3 life vest. I inflated the left side first, then couldn't find the right toggle with my left hand. I groped around for a few seconds, then forgot about the right toggle. I unfastened the left rocket jet fitting and let the seat pack fall to the right. Actually, it seemed to hang between my legs. I attempted to get at the lanyard to the life raft but with my left hand, all I could reach was the D-ring for the bail-out bottle so I forgot about that too. I went back to squeezing my stump and noticed I was still wearing my left glove. I pulled off the glove with my teeth, let it drop, and went back to squeezing the stump.

I watched the glove falling lazily a few feet away from me for a while, then shifted my gaze to the DD. I didn't have any vertical reference points, and for a while it seemed I was not falling. I noticed the DD had a boat rigged out and suspended a few feet above the water. I couldn't think of anything else to do so I just kept applying pressure to the stump and watched my wingman flying in a tight circle around my position. I recognized relative movement when I was just a few feet above the water. I crossed my legs, held my breath, and almost immediately hit the water. When I bobbed back to the surface, I floated for a few seconds before I remembered to disconnect myself from the chute. The water was warm, with a gentle swell, and there was no discernible wind. The chute had collapsed behind me and all I could see were some shroud lines over my shoulder. I unlocked both Koch fittings and the risers fell away behind me. The SAR DD was about a half mile away and the whaleboat was already in the water. I saw someone in khaki point in my direction. I muttered a few encouraging curses to speed them on. I had lost the sense of time passage but it seemed that the whaleboat got to my vicinity quite rapidly.

As the whaleboat neared me, the coxswain throttled back and turned away. Apparently he was concerned about running over me. I yelled to the boat that I was bleeding badly, and to drive right in, which the coxswain did. When the boat was alongside, numerous hands reached out to grab me. I told them to be careful of my right side. After I was resting safely in the whaleboat, my right arm became painful for the first time. Up to that point, I had had just a mild stinging sensation. Someone removed my helmet and cradled my head in his lap. There was a corpsman in the boat and, although I didn't feel him puncture my arm, I was receiving Dextran from a bottle within seconds. The pain was severe, so I asked the sailor holding my head to break out the morphine syrettes I carried in my left sleeve pocket. He said he had never given morphine so I mumbled step-by-step instructions. I told him to unscrew the plastic cap and throw it away, push the wire plunger all the way into the syrette, then pull it out and throw it away. The sailor was obviously shaken because he pulled out the plunger and threw the syrette over the side. We went through the whole thing again with the second syrette, this time successfully, and the sailor got the morphine into my arm. I thought I was going to pass out so I told the sailor to remember to tell the doctor that I had been given morphine. Shortly thereafter we came alongside the SAR DD.

The bow and stern hooks were sharp; we latched on smoothly, and almost in one motion, were hoisted to deck level. I was taken down to sick bay where the ship's doctor began working on me. After a few minutes, another doctor from another carrier arrived and introduced himself. In my drowsy state that confused me somewhat. After pondering the thought, I announced that my carrier was closer than his and that I wanted to be returned to my ship. I have no idea how long I was aboard the DD, but recall someone saying "about an hour ago," apparently in reference to my accident. That would have made the time about 0930. Shortly thereafter, I was placed on a stretcher, taken on deck and hoisted into a helicopter. Just before I left the DD sick bay, I insisted that my flight boots go along with me. A couple of my officers had dyed the boots bright blue—the squadron color—a few days previously as a joke. This was the first mission I'd flown wearing my blue boots and I didn't want to lose them. The carrier surgeon assured me that all my gear would accompany me.

I don't recall how long the helo trip back to my carrier took. I was pretty well doped up on morphine and quite weak. When we set down on the flight deck I recall two things distinctly: the air boss announced on the 5MC, "163 returning," which made me feel better and our flight surgeon spoke to me. Hearing a familiar voice also made me feel better. His comment was, "Boy! Some people will do anything to get out of a little combat!" With friends like that, who needs enemies? I was taken below and into surgery, where among other valiant efforts (eight units of blood) what was left of my right arm was surgically amputated, leaving me with about a six-inch stump. In retrospect, I can think of some survival procedures I could have followed to more closely coincide with "the book."

But it is encouraging to note that the essential things worked. The A-4 RAPEC seat, which is famous for its simplicity and reliability, worked as advertised. My wingman stated that, in addition to the frag that went through the cockpit, my aircraft was "full of holes" and streaming fuel from several places. It is logical to assume that frags could have penetrated the fuselage and damaged the seat mechanism, since my wingman stated the AAA burst was "close aboard" my aircraft. However, it never crossed my mind that the seat would function other than as advertised when the time came to use it. One half of the C-3 life vest is sufficient to keep afloat a pilot with full combat gear (.38 revolver, ammo, survival vest, RT-10 radio, etc.). The Koch fittings worked correctly after water entry. I merely unlocked them and the riser straps fell away. My .38 revolver and pencil flares, carried in a front pocket of my survival vest, were readily accessible although in the circumstances of my rescue they were not used. I retained my helmet with visor down throughout the incident until I was in the whaleboat. With the visor down, oxygen mask on, and chin strap cinched, I experienced no facial injuries or discomfort from wind blast, even though the canopy and part of the windscreen had been carried away by the frag.

I experienced no difficulties in doing essential things with only one arm, except for access to my morphine syrettes. I carried them in the left sleeve pocket of my flight suit and could not get at them. I recommend that morphine syrettes be carried in a more accessible one-handed location, possibly in a front pocket of the survival vest. I could not reach the life raft lanyard with my left hand after releasing the left rocket jet fitting and letting the seat pack fall to my right side. During my flight from the beach to the SAR DD, I thought of applying a tourniquet to my right arm stump. I had the nylon cord lanyard attached to my .38 revolver handy, but reasoned that the effort to untie it, get it around the stump, and secured (with one hand and my teeth, no doubt), coupled with flying the aircraft was a tenuous prospect at best. Some thought might be given to a simple, one-hand-operable tourniquet as an addition to combat survival gear. Not everyone will have his arm blown off, but there have been several pilot injuries in the Vietnam War where such a tourniquet would have been handy.

13

LT. JACK L. FRUIN—1949

It happened on August 9, 1949. Lt. Jack L. Fruin of VF-171 was on a routine training flight after picking up a new F2H Banshee at Cherry Point. Flying at thirty-eight thousand feet, Lt. Fruin, "Pappy" to his squadron mates, noticed a spot of frost forming inside his canopy. Soon, the entire inside of the canopy was covered with ice, some of it nearly an inch thick. The cockpit was nearly pitch black.

Pappy brought the Banshee down, thinking the warmer air would defrost the canopy, but suddenly, the rate-of-climb indicator began oscillating and quickly stopped altogether. Then, the whole instrument panel went crazy. Pappy guessed that ice had clogged the outside ports for the pitot-static instruments.

He knew he could keep his wings level, but he couldn't tell whether he was in a dive or climb. The Banshee began buffeting wildly, slamming him around the cockpit. The aircraft was approaching supersonic speed, outside the design limits for the straight-winged F2H.

The young pilot knew he was facing a critical decision: stay with the plane or use the newfangled ejection seat. Many of the first-generation jet aviators were reluctant to use the seat. The idea of being shot out of their warm comfortable cockpit was not appealing. In addition, Fruin's plane was fresh from the factory. He wasn't sure if the complicated ejection seat mechanism was even installed correctly.

As the plane's buffeting increased, he made his decision. He put his legs in the stirrups and pulled up the pre-ejection leg braces. Then he reached for the face curtain and pulled, triggering the catapult.

The next thing he knew he was hurtling out of the plane at nearly 600 mph. He knew he had to free-fall for quite a distance to get out of the rarified atmosphere before freezing to death or dying from lack of oxygen. The rip cord was next on his mind, but he couldn't find it. At fifteen thousand feet, with the ground rushing up at him, he finally found the cord dangling over his side.

With great effort, he yanked the cord with all his might, as the chute opened, jerking him back a few feet. Lt. Fruin floated into a swampy inlet, a few miles from the ocean. He inflated the life raft attached to the chute and climbed in. He then used his hands to paddle to within a hundred feet of the marshy ground and began calling for help.

Fortunately, his weak cries were heard by three boys in a rowboat who came to his rescue. They pulled the aviator into their boat and brought him to shore where they had their horses tied. While two rode for help, the third remained with Fruin. A cattle rancher came to his aid and drove him to a hospital twenty-two miles away.

Besides making the first operational use of an ejection seat in the United States, Lt. Fruin—who later retired as a captain—may also hold the record for the longest free fall.

14

LT. KEITH GALLAGHER—1991

Murphy's Law says, "Whatever can go wrong, will, and when you least expect it." (And, of course, we all know that Murphy was an aviator.) Murphy was correct beyond his wildest dreams in my case. Fortunately for me, however, he failed to follow through. On my twenty-sixth birthday I was blindsided by a piece of bad luck the size of Texas that should have killed me. Luckily, it was followed immediately by a whole slew of miracles that allowed me to be around for my twenty-seventh. Not even Murphy could have conceived of such a bizarre accident (many people still find it hard to believe), and the fact that I am here to write about it makes it that much more bizarre.

We were the overhead tanker, one third of the way through cruise, making circles in the sky. Although the tanker pattern can be pretty boring midway through the cycle, we were alert and maintaining a good lookout doctrine because our airwing had a midair less than a week before, and we did not want to repeat. We felt we were ready for "any" emergency: fire lights, hydraulic failures and fuel transfer problems. Bring 'em on! We were ready for them. After all, how much trouble can two JOs get in overhead the ship?

After my third fuel update call, we decided that the left outboard drop was going to require a little help in order to transfer. NATOPS recommends applying positive and negative G to force the valve open. As the pilot pulled the stick back I wondered how many times we would have to porpoise the nose of the plane before the valve opened. As he moved the stick forward, I felt the familiar sensation of negative "G," and then something strange happened: my head touched the canopy. For a brief moment I thought that I had failed to tighten my lap belts, but I knew that wasn't true. Before I could complete that thought, there was a loud bang, followed by wind, noise, disorientation and more wind, wind, wind. Confusion reigned in my mind as I was forced back against my seat, head against the headrest, arms out behind me, the wind roaring in my head, pounding against my body.

"Did the canopy blow off? Did I eject? Did my windscreen implode?" All of these questions occurred to me amidst the pandemonium in my mind and over my body. These questions were quickly answered, and replaced by a thousand more, as I looked down and saw a sight that I will never forget: the top of the canopy, close enough to touch, and through the canopy I could see the top of my pilot's helmet. It took a few moments for this image to sink into my suddenly overloaded brain. This was worse than I ever could have imagined—I was sitting on top of a flying A-6!

Pain, confusion, panic, fear and denial surged through my brain and body as a new development occurred to me: I couldn't breathe. My helmet and mask had ripped off my head, and without them, the full force of the wind was hitting me square in the face. It was like trying to drink through a fire hose. I couldn't seem to get a breath of air amidst the wind. My arms were dragging along behind me until I managed to pull both of them into my chest and hold them there. I tried to think for a second as I continued my attempts to breathe.

For some reason, it never occurred to me that my pilot would be trying to land. I just never thought about it. I finally decided that the only thing that I could do was eject. (What else could I do?) I grabbed the lower handle with both hands and pulled—it wouldn't budge. With a little more panic-induced strength I tried again, but to no avail. The handle was not going to move. I attempted to reach the upper handle but the wind prevented me from getting a hand on it. As a matter of fact, all that I could do was hold my arms into my chest. If either of them slid out into the wind stream, they immediately flailed out behind me, and that was definitely *not* good.

The wind had become physically and emotionally overwhelming. It pounded against my face and body like a huge wall of water that wouldn't stop. The roaring in my ears confused me, the pressure in my mouth prevented me from breathing, and the pounding on my eyes kept me from seeing. Time had lost all meaning. For all I knew, I could have been sitting there for seconds or for hours. I was suffocating, and I couldn't seem to get a breath. I wish I could say that my last thoughts were of my wife, but as I felt myself blacking out, all I said was, "I don't want to die."

Someone turned on the lights and I had a funny view of the front end of an A-6, with jagged Plexiglas where my half of the canopy was supposed to be. Looking down from the top of the jet, I was surprised to find the plane stopped on the flight deck with about hundred people looking up at me. (I guess I was surprised because I had expected to see the pearly gates and some dead relatives.) My first thought was that we had never taken off, that something had happened before the catapult. Then everything came flooding back into my brain—the wind, the noise, and the confusion. As my pilot spoke to me and the medical people swarmed all over me, I realized that I had survived, I was alive.

It didn't take me very long to realize that I was a very lucky man, but as I heard more details, I found out how lucky I was. For example, my parachute became entangled in the horizontal stabilizer tight enough to act as a shoulder harness for the trap, but not tight enough to bind the flight controls. If this had not happened, I would have been thrown into the jagged Plexiglas during the trap as my shoulder harness had been disconnected from the seat as the parachute deployed.

There are many other things that happened, or didn't happen, that allowed me to survive this mishap, some of them only inches away from disaster. These little things and an s-hot, level-headed pilot who reacted quickly and correctly are the reason that I am alive and flying today. Also, a generous helping of good old-fashioned Irish luck didn't hurt.

15

LT. KEITH GALLAGHER/
LT. MARK BADEN—1991

As we finished the brief, my BN (bombardier navigator—Lt. Keith Gallagher) told me that it was his birthday and that our recovery would be his 100th trap on the boat (the USS *Abraham Lincoln*). To top it off, we were assigned the plane with my name on the side.

As we taxied out of the chocks, I was still feeling a little uneasy about all the recent mishaps. To make myself feel better, I went through the "soft shot/engine failure on takeoff" EPs (emergency procedures), touching each switch or lever as I went through the steps.

"At least if something happens right off the bat, I'll be ready," I thought.

The first few minutes of the hop were busy. Concentrating on the package-check and consolidation, as well as trying to keep track of my initial customers, dispelled my uneasiness.

[NOTE: The KA-6D is a tanker version of the A-6 Intruder. A total of 90 KA-6Ds were produced by Grumman for the Navy by modifying existing Intruder airframes. To make the conversion, certain radar and bombing equipment is removed and replaced with an internal hose-and-reel refueling package, with the drogue fairing protruding from underneath the rear fuselage. The KA-6D retained a visual bombing capability (which was seldom exercised). The A-6 had a long and outstanding record of reliable service for the Navy from 1963 to 1997.]

AS we approached mid-cycle, that most boring time in a tanker hop, we kept ourselves occupied with fuel checks. We were keeping a close eye on one drop tank that had quit transferring with about a thousand pounds of fuel still inside. I had tried going to override on the tank pressurization, but that didn't seem to work.

My BN and I discussed the problem. We decided it was probably a stuck float valve. Perhaps some positive and negative G would fix it. We were at eight thousand feet, seven miles abeam the ship, heading aft. I clicked the altitude hold off and added some power to give us a little more G.

At 230 knots I pulled the stick back and got the plane five degrees nose up. Then I pushed the stick forward. I got about half a negative G, just enough to float me in the seat.

I heard a sharp bang and felt the cockpit instantly depressurize. The roar of the wind followed. I ducked instinctively and looked up at the canopy, expecting it to be partly open. Something was wrong. Instead of seeing a two- or three-inch gap, the canopy bow was flush with the front of the windscreen. My eyes tracked down to the canopy switch. It was up.

My scan continued right. Instead of meeting my BN's questioning glance, I saw a pair of legs at my eye level. The right side of the canopy was shattered. I followed the legs up and saw the rest of my BN's body out in the windblast. I watched as his head snapped down and then back up, and his helmet and oxygen mask disappeared. They didn't fly off; they just disappeared.

My mind went into fast forward. "What the hell happened?" I wondered. "I hope he ejects all the way. What am I going to do now? I need to slow down."

I jerked the throttles to idle and started the speed brakes out. Without stopping, I reached up, de-isolated, and threw the flap lever to the down position. I reached over and grabbed for the IFF selector switch and twisted it to EMER. I was screaming, "Slow down! Slow down!" to myself as I looked up at the airspeed indicator and gave another pull back on the throttles and speed brakes. The airspeed was passing 200 knots.

I had been looking back over my shoulder at my bombardier the whole time I was doing everything else. I felt a strange combination of fear, helplessness, and revulsion as I watched his body slam around in the windblast. After his helmet flew off, his face looked like the people who get sucked out into zero atmosphere in some of the more graphic movies. His eyes were being blasted open, his cheeks and lips were puffed out to an impossible size and the tendons in his neck looked like they were about to bust through his skin as he fought for his life.

At 200 knots I saw his arms pulled up in front of his face and he was clawing behind his head. For a moment, I thought he was going to manage to pull the handle and get clear of the plane. I was mentally cheering for him. His arms got yanked down by the blast and I cursed as I checked my radio selector switch to radio 1.

"Mayday, Mayday, this is 515. My BN has partially ejected. I need an emergency pull-forward!" The reply was an immediate, "Roger, switch button six." I switched freqs and said (or maybe yelled), "Boss (Air Officer), this is 515. My BN has partially ejected. I need an emergency pull-forward!"

I slapped the gear handle down and turned all my dumps on (in an effort to get slower, max trap never crossed my mind). The Boss came back in his ever-calm voice and said, "Bring it on in."

As I watched the indexers move from on-speed to a green chevron, I worked the nose to keep the plane as slow as possible and still flying. The plane was holding at around 160 knots and descending. My BN's legs were kicking, which gave me some comfort; he was not dead. But watching his head and body jerked around in the windblast, being literally beaten to death, made me ill.

I had been arcing around in my descent and was still at seven miles. The boss came up and asked if the BN was still with the aircraft. I think that I caused a few cases of nausea when I answered, "Only his legs are still inside the cockpit." It made sense to me, but more than a few people who were listening had visions of two legs and lots of blood and no body. Fortunately, the Boss understood what I meant.

As I turned in astern the boat, I called the Boss and told him I was six miles behind the boat. I asked how the deck was coming. He asked if I was setting myself up for a straight-in. I told him "Yes." He told me to continue.

It was then I noticed that my BN had quit kicking. A chill shot through my body and I looked back at him. What I saw scared me even more. His head was turned to the left and laying on his left shoulder. He was starting to turn gray. Maybe he had broken his neck and was dead. Bringing back a body that was a friend only minutes before was not a comfortable thought. I forced myself not to look at my bombardier after that.

The front windscreen started to fog up about four miles behind the boat. I cranked the defog all the way and was getting ready to unstrap my shoulder harness so I could wipe off the glass when it finally started clearing.

I saw the boat making a hard left turn. I made some disparaging remarks about the guys on the bridge as I rolled right to chase centerline. I heard CAG paddles (landing signal officer) come up on the radio. He told the captain he would take the winds and that he needed to steady up. My tension eased slightly as I saw mother begin to leave her wake in a straight line.

I was driving it in at about three hundred feet. I had been in a slight descent and wasn't willing to add enough power to climb back up to a normal straight-in altitude for fear I would have to accelerate and do more damage to my already battered BN. I watched the ball move up to red and then move slowly up toward the center. Paddles called for some rudder and told me not to go high. My scan went immediately to the 1-wire.

I had no intention of passing up any "perfectly good wires." I touched down short of the 1-wire and sucked the throttles to idle. The canopy shards directly in front of the BN's chest looked like a butcher's knife collection. I was very concerned that the deceleration of the trap was going to throw him into the jagged edge of the canopy.

I cringed when I didn't immediately feel the tug of the wire. I pulled the stick into my lap as paddles was calling for attitude. I got the nose gear off the deck and then felt the hook catch a wire. I breathed a sigh of relief. Testing the spool-up time of a pair of J-52s as I rolled off the end of the angle was not the way I wanted to end an already bad hop.

As soon as I stopped, I set the parking brake and a yellow shirt gave me the signal to kill my no. 2 engine. Immediately after that, I heard a call over the radio that I was chocked. I killed no. 1 and began unstrapping. As soon as I was free of my seat (I somehow remembered to safe it), I reached over and safed the BN's lower handle, undid his lower Koch fittings, and reached up to try to safe his upper handle.

As I was crawling up, I saw that his upper handle was already safed. I started to release his upper Koch fittings but decided they were holding him in and I didn't want him to fall against the razor-sharp Plexiglas on his side.

I got back on my side of the cockpit, held his left arm and hand, and waited for the medical people to arrive. I realized he still was alive when he said, "Am I on the flight deck?"

A wave of indescribable relief washed over me as I talked to him while the crash crew worked to truss him up and pull him out of the seat. Once he was clear of the plane, they towed me out of the landing area and parked me. A plane captain bumped the canopy open by hand far enough that I could squeeze out. I headed straight for medical without looking back at the plane.

Later, I found that ignorance can be bliss. I didn't know two things while I was flying. First, the BN's parachute had deployed and wrapped itself around the tail section of the plane. Second, the timing release mechanism had fired and released the BN from the seat. The only things keeping him in the plane were the parachute risers holding him against the back of the seat.

[NOTE: Lt. Mark Baden was awarded the Air Medal for his decisive action on that day. The LSO, LCdr. Mike Manazir, received the "Bug Roach Paddles Award" for his part in the recovery.

The crew of the *Lincoln* was recognized for a well-executed emergency pull-forward—Lt. Baden had the jet on deck about six minutes after the emergency began. The captain of the *Lincoln* would later read over the PA system a portion of a letter written by Michelle Gallagher (Lt. Gallagher's wife) where she thanked the crew of the *Lincoln* for saving her husband's life.]

RADM PAUL T. GILLCRIST—1966

In the Gillcrist household, 9 November 1966 began as did most workdays. The alarm rang at 0530, and I shut it off after the first ring. I had been lying there waiting for it to go off. This morning I was tired. I hadn't slept well. My left knee prevented me from lying in any other position but on my right side. However, my left hip had arthritis, which was beginning to give me some trouble. Also, my back began to hurt after about five hours in bed. The net result was the same each night—I usually slept for about four hours. After that, the night was spent changing positions every fifteen minutes. As a result, I do a lot of thinking at night.

On this particular morning in our quaint but modest home in La Jolla, the routine was just a little different. Nancy had driven up to San Francisco with our youngest child, Peter, the five-year-old, the day before. I got the three older children up, fed them their breakfast, and saw them off to school with the admonition, "Mrs. Linkletter [the babysitter] will be here when you get home tonight. Do as she says. I'm going to be night flying and won't be home till late." Little did I realize how late I would really be that night!

By now I was getting used to the scrambled eggs on the visor of my cap. I liked being a senior officer (a commander). I liked being the executive officer of a fleet fighter squadron, with the almost certainty of succeeding to its command in a year's time. Furthermore, I liked the fact that I was now a combat veteran, had been shot at, and had responded well. The air wing was getting ready to deploy on its next combat deployment on USS *Hancock* in a few months. Fighter Squadron 53 had done well during the workups and would deploy with not only a goodly percentage of seasoned combat pilots but, just as important, seasoned enlisted maintenance personnel.

It was with these good feelings that I sat down that evening in the ready room at NAS Miramar and briefed a rather unexciting night intercept training mission with one of those seasoned veterans, Lt. Randy Lanford, as my wingman. The night flight would be relatively simple. We would taxi out, take off singly, and go to our assigned stations in the offshore training area, and run broadcast control intercepts on each other. Each would take turns being the target and interceptor airplane until we reached bingo fuel. At that point the intercept in progress would be completed with a rendezvous, a two-plane (section) visual return to Miramar, and a final landing. It was not a difficult mission, but it was important because this was the final opportunity to practice this intercept mission before being given the competitive exercise by the air wing observer. Doing well in all of the competitive exercises is very important for a hard-charging, seasoned lieutenant. But for the squadron executive officer, it is essential. I had learned long ago that in naval aviation, one leads by example, not precept.

The departure from NAS Miramar was uneventful. It was a crystal clear, moonless night with plenty of starlight. As my F-8E climbed to the assigned altitude of forty thousand feet for the intercept, the stars kept getting brighter and brighter. Passing through twenty thousand feet, I was above 75 percent of the man-made pollution through which earthbound people view the heavens. The difference was always startling to me. The exquisite view of the heavens from a high altitude made me feet somehow disconnected from Earth.

As I passed through thirty-seven thousand feet, I noted Firefighter Two about twenty miles in trail, about five thousand feet below, and reporting his radar was good and that he beheld me in radar contact. I scanned the engine instruments and everything seemed normal. Directing my attention back to my own radarscope for a minute, I fine-tuned the radar in preparation for my turn as interceptor.

BANG! A tremendous compressor stall jolted the airplane. It sounded as loud as a 20mm shell exploding inside the cockpit. Quickly rescanning the engine instruments, I saw the exhaust gas temperature needle climbing toward the redline and the engine RPM needle unwinding. Then the lights went out and it got ominously silent. Damn! A goddamned flameout. Shutting down the throttle, I reached over in the dark and deftly pulled the ram air turbine handle as I banked the airplane gently toward the distant lights of the Los Angeles area. I flipped the generator switch to EMERGENCY, and the lights in the cockpit came back on. "Priorities," I told myself. "Fly this airplane first, talk later. Get the engine started. Get on best restart speed." I attempted several engine starts in primary, then shifted to emergency fuel control and tried again. My God, it's quiet in here, I thought. All I could hear was the steady chirping in my earphones, which told me that the engine igniters were firing, but the engine RPM needle never flickered. No dice!

"We'll keep trying, but now I better tell somebody I've got a problem. Keep flying it smoothly. Got to hold the best glide angle of attack. It's a long way to those white lights and that water is very cold." I kept talking to myself. I thought about the cold water. Without an exposure suit I would be good for about twenty minutes before becoming too numb to function well. Death would come fifteen or twenty minutes later.

"Mayday, Mayday. This is Firefighter Two Zero One." The calmness of my voice surprised me as I transmitted on the emergency frequency. "Seven-five miles on the two seven five radial of Miramar TACAN, at three-five-thousand feet with a flameout. Gliding toward El Toro area, unable to restart. Anticipate ejection when I get to ten thousand. Request any assistance for a water recovery near the coastline. Over."

The response was startlingly clear and immediate. "Roger, Firefighter, this is El Toro Tower. I have a helo in the air. Approach Control picked up your emergency squawk a few moments ago and has you in radar contact. Also there's a Navy Sierra Two in the area equipped with flares. Keep it coming. Over. "

Wow, I thought, that's what I call quick service. I figured that with my present load of fuel, the best lift-over-drag ratio would be fifteen units on the angle of attack gauge. It was giving me a glide speed of 215 knots as I passed through 25,000 feet. Quickly calculating, with a rate of descent of 2,700 feet a minute, I would have six or seven minutes more before I got to 10,000 feet. That's where the book says to jump out. But to hell with the book, I thought. Let's see where the coastline is by then, and the S-2 and the helo, for that matter.

There was one thing I was certain of—I didn't want to eject over land. The impact of a normal parachute descent would be disastrous. All the pins, wires, and screws in my legs would be reduced to a shambles, and I was fairly sure I would never walk again. I must land in the water.

"Firefighter One, this is Firefighter Two. I have you in sight. There are sparks coming out of your tailpipe. I recommend no more air start attempts. Over." Good old Randy. He was his usual competent self. He had apparently run an intercept and was closing from astern.

Descending through twenty thousand feet, I could see the lights of the Los Angeles area much more clearly and began to think I might make it to the beach. It was deathly quiet in the cockpit. There were no engine instruments to monitor. However, that emergency ram air turbine was turning in the airstream, providing electrical and hydraulic power to give me flight instruments to fly by, lights with which to see them, and power to the hydraulic flight control systems.

The S-2 aircraft had announced that it had my F-8's lights in sight, and so also did the helicopter. They were orbiting just off the coast near Newport Beach. Passing 15,000 feet, I sensed a fair degree of concern on the part of El Toro Approach Control about the 28,000 pounds of inert aluminum, steel, and fuel that was descending at 275 miles an hour toward one of the world's largest cities. As the airplane passed through 11,000 feet, I estimated that it was about three miles off the coast. I decided to make a right turn to a direction directly away from the coastline, and at a point about three miles off the beach, trimmed up at 250 knots and at about 8,000 feet, I would eject. "El Toro Approach Control, this is Firefighter One. I'm turning starboard, heading it out to sea, and will eject when I'm steadied up on one eight zero. Over."

The reply was immediate and the voice sounded relieved. "Firefighter One, this is El Toro Approach Control. Roger, call just before ejecting. Over."

I had about two minutes to get set. The airplane was all trimmed up for hands-off flight at 250 knots, just like the book said. I took off my kneeboard and set it up on the left corner of the instrument panel. Then I did something I knew was against the rule book—I disconnected the leg restraint garter on my left leg. The F-8E escape system includes ankle and lower-leg garters with a lanyard connecting them to the ejection seat. Their purpose was to forcefully pull the feet back to keep the bottom corner of the instrument panel from cutting off the toes of the boots as the ejection seat rose up the sails and cleared the fuselage of the airplane. My left knee wouldn't bend past about 95 degrees. Indeed, it had taken me sixteen months of agonizing physio- and mechano-therapy to get it to bend that far after three extensive knee operations to repair the damage done when I hit that plowed field near Cambridge, Maryland, seven years earlier. I had known that I would have to make a decision if faced with ejection. It was something the flight surgeons hadn't thought of. If they had considered it, I would never have been allowed to fly again. If the lanyard drew my lower legs back forcibly, the movement would tear everything loose in my left knee and I would probably never walk again. Better to lose my toes, I thought to myself as I disconnected the lanyard.

By this time I had rolled the airplane out on a heading of one-eight-zero degrees now heading directly away from the lights on the beach. Everything was black out in front of me. I thought about the cold water down there.

"El Toro Approach Control, this is Firefighter One. Steady up one eight zero, I am ejecting. Out." As I grabbed the face curtain handle and yanked down hard, I thought about what the babysitter would do when I didn't show up. Would I ever see my kids again? God-damn, here I am looking at the inside of this face curtain for a second time. There was a tremendous explosion as the Martin-Baker escape system fired the seat up the rails and out into the night.

I felt the impact of the seat on my spinal column and silently prayed that it wouldn't make my already-screwed-up back any worse. As the windblast hit me, I felt myself complete one forward tumble, and then there was the opening jolt of the parachute deploying. It was deathly still. The quietest place in the world is descending in a parachute over water at night. I raised my helmet visor and knew immediately that something was terribly wrong. The web of the parachute shroud lines was wrapped around my neck, helmet, and upper body. "Jesus Christ," I muttered, "I can't go into the water like this. I'll drown for sure." The history books of naval aviation are filled with the names of aviators who drowned by entanglement in the shroud lines that connect the parachute canopy to the pilot's shoulder harness. Although it was contrary to recommended procedure, I took off the helmet and threw it away. Then I got out my parachute shroud cutter, a switchblade jackknife with a razor-sharp hooked blade welded in the extended position just for this purpose. I cut one of the shroud lines wrapped around my neck and looked up to see what effect it had on the shape of the parachute canopy twenty feet above. I sure didn't want to cause the canopy to collapse, making me a "Roman candle" (parachuter name for a collapsed parachute, the result usually being death). Once seven years ago was enough in one lifetime.

My eyes widened in horror as I saw the ejection seat, all two hundred pounds of it, tangled in shroud lines about fifteen feet above my head. How the hell did that thing get up there? If it came down on my now-unprotected head when I hit the surface of the water, it would kill me. I also wondered what all this messed-up equipment was doing to my rate of descent. "Jesus, this is not a good day for me," I muttered. "What next?"

What was next was the life raft. Looking down, I saw that the lower half of my seat pan shell had not opened. It was supposed to open automatically, allowing the life raft to fall away about fifteen feet until the attaching lanyard came taut. The opening jerk was then supposed to inflate the one-man life raft. It didn't work. The seat pan lower shell was still attached to its upper half. Ready for this contingency, I pulled on the handle located on the upper shell of the seat pack. It still didn't open. Almost in a rage, I shouted out loud, "Goddamn it, what next?" Then I saw the reason. There was a parachute shroud line wrapped around the seat pack, keeping it shut. I grabbed the shroud cutter, pried the lower shell away from the upper, and the life raft tumbled out. It fell to the end of the lanyard and was jerked to a halt about fifteen feet below me, but there was no familiar hiss of the carbon dioxide bottle inflating the raft.

"I can't believe this!" I screamed. "Nothing at all is working right tonight." My throat was dry. There wasn't enough time to haul up the life raft pack and try to troubleshoot what was wrong with it in the dark. "Screw it," I said, "I've got to get set for water entry." I hoped there'd be some surface wind to carry the heavy ejection seat downwind, so it would hit the water behind my head, not on it.

I knew I had to get unsnapped from the shoulder harness as soon as my feet touched the surface of the water. It was important not to release the two shoulder snaps prior to actually touching the water. It is easy, under certain wind and sea conditions, for an aviator descending in a parachute to misjudge his height above the water by hundreds, even thousands, of feet. It was especially easy to make that miscalculation at night, I was taught. In actual fact, even with no moon and only starlight, I could tell precisely when I was going to hit, and I had each hand on a shoulder harness release snap as I did.

I was surprised how far below the surface I went. Coughing out a gulp of seawater that had gotten into my lungs as I surfaced, I found that the right shoulder harness hadn't released. I felt the first fluttering of panic stir in my stomach "Don't panic, keep cool, old buddy," I muttered to myself. "New priorities." The ejection seat was now fifteen or twenty feet below me and still connected to me at two points—the right shoulder harness and some shroud lines that I could feel wrapped around my right ankle. Oh God, I'm going down! I was being inexorably pulled below the surface.

Just before I went under, I took a deep breath, reached down, and pulled the two toggles on the flotation vest. The positive buoyancy it gave me was barely balanced by the weight of the ejection seat somewhere below. Kicking mightily with my free left foot and stroking with both hands, I got back to the surface, choking on seawater and gasping for air. With both hands I still couldn't release the right shoulder harness. In desperation I found the shroud cutter and in about ten mighty strokes cut through all four layers of nylon in the shoulder harness. I was now free on top but still attached to the parachute by the right ankle. There was a gentle two- or three-foot swell. Each time a swell went by, the parachute pulled me under the surface. Jesus, I'm not making it, I thought, visualizing my kids snug in their beds.

Clawing and kicking my way back to the surface, I took a deep breath of air and reached down with the shroud cutter, frantically slashing at the lines around my ankle. Until now the adrenaline had kept the fifty-two-degree water from numbing me, but my arms were beginning to feel like lead.

Suddenly, I became aware of a brilliant light. As I clawed my way back to the surface again, I saw that the S-2 had dropped a pattern of flares in the water around me. To my horror, one of the flares was drifting directly toward me. It was about three feet long and five inches in diameter, with a full twelve inches of it above the surface. The flare itself was a blinding white jet of flame about a foot high, making a roaring sound like a huge blowtorch. It was now about four feet away and drifting right toward my body. I kicked at it with my free left foot. My heel struck the underside of the flare, and the blowtorch tilted toward the toe of my boot. Just before I was yanked under the next swell, I caught a glimpse of smoke coming off the singed toe of my boot. Jesus Christ, I thought, still choking on seawater, I really don't need any more of this kind of help!

Finally I was able to cut away most of the shroud lines wrapped around my right ankle and was floating higher in the water, although still going under a little bit with each passing swell. I had kicked away the flare as it drifted by. I heard the sound of a motor and looking up saw a Navy rescue helicopter pass about fifty feet overhead. It was dragging a rescue horse collar in the water at about five miles an hour. It was just out of reach. Letting go of the shroud cutter, I reached into the pocket of the survival vest and pulled out a day-and-night signal flare. Maybe he can't see me, I thought.

I remembered being taught to use the day-and-night flare by feel. The night end of the flare had bumps on it. The water survival instructor had told us, "The end with the bumps is the night flare; the end without bumps is the day flare—orange smoke. Just remember, bumps make you think of tits at night." No naval aviator ever has any trouble remembering which end of the flare to use. I pulled the tab up, bent it over, and hit it with the heel of my hand, just like the instructor said. Then I yanked on the tab and it came away in my hand, but for some reason the flare didn't light. In utter frustration I threw away the useless thing and reached down the shroud line lanyard (on my vest) for the shroud cutter. I came up with the bitter end of the lanyard.

I must have accidentally cut the line itself, and when I let the shroud cutter go to grab for the flare, the cutter had begun its three thousand-foot descent to the floor of the Pacific Ocean. I was still being pulled underwater every fifteen seconds or so, so I dragged my survival knife out of its leather sheath and finished cutting the remaining shroud lines free from my ankle.

Heaving a tremendous sigh of relief, I found myself floating clear of the tops of the swells, but I had swallowed a lot of seawater and was getting terribly cold. Again, I heard the helicopter coming and saw the rescue horse collar skipping along the top of the water just out of reach in spite of my last-minute lunge at it. It suddenly dawned on me that the helicopter couldn't hover! It was a dark, moonless night with no horizon, and with no automatic hovering mode in his flight control system, he physically could not stay motionless over one particular spot in the ocean.

I drew out my thirty-eight-caliber revolver and loaded it with six flare rounds. "Next time he comes by," I said out loud, "I'm going to give him his first night over-water hovering lesson." As the helo approached, I judged the horse collar would pass about ten feet from me. This was probably my last chance. I realized that I had been in the water about twenty minutes and I couldn't feel anything below the waist. I was running out of time.

When the helo was nearly overhead I aimed at a point a few feet in front of the pilot's windscreen and fired all six tracer rounds as fast as I could pull the trigger. The helo came to a screeching halt, the horse collar stopped about ten feet away, and I took three or four frantic strokes, grabbing the horse collar just as it started to drift away again. There wasn't any way I could get into the collar properly because it was being pulled away from me, so I climbed into it backward, locked my arms together, then gave the crewmen the thumbs-up signal to hoist away.

About thirty feet above the water's surface I felt my whole weight slide to the bottom of the sling. My one arm was locked around the horse collar above the protective padding, and as my weight shifted, a swaged cable fitting ripped a two-inch gash into my bicep. I didn't even care. I was hanging on for dear life when I felt hands grab me and haul me into the cabin of the helicopter.

"How do you feel?" shouted the aircrewman as I sprawled exhausted on a bucket seat attached to the side of the helo.

"Okay," I replied hoarsely.

Nothing else could possibly go wrong, I thought to myself as the flight surgeon took my vital signs in the medical dispensary at Marine Corps Air Station, El Toro. I had just gone into shock, and despite the blanket wrapped around me, I was shaking violently and uncontrollably. The flight surgeon went to the medicine locker to get a shot of brandy.

He was gone for what seemed like an eternity. Finally, he came back to his shivering charge and very sheepishly admitted that he didn't have the right combination to the safe where the brandy was kept. Still shivering uncontrollably, I looked at him and said, "Hell, Doc, don't sweat it. Nothing else worked right tonight."

The ride back to Miramar in a Marine Corps sedan took about an hour. When I arrived at my office, still in my skivvy drawers and wrapped in a blanket, the CO had long since gone home for the night. I called the babysitter, apologized for being late, and told her I'd be home in twenty minutes. It was midnight when I walked the babysitter to her apartment behind our house. I took a long, hot shower, then sat down and poured myself a well-earned three fingers of good brandy. It was the perfect nightcap.

As the warmth of the brandy spread inside me, I examined my "go-to-hell" flying watch lying on the kitchen table. It was a cheap Timex I used for flying. Someone at the squadron had told me while I was getting back into uniform that I could save the water-soaked watch by putting it in the oven and steaming it dry for fifteen minutes at three hundred degrees Fahrenheit. I had just removed it from the oven. The crystal was made of plastic, however, and the heat had melted it onto the dial. It was now hard as rock, with the hands permanently set at 9:17. The clock on the instrument panel was the last thing I saw in the cockpit before pulling the face curtain—it said 9:17. Apparently the shock of ejection was too much for the watch. I chuckled to myself. "And I thought everything had gone wrong that could possibly go wrong." After kissing the three children good night as they slept blissfully unaware of the events of the evening, I thought to myself, I guess I don't know how lucky I really am.

AS a postscript to the events of the previous evening, Fighter Squadron 53's safety officer, LCdr. Bob Rice, walked into my office the following afternoon. He ceremoniously laid two things on my desk: an airplane eight-day clock and a pilot's kneeboard slightly charred. The clock was still ticking away. It seems that even though I had trimmed the stricken F-8E for hands-off flight and pointed it out to sea, the shock of the ejection must have disturbed that delicate balance. After I ejected, the El Toro Approach Control radar operator watched with growing horror as the airplane started a gentle right turn, flew a complete reversal of course, and touched down in an empty field alongside Leisure World, a row of houses near El Toro. The aircraft had burned, but the cockpit remained intact. My kneeboard was sitting exactly where I had stowed it just prior to ejecting.

17

WESLEY GISH—1956

In 1956, I was a Navy pilot with VF-33 at Oceana Naval Air Station. Shortly after my arrival, William "Bill" Mamby, our XO, was promoted to commander and given command of a new F7U squadron. Bill was a great guy and superb pilot. Before he left VF-33, he set an unofficial climb record in our FJ-3 Fury, 0 to 10,000 feet in 72.3 seconds. Later that year, Bill and his wingman were killed in F7Us near Chattanooga, Tennessee, when they encountered turbulence and the F7Us went into "the thing"—post-stall gyration—and crashed. [The force of these gyrations became infamous for another effect: the pilots could not raise their hands to their helmets to activate the ejection sequence, and many were lost as a result—Ed.]

Several Chance Vought pilots and naval aviators were killed by "the thing," during which the airplane flip-flopped and gyrated violently, totally unlike a normal stall. The hydraulic control systems in the F7U were notorious for their failure and resulted in many ejections. To make matters worse, the gun ports were in front of the engine intakes, and when the guns were fired, their gases flamed out the engines. The fourteen-foot nose gear sometimes failed on carrier landings and slammed the cockpit to the deck, causing a compression fracture of the pilot's spine. This injury was referred to as "the Cutlass back." I also saw an F7U crash shortly after takeoff at NAS Oceana. The pilot somehow escaped and was found by the crash crew running "like hell" back toward the runway.

The only thing that worked well on the F7Useless, as we called it, was the ejection seat.

18

MAJ. JAMES HALL—1965

"I've been kicked in the ass harder than that . . ."

—Jim Hall

Zero-Zero: just about the lowest point in the Ejection Envelope. Sitting on the ground, with the aircraft immobile. An emergency arises and you don't have time to hop out of the cockpit and run. What can you do? How do you know the seat will work? Will it launch you high enough for the parachute to open? Will you be injured by the force of the launch?

These questions led to a unique test. In the mid-1960s a firm that had made its name providing ejection seats and egress technology to both the military and to NASA decided that instrumented dummies did not provide all the information needed. They felt that certain questions of human physiology needed to be answered by a test of a live human. Weber Aircraft's seats had saved over five hundred lives by this time. They had been fitted to such varied craft as the F-106 and the Gemini Space capsule. The F-106 seat included the latest technologies available to allow for a clean ejection, including a gun-deployed parachute, rocket motor, and self-deploying survival equipment.

In late 1965, Jim Hall, a professional parachute safety instructor and major in the Air Force Reserve, volunteered to act as the human guinea pig for the 0-0 seat package. He was instructed in all facets of the seat operation. He viewed films of the forty-three sequential successful tests of the F-106 0-0 system. He also was measured for center of gravity in order to align the rocket exhaust with the center of mass of the man-seat package. In the tradition of the day, he visited the assembly line and selected the particular seat he would later ride.

The engineers checked and verified all functions of the particular seat. They selected a lake not far from the factory for the test. A set of seat rails were attached to a test stand. The date and time were selected. And then it was time.

Jim Hall, accompanied by a platoon of engineers, arrived at the site and was shown the seat. Now it was mounted on the rails, wired and ready to fire. Every mechanical function had been checked and double-checked. Major Hall was attired in an orange flight suit. Its arms were cut away at the shoulder to reveal a small area of skin that had been marked by pigment. He was strapped into his chute and assisted into the seat. All the straps were connected and tightened. The engineering cameras were armed to record every aspect of the test, even the slump of Jim's shoulder markings under launch acceleration. Then the engineers withdrew to a safe distance. The rescue launches on the lake were signaled, and the countdown began . . .

Major Hall gripped the handles built into the sides of the seat bucket and pulled them up to the firing position . . . and nothing happened . . . for one long second. The delay cartridge allowed the high-speed cameras to get to speed and then the hot gas was unleashed into the catapult initiator. The major rose up the rails with an onset rate of 150 G's/second with a maximum of about 14 G's. The rocket ignited as the seat cleared the rail, providing a huge jet of flame. One second and almost four hundred feet later, seat separation occurred. The parachute gun fired, and two seconds later the parachute was fully inflated. The survival kit automatically released and dropped to the end of its lanyard. The rubber raft, suspended from the same lanyard, immediately inflated.

Approximately twenty-six seconds after Major Hall pulled the handles he landed in the lake. A journey of only a few dozen yards had taken him to an altitude of about four hundred feet and into the history books (albeit only a few obscure ones). To this day, Jim Hall's zero-zero ejection test remains the only 0-0 test that was executed with a human subject in the United States by an American company. (The first known live 0-0 test was executed in 1961 by Martin-Baker Aircraft Co. Inc. Doddy Hay, an M-B employee, was the "Man in the Hot Seat" for that first test. There have been several other live tests, most of which have been at altitude, or with some airspeed.)

19

CAPT. RALPH HARRISON—1980

This ejection occurred at the end of a three-day local exercise. On returning for a full-stop landing, IFR recoveries were in process and I was cleared for a radar-vectored Ground Controlled Radar Approach (GCA). GCA called me one mile from the glide path and I lowered full flaps and increased fuel flow because of the extra drag, and then that's when the banging started, really loud clanging, banging. It didn't feel like explosions—more like as if someone was hitting the aircraft with a sledgehammer, and at the same time the CF-104 rolled violently left and right three or four times. There were about three to five bangs and with each bang the Starfighter rolled back and forth.

At the same time the warning panel lights and the master caution light would flash like a pinball machine, but the only one that stayed on was NUMBER 2 GENERATOR FAILED. With each bang the panel would light up and then go out but I couldn't catch up with it to see what lights were flashing, and that moment I declared an emergency. The engine instruments looked normal to me and no fire warning lights came on. Then almost immediately there was a tremendous explosion which really vibrated the aircraft and fumes entered the cockpit. I called GCA that I was ejecting. I would estimate the time from the start of the banging to ejection was between ten to fifteen seconds.

As I was IFR and in cloud I kept the 104 steady with my right hand and pulled the D-ring with the other hand. As the D-ring was travelling up I released the control stick and used both hands to continue pulling. The canopy blew off with a very loud bang and the shoulder straps pulled me back quite quickly. I saw the instrument panel and the canopy bow flash by and at the same time there was a very, very loud roar probably caused by the windblast and the rocket motor in the ejection seat. I felt I was tumbling backward. The roaring ceased and I remember thinking this is where the chute should open. I felt a gentle tug and I could see I had a good chute.

Almost immediately I came out of the clouds. I was sitting straight up and down with no oscillation of the chute. I would estimate I was about fifteen hundred feet above ground. At this time I was aware my knees were hurting and the flying suit was torn around the knees. I don't remember how I received these injuries. I was having difficulty in breathing and I realized the problem was my mask was still on, and then I removed it from my face. Knowing I would be landing soon, I released the seat pack, which is attached to the parachute and to the Mae West by a lanyard, and I felt a tug when the seat pack reached the end of the lanyard and deployed. But the line broke and I helplessly watched the pack fall to earth with the dingy opening. The wind started to drift me toward woods which were near a freshly ploughed field. I pulled on the back parachute lines, which set a drift away from the trees. About two hundred feet I started to go right toward that ploughed field. The drift was slow and I managed a soft landing. I released the chute right away. I laid there for a few minutes rubbing my knees until the pain went away.

By this time I was drawing a crowd. The aircraft explosions had alerted their attention to me. Two nice ladies found my seat pack and brought it to me but they didn't stick around. A gentleman from the local village came to me and put his hand on my shoulder, and in German told me I was going to be all right—but he didn't stay either. I think they were trying to tell me something. Then I realized I had on a shoulder holster with a pistol in it (the pistol was carried as a part of the exercise, but it was unloaded and the firing pin had been removed). Perhaps that's why they didn't want to keep me company! I opened the seat pack and found the emergency radio but the container for the radio had been bent on impact and I couldn't get it out. About fifteen minutes later a German ambulance arrived and took me to the base. I believe someone in the local village must have called for the ambulance. I ended up with contusion/abrasion to each knee, with a right chip fracture of the patella and a marked hemarthrosis. I had no other bruises, not even from the parachute straps. As for the cause of the accident, the Board of Inquiry found that during a routine check prior to 807's last flight a tech did not properly torque the fuel reference pressure line hose fitting which had been disconnected during this maintenance check.

As a result, due to aircraft vibration this fuel line fitting worked loose somewhere during the last phase of my flight and fuel pooled between the fuselage and engine. To give the Starfighter more lift on landing when full flaps are selected, hot compressed air from the last stage of the engine compressor is directed over the flaps. The temperature of this hot air is 900° Farenheit. When I lowered full flaps this hot air probably ignited the fuel/air mixture, which in turn ruptured other fuel lines. The explosion probably blew out the first fire but as other fuel lines were ruptured more explosions occurred and the fate of the aircraft was sealed. Witnesses on the ground who were directed to the Starfighter because of the explosions stated there was a large plume of fire at the tail end of the 104. The aircraft flew for another two nm where it flamed out due to fuel starvation and crashed in an open field. As for my injuries, they were caused by either coming in contact with the canopy bow or a collision with the seat during man/seat separation. The Board found that the D-ring cable should have been cut as soon as the ejection seat ejector straps functioned, but there was enough of a delay to cause a man/seat collision. In other words, I was still holding the D-ring when I was pushed out of the seat and then I could have swung around and made contact with it. (I still have the D-ring and it hangs on the wall in my computer room.) A modification to the timing of the D-ring cutting was ordered but I have no idea if it was actioned. Also modes were ordered for the seat pack lanyard and the container for the emergency radio. Again, I am not aware if this was done too.

20

CAPT. JOSEPH M. HARTER—1963

If you have the idea that accidents always happen to the other person, discard it. Accidents are no respecter of persons and when you are in an emergency situation which calls for bailing out of an aircraft you find this out the hard way.

At the time I had been sent TDY to Forbes Air Force Base for aircraft commander upgrading. With the usual ground school preparation completed I eagerly started the flying phase and found the first six missions to be very routine. On the seventh mission, however, the routine was left at home plate.

Our instructor, another student pilot, a crew chief and I took off on a refueling jaunt. We were proceeding to our refueling area when I noticed two amber power control unit lights glowing to my right, indicating a malfunction in the hydraulic boost of the ailerons. Believing the instructor pilot may have been "testing," as some have done, I asked him to check all circuit breakers. When he told me they were all in, I explained my trouble.

Our next step was to follow the Standard Operating Procedures and call the Command Post to advise them of our difficulties. Apparently, we were out of radio range as the Command Post could not be reached. We then contacted our tanker and asked them to call. Still no luck. We continued our mission and chased our tanker around cloud formations for a short while.

From the corner of my eye I noticed a red light come on that was beside one of the two amber lights. I notified the instructor pilot and we made an immediate disconnect from the tanker. The malfunction was not difficult to diagnose; it definitely meant a control problem that we could not remedy in the air. I relinquished control of the aircraft to the instructor pilot and received clearance from Kansas City to return to home plate, while the third pilot figured our optimum altitude to be thirty-five thousand feet. We realized we could not stay in the clear at this altitude because of a cirrus deck of clouds, but without a navigator aboard to operate our radar it was impossible for us to know that on the other side of the cirrus clouds was one of Kansas' typical thunder bumpers.

The aircraft started to vibrate from the turbulence. It became more violent—too violent for cirrus clouds! I stared at the instruments: altitude, about 35,000 feet; airspeed, oscillating between 220–240 knots; attitude, right turn, then a sharp left turn. I looked in the mirror that was focused on me. "Harter," I said, "remember, this type of situation always happens to the other person." I should have saved my breath. At this moment the instructor pilot was turning the aircraft to head back on our reciprocal course, and I realized that at any time we could lose complete control of our aircraft.

The turbulence became unbearable. I noticed the attitude indicator go crazy—90 degrees of bank, then 135 degrees of bank in the opposite direction. The instructor pilot was trying desperately to talk to Kansas City about our situation: "Kan—Kansas City, we're in a spin, we're in a spin!" In the same breath: "Bail out, bail out! . . . Depressurize! depressurize!"

I will never know how long I took to squeeze the trigger, but evidently not too long. The canopy departed and I followed. But to this day I do not remember squeezing the trigger. There was an unknown number of seconds that had departed my life, because I had blacked out during my ejection. I did not have the time to think out a decision when I regained consciousness; in fact I am still vague about the act of opening my own parachute.

The opening shock made me pass out again. After a few seconds I realized I did not pull my bailout oxygen bottle. Frantically I pulled at the green apple and managed to sever the line. With a significant sigh of relief I started to think about other problems, and found one quick: I had lost my helmet from the windblast so my oxygen bottle did not help. From my training I feared that soon I would get hypoxic since I had no idea of my altitude. Moments passed but I did not get the symptoms of passing out. I realized then that I was at least low enough not to suffer from hypoxia.

I was still trying to survey my situation but the numbness from the bitter cold dulled my senses. I wrapped a scarf around one hand in an effort to stop possible frostbite. The sky was filled with white swirling patches of clouds and thunder roared with deafening pitch around my bare head. The shroud lines of my parachute were snapping from updrafts and downdrafts. I was swinging like a pendulum on a grandfather clock, not knowing when I would stop oscillating. In between my thoughts I prayed like no man has ever prayed. Words came to my mind that I didn't know existed. I could only hope if God ever answered my prayers, please let it be now.

Soon I knew my prayers had been answered. For the first time since I hit the silk I knew I was descending. I finally broke through the overcast and calculated the ground to be three thousand feet below.

Now I was faced with further problems. Where am I going to touch down? The area was sparsely populated but the small towns passed by very rapidly. I was moving horizontally much faster than vertically. This situation made it extremely difficult to decide my impact with the ground. I tried to judge carefully, from my line of travel, the possible area of landing. Time was growing short. My descent was faster than I had judged it to be. My decision on possible areas of landing could not have been more undesirable if I had had time to judge them: a farmer's cattle drinking pond, or a small forest of irregular looking trees.

Frantically I tried to remember my survival training in how to juggle the parachute risers to land in a predetermined site. It didn't work, for I was too weak from fright and panic to manipulate my hands correctly. Due to the violent winds, the rate of descent became faster than the rate reckoned with in our training. I was suddenly submerged in smelly, stagnant water. After a few sickening swallows of water, I came to the surface. My parachute canopy was still billowed from the fast-moving wind. Gliding on the surface of the pond I reached for my harness quick-disconnect. Simultaneously the canopy deflated as it struck a wharf in the pond. Even though I was in shock, I distinctly remember spending fifteen minutes of hell under an orange and white canopy of silk.

My panic and fear very slowly began to subside. I was able to stand on my feet while I proceeded to unhook my harness. But because of my unstable legs, I fell down numerous times, again swallowing more stagnant water. I struggled breathlessly to reach the shore, falling, swallowing more water. Only ten steps were needed to reach the shore but I must have taken thirty. Lying exhausted, trying to regain my strength, I said another prayer of thanks.

With effort I managed to stand, but not too erect. I looked about my surroundings deciding which direction to travel. All I could see in the distance, silhouetted by brilliant flashes of lightning, were a few cattle. I remember hoping the herd did not include an angry bull, for in my weakened condition I could not have outrun a turtle. To my surprise I stumbled in the right direction, as I met a vehicle along a nearby dirt road. The occupant of the car had noticed my descent and had driven in my general direction. When we arrived at the hospital I was asked if I needed a wheelchair and I bravely uttered no. It wasn't until I was inside the hospital that the full impact of shock struck me. I began shaking so terribly that it took four people to undress me. I learned a short time later that the crew chief and I were the only survivors.

I am not necessarily a superstitious individual, but this accident happened on the 13th day of the month, at 1300 hours, and I was assigned Room 13 in the hospital. Another 13 and the men in the little white coats would be asking for me.

21

CAPT. **RICHARD HAUCK—1973**

I hope this thing doesn't blow up! I remember having that thought as my crew and I accelerated through Mach 16 aboard *Discovery*, 60 miles above the Atlantic.

Dick Covey, Dave Hilmers, Pinky Nelson, Mike Lounge and I were strapped into our seats, upside down, blasting downrange inside 150 tons of hardware. It was September 29, 1988—just 32 months after the loss of *Challenger*. Was I scared? Many years before, I'd flown a machine that had blown up underneath me. You bet I was scared. But I also knew that a certain amount of fear is good, maybe even necessary, for sharpening one's survival skills.

As a student at the Naval Test Pilot School in the early 1970s, I had a very disturbing dream one night—a nightmare, in fact. I dreamt that I was taking off in an A-4 Skyhawk. Right after takeoff the aircraft pitched up out of control, stalled, and plunged to Earth, where it exploded in a gigantic fireball. Even though I could see the billowing flames as if I were a bystander, I knew I was dead. I woke up suddenly, incredibly relieved to find myself safe in bed.

Lying there trying to get back to sleep, I remembered that I was on the flight schedule that morning—to fly an A-4 Skyhawk. I've never been a superstitious person, and I was determined to fly that flight. It wasn't a matter of being fearless—I'd simply learned to manage my fear by taking each additional risk incrementally. After carefully reviewing the test objectives and my emergency procedures, I headed out to the flight line. As I climbed into the cockpit I chuckled nervously to myself, eager to conquer the hobgoblins dancing around in my subconscious. Thankfully the flight was routine—not a flicker of a problem.

Unfortunately the test flight I flew on July 23, 1973, didn't have such a happy ending. The aircraft was an RA-5C Vigilante, a Navy photo reconnaissance aircraft capable of speeds up to Mach 2. The test objectives were simple: Verify the Vigi's response to commands sent by an automated carrier landing system on the ground. Shortly after takeoff from the Patuxent River Naval Air Station in Maryland, I climbed to twelve hundred feet and turned downwind to set myself up for a hands-off approach and landing. It was a hazy summer day with no definable horizon. Looking straight down, I could barely see the ripples on the surface of the Chesapeake Bay. Shortly after lowering the landing gear and flaps, I heard and felt an ominous *thrunk*. Several seconds later, my hair bristled as another shuddering sound shook the Vigi. Turning my attention back inside the cockpit, I saw a "RAMPS" warning light flash on, then off. This confused me, as that light indicated that the engine inlets were somehow out of configuration—and the ramps shouldn't even move when the aircraft is subsonic. Then the left engine RPM gauge started unwinding rapidly, signaling a flameout and loss of thrust from that engine. The situation was deteriorating rapidly!

Looking up, I saw that the Vigi's nose had pitched down dangerously, to about 20 degrees below the horizon. The water was racing toward me, and the surface waves were now alarmingly well defined. I grabbed the ejection handle next to my left thigh and pulled. Hurled upward by the rocket seat, the next thing I knew I was looking down at a fireball instead of water. I assumed the plane had exploded on impact. Later, an investigation of the wreckage showed that the airplane had already been on fire when it hit the water. In other words, I had ejected *after* the fuel tank exploded.

Yes, as *Discovery* accelerated into orbit, I was scared.

The obvious question is: Why do people take such risks, willingly exposing themselves to certain, palpable danger? It isn't just astronauts. You might ask the same question of firefighters, police officers, and combat troops. Most have doubts, and are well aware of the risks inherent in their jobs. In fact, intelligent people will extract themselves from these professions when they recognize that their personal risk/reward ratio has tilted too far in the "risky" direction.

I'm reminded of the story of the carrier pilot who found the stress of night carrier landings overwhelming. I can testify from my own experience that landing a jet on the deck of an aircraft carrier at night, in instrument conditions, is the most demanding piloting task I ever had to cope with. Even though I had my heart in my throat the first time I piloted a space shuttle to a dead-stick (un-powered) landing in November 1984, it was on a clear day, the surface winds were benign, and the two-and-a-half-mile-long runway that I could see from a hundred miles away didn't move an inch. That was tough, but it wasn't a night carrier landing.

Navy legend has it that on one inky night, approaching the ship, this particular pilot glanced out the left window and saw his wife and children sitting on the wing, staring at him with vacant eyes. Summoning all his courage, he focused intently on his instruments and brought his airplane down to the deck safely. Then he immediately strode down to his squadron commander's cabin and handed in his golden Navy wings. Rather than disparage this man as a quitter, I admire him for recognizing his limits. It's very likely that many aviators have died because they didn't have the courage to admit to themselves—and to their colleagues—that they had reached that personal boundary.

Back aboard *Discovery*, as the shuttle thundered into orbit, I was able to reject the awful speculation that would naturally spill out if I let it. At that point, we astronauts were along for the ride, with no real options other than to enjoy the thrill. I had launched twice before on the space shuttle, but was acutely aware of a key difference on this STS-26 flight. This time I couldn't take comfort in the fact that NASA had never lost a crew to an in-flight accident. *Challenger* was on all of our minds.

Still, I was convinced that this would be the safest shuttle flight ever, and had told my family so before the launch. NASA had spent the previous thirty-two months fixing not only the particular O-ring seal problem that caused the *Challenger* accident, but studying in minute detail other shuttle systems to minimize the likelihood that some other serious problem was lurking in the shadows. The agency's safety and quality control programs had been overhauled. Astronauts had been placed in key management positions to ensure that the crew's voice was heard throughout the decision process. And the shuttle's hardware and software had been re-verified.

For me anyway, there was a personal element to this sense of confidence. I was comforted that my good friend Dick Truly had painstakingly overseen the reconstruction process, and that Bob Crippen, who had commanded my first shuttle flight, was head of the flight readiness review panel that certified our mission as ready for flight just the day before. Tens of thousands of NASA and contractor employees had dedicated themselves to resurrecting the shuttle program. This *would* be the safest flight ever, or as safe as possible given the constraints of time and budget. At the same time, I knew that there's no such thing as perfection. Our safe return was not guaranteed. So, as we accelerated past Mach 16, I couldn't escape the reflection that this incredible machine was crafted by fallible humans. *I hope this thing doesn't blow up!* Just as quickly, I suppressed the thought—nothing to be done about it now anyway—and got back to monitoring the instruments.

That mission of *Discovery* was designed to be as benign as possible. Get up and back safely, proving that NASA was back in the spaceflight business. And so we did.

Now, in the wake of the *Columbia* tragedy, we once again hear the question: Is spaceflight worth the risk? I've been asked that several times since February 1, but I'm never quite certain what it means. What risk are we talking about? As a taxpayer who shoulders part of the financial burden of this grand enterprise, you should certainly get a vote on how the money is spent. But are you questioning whether I should risk my own life? My family has a right to weigh in on that—after all, they have a huge emotional, even financial, stake in my decision. But why should you get a vote? Please leave matters of risk up to the astronauts and their families. They've made their choice.

The families of the *Columbia* crew said it eloquently in a joint statement written under the most difficult of circumstances, just days after their tragic loss:

> "Although we grieve deeply, as do the families of Apollo 1 and *Challenger* before us, the bold exploration of space must go on. Once the root cause of this tragedy is found and corrected, the legacy of *Columbia* must carry on—for the benefit of our children and yours."

The authors of that statement are painfully aware that astronauts take risks. They also know the real rewards of participating in a great adventure, of advancing frontiers and serving one's country in the company of extraordinary colleagues. Only by taking such risks is society rewarded with increased knowledge and a sense of forward motion. And that, in the end, is what makes the risk worthwhile.

22

LT. NEIL P. JENNINGS—1995

September 20, 1995 was a standard day aboard the Navy aircraft carrier USS *Lincoln*, except for only one noteworthy exception. On that particular day we were headed eastbound, and we were on our way home from a six-month deployment to the Persian Gulf. We were about halfway through a transit that would take us back to our home base in San Diego. We had spent most of our deployment flying missions over Iraq in support of Operation Southern Watch, and we were finally on our way home to our waiting families.

It takes approximately six weeks for an aircraft carrier to travel from the Mideast to the West Coast. On the trip to the Mideast there is a lot of excitement and anticipation regarding the mission that you are on and the ports that you will see. In contrast, the trip home is marked by long days and sleepless nights, and much of the crew has "channel fever," longing to be home but not getting there quickly enough.

September 20 was a Wednesday, and the day began like any other day on the ship. I woke up at around the crack of ten, crawled out of the rack, showered, dressed, and then headed down the narrow passage to the ready room, where aircrew congregated in between training, working, and flying events.

On the flight schedule I was crewed with my Radar Intercept Officer (RIO), Lt. "Buga" Gusewelle. I enjoyed flying with Buga. He was a great officer and a great RIO, and he had a spark of enthusiasm that set him apart from the crowd. He loved flying the Tomcat, and that made me love flying it too. The deployment we were on was Buga's first and my third.

The flight schedule had us down for a 1400 brief and a 1600 launch. Our mission was to fly a ship's service hop in support of the USS *John Paul Jones* (*JPJ*). We would be flying a cruise missile profile, while simulating an attack on the *JPJ*. Neither Buga nor I were particularly interested in either the brief or the mission, because we were designated as the "spare" for the flight. This meant that we would not get airborne unless one of the "go birds" had a maintenance problem and was unable to launch. We had the less than enviable task of getting our aircraft ready to launch, but there was no assurance that we would get to go flying. Being the spare was usually a lot of work with no reward.

Buga and I met in the ready room just before 1400, checked the weather, looked at the list of divert fields, sat through a flight brief, compared notes, did a quick crew brief, and then had about ten minutes to take care of administrative tasks before we headed out the door.

A little after 1500 we left the ready room and stepped into the passageway where Maintenance Control was located. The maintenance chief handed us the Aircraft Discrepancy Book for Lion 112. We read through the binder of recent maintenance actions and noted that our jet had a marginal radar but that all the other systems were up and working. We left Maintenance Control, cut back through the ready room, and headed down a passage that took us to the Para Rigger Shop. We then suited up into our flight gear and headed outside. At around 1515 we arrived on the flight deck and walked aft, looking for our assigned F-14, Lion 112.

One hundred twelve was parked all the way aft on the starboard side of the flight deck, and it had been chained down at the edge of the deck with the tail hanging out over the water. Considering that we had been on cruise for five months, 112 still looked remarkably good. Our plane captain had taken pride in the aircraft, and he had worked hard to get the exterior of the jet clean. The flight deck is a greasy, grimy and crowded environment, and it takes extra effort to keep the jets looking good while they are continuously being used to fly missions. I was always glad to man-up a jet that looked as good as 112 did, because it gave me confidence that the jet was ready to go.

It was a beautiful day with great visibility and a thin cloud layer at around ten thousand feet. The temperature was quite bearable compared to the Persian Gulf that we had just recently left. It was only 87 degrees outside, not the normal 100 to 110 that we had become used to.

I didn't pay much attention to the preflight of the aircraft. When I got to my ejection seat, however, I inspected my Martin-Baker GRU-7A like it was the most important piece of equipment on the planet—which it pretty much was. For most of my career I had been in the habit of double- and triple-checking every cotter key, pin, fastener, nut, bolt, clip, and strap on the seat. Even though I was in the spare aircraft, I took my time making certain that my seat was ready to use, and it was.

We started the engines on our F-14 Tomcat, got the generators on line, powered up the systems, and completed the required checklists. We had just finished when we saw a "yellow shirt" heading in our direction, giving our plane captain the signal to remove the chocks and chains that held us firmly in place. Hey, maybe we were going to get to go flying after all.

All of a sudden there was a flurry of activity as our young plane captain and his two assistants pulled the chains off, kicked the chocks out from under the tires, and did a final visual check of 112 to make sure we were ready to taxi. Buga jumped on the radio and verified that Lt. "Haggis" Karger and Lt. "Smoke" Stinson were having problems with their F-14. The launch had already started, and airplanes were roaring off the catapults. Whatever issues they were having, there was no time to fix Haggis and Smoke's Tomcat before the launch would be complete. This meant that Buga and I were definitely getting into the air.

Any opportunity to go flying is relished. We were both psyched that we were taxiing to the catapult, because it meant that we were going to escape the floating gray prison that had been our home for the better part of half a year. Buga used the opportunity to poke fun at Haggis and Smoke on the radio, which was standard fare. It was to be expected when you went "down" and there was a spare ready to replace you.

Takeoff checklists complete, engines at full power, final checks done, afterburners lit, and I saluted the catapult officer. He completed his last look-over, touched the deck, pointed forward, and waited for the catapult to fire. Another catapult officer below the deck pushed a button on a console, steam pressure was ported through a complex launch system, and we were roaring down the catapult, going from 0 to 150 knots in two seconds.

The catapult shot takes your breath away. As the jet accelerates you get tunnel vision, and you feel a rush of adrenaline that cannot be described. It is both exhilarating and addicting, and there is nothing in the world that matches it.

Once we were clear of the flight deck I did a clearing turn, got the gear and flaps up, disengaged the afterburner, and leveled us off at five hundred feet. Compared to the helter-skelter world on the flight deck, being airborne was quiet and relaxing. The air was smooth, our jet was flying crisply, and we were lucky to be alive.

At seven mile we started our climbing left turn to eight thousand feet. We leveled off at assigned altitude, and I initiated a sharp left turn inbound to go find the ES-3 tanker that was waiting for us overhead the ship. We visually spotted the ES-3 at about seven miles and proceeded to rendezvous from the left side. The ES-3 was holding overhead the ship in a continuous left-hand turn, waiting to pass us the three thousand pounds of fuel that would give us enough gas to complete our mission.

A couple of our squadronmates in another F-14 had gotten to our tanker just before us, and we watched as they completed refueling. Lcdr. "Stash" Fristachi and Lt. "Stinkin" Cassole were in the only other F-14 airborne during our cycle, and they were assigned the same mission as we were. Within a few minutes they disconnected from the fuel hose and departed off the right side of our ES-3. The tanker pilot then gave us a signal that we were cleared to move aft and plug in.

Per the brief we were scheduled to get three thousand pounds of fuel from our tanker, which was enough to pump us back up to a full load of twenty thousand lbs. of fuel. It only took a few minutes to get our allocated gas. I then moved over to the right side of the tanker, the ES-3 pilot and I exchanged hand signals, we watched his fuel hose retract, and we departed off his right side and proceeded outbound. Buga checked us out with the USS *Lincoln* controllers as we proceeded on mission.

The crew of the USS *John Paul Jones* had recently upgraded their weapons system software, and our mission was to make several low and fast flights by the *JPJ* to allow them to check the functionality of their radar and weapons system. The *John Paul Jones* was only seventy miles from the *Lincoln*, and it didn't take us long to transit to our assigned holding fix, which was forty miles south of the ship at twenty thousand feet.

We caught sight of Stash and Stinkin and rendezvoused on them briefly. They had arrived at the holding fix a few minutes ahead of us. Buga checked us in with our controller, and shortly after that Stash and Stinkin departed the holding point, starting their first run on the *JPJ*. Our goal was to follow them in a ten-minute trail.

Within a few minutes we got a call on the radio to turn inbound to the *JPJ* and start our run. I pushed the nose of our F-14 over in a descent, unloaded the wings, and willed our fuel-heavy Tomcat to accelerate as quickly as it could.

At sea level the speed of sound is more than 600 knots. The *John Paul Jones* controller had asked us to do our flyby as fast and as low as we could go, and our goal was to arrive at the ship at 500 feet doing just over Mach. At 30 miles out we could see a small dot on the smooth ocean surface that was our target for the flyby. We continued to accelerate and descend, and somewhere around 10 miles we leveled off at 500 feet doing almost 600 knots indicated.

We got closer to the ship, and I briefly glanced in the mirrors on the canopy bow. I saw that a large vapor cloud covered the back half of our aircraft. At high speeds, and especially on humid days, it was not uncommon to see the "shock wave" that attached itself to the aircraft.

A couple of miles from the *John Paul Jones* we could see several dozen sailors standing in various places on the deck, waiting to watch us fly past. The *JPJ* had been at sea with us for the entire deployment, and their mission was to provide a defensive capability to the battle group through their AEGIS radar and SM-2 surface-to-air missiles. As we flew past the ship we could see the faces of some of the crew. They were excited to be getting their own personal air show.

The ship passed behind us, and I initiated an aggressive right-hand climbing turn that would carry us back up to our holding altitude. As I pulled the stick back and nudged it slightly right I set a little more than six G's for the climb.

As soon as I loaded the aircraft up with G there was a trouble-some "bang" and the jet rolled dramatically and uncontrollably left. Instinctively I countered the left roll by moving the stick right, but despite my best attempts we kept rolling hard left. In an instant it felt like the nose snapped downward in full left yaw, and I was certain we were headed down toward the water. My head banged hard off the canopy and all of a sudden time stood still.

In a span that was perhaps a few hundredths of a second the comfortable air-conditioned cockpit of our Navy fighter became foreign and hostile. I was confused about what had happened, and I was desperate to sort our situation out. I stared at the engine instruments and flight instruments, but the gauges held no usable information. In short, the instrument panel was a blank slate.

I attempted to regain control of our tumbling aircraft by centering up the stick and pulling the throttles back out of afterburner. I noticed fire off the right side of the aircraft, somewhere aft. I could not discern the horizon. There was no differentiation between sea and sky. Nothing made sense, and I was sure that we were not going to make it.

The next second and a half lasted for what felt like forty-five minutes. My mind accelerated to hyperspeed as I recalled experiences with my wife and children. My memories were vivid with scenes from home played out in incredible detail. I recalled countless random thoughts all the way back to my childhood. I had a deep sense of peace, and there was no fear. My thoughts of my family were of sadness for my young children, who I imagined growing up without a father.

Watching the canopy come off snapped me back to real time, and everything slowed down to normal speed. Less than two seconds had passed, but I had relived a lifetime of experiences.

The "ejection decision" is a topic that is often discussed by aircrew that ride on ejection seats when they fly. In the Navy ejection is a standard briefing item that is discussed during every flight brief. Most aircrew have similar decision points as to when they would reach down and pull the yellow and black handle; however, every aviator puts their own twist on when and why they would make the decision to get out. For better or worse, when an aircrew pulls an ejection handle, it sets off an unstoppable chain of events that guarantees that a sleek and beautiful aircraft will be turned into a pile of unrecognizable trash.

Sitting just eight feet behind me, Buga knew the situation was dire. There was fire in his cockpit, and he knew that regardless of the consequences we were going to have to give this jet back to the taxpayers and find another way home.

Right after the canopy came off, for an instant I thought, "Good on you, Buga." Even though I didn't think we could survive, I was proud of Buga for pulling the handle. The last time I had looked we were doing more than 600 knots, which was not good. It was generally known that high-speed ejections were deadly, and we were going way too fast to eject safely. It didn't matter. Our odds outside the aircraft were better than staying with it.

With our fighter turned into a convertible there was nothing more to do, so I let go of the stick and throttles. I crossed my arms, grabbing tightly on the webbing on either side of my survival vest, and I wondered if the windblast was going to hurt. I squinted through the hot fire that surrounded me, and I mentally prepared to ride my seat up the rails.

There was a bright flash as Buga's seat fired, and it suddenly became very hot where I was sitting.

A few hours after the crash Buga told me that he looked down as he punched out, and all he could see was the cockpit of the aircraft. The front part of our jet had broken off somewhere forward of the wings.

I didn't have long to contemplate the disadvantages sitting by myself in the middle of a gigantic fireball. My seat fired with a gigantic kick, and I rocketed up and away from the burning wreckage. Strangely, as I cleared the cockpit there was not even a wisp of wind. There was no windblast, no flailing limbs, no blunt force trauma, nothing.

I had barely accelerated away from the jet when I felt my seat fall away. My parachute then opened with an explosive force. I was incredulous that I was still alive. I had expected the worst, but by the grace of God I had survived.

The terminal velocity of a Martin-Baker ejection seat is around 180 knots. Something interesting happens when you are hurtling along at race-car speeds and then are rapidly decelerated to nearly a standstill. At that moment the straps on your parachute harness cause friction burns in all the places where they are close to your skin. Your flight suit offers very little protection as the heat is transmitted through the material. It's amazing to think that the friction created from just a couple of inches of strap movement is enough to cause burns that last several days.

Immediately after my parachute opened I saw a large splash in the water directly below me. I looked down and to my right and saw the burning wreckage of our F-14 Tomcat, as it spiraled down toward the water in a left-hand death roll. It was almost completely engulfed in flames. Panels were missing, I couldn't tell the top from the bottom, and what was left was nearly unrecognizable. Hanging in my parachute watching the scene unfold was surreal. It was like watching a movie.

I conducted a quick body-parts inventory and verified that all my toes and fingers still wiggled. I was thankful to have all the same pieces attached to me that I started the day with. As I coasted downward, I thanked God a hundred times. I also wondered what the salt water was going to feel like on my burned face and neck. I knew it was not going to be pleasant.

My next set of actions all mirrored what I was taught in Physiology: inflate the life preserver, connect the lobes, deploy the parachute four-line release, drop the raft, and locate the parachute release fittings. Initially I attempted to steer over toward Buga, but as I started turning toward him I became concerned that I might actually hit him. I gave up on trying to land near wherever Buga landed in the water, and I prepared for water entry.

I'm not sure what I was expecting, but when my feet hit the water I went at least three or four feet under. It was an uncomfortable feeling, but my life preserver popped me back up to the surface within a couple of seconds. My parachute fell into the water in front of me, and I never saw it again.

I retrieved my raft, which was attached to my seat pan via a lanyard. I climbed in and wondered if the warm water meant that there might be sharks nearby. I pulled my feet safely into my cramped raft, but then I thought that if a shark attacked me after I had just survived an aircraft crash, then it just wasn't my day. I put my feet bravely back into the 85-degree water and didn't think another thought about sharks. I was right about the salt water and the burns. My face and neck stung like hell.

As I sat in my raft, taking inventory of what had happened, the *John Paul Jones* was bearing down on my position at flank speed. I could see that I didn't have much time left in the water, so I removed my flare gun from my life vest and started firing off my pencil flares as quickly as I could get them loaded. I figured I would only have one chance in my lifetime to use some of the equipment that I had been lugging around, and I wanted to light off all of my pyrotechnic devices before I was rescued. Before I could get my last flare loaded a motor whaleboat from the *JPJ* was sitting next to me in the water, and strong hands were pulling me safely inside.

The boat crew gunned the engine and raced over to pick up Buga. I was happy to see that he was alive and looking good, except he was oddly holding his hands above his raft, showing that he had severely burned fingers. Apparently the fire was much more intense where he was sitting.

Within minutes the entire motor whaleboat was hoisted back aboard the *JPJ*, with me, Buga, and our three rescuers still in it. We had no training to prepare us for what was next, and from this point on we were just making it up as we went.

We were first directed to a small broom closet that had a sign on the door that announced that we had arrived at *JPJ*'s sick bay. Someone treated our burns with a white cream, and we chatted briefly with a few of the crew. The captain met us in his small sick bay, and he graciously presented us with two hats and two shirts that had *JPJ*'s logo on them. We were thrilled to receive a souvenir from our unannounced visit.

A couple of guys then led us down to the mess deck where we addressed a large number of the crew on a PA system that had been hastily set up for us. We thanked the crew for pulling us out of the water and apologized for dripping salt water on their clean decks. A couple of minutes into our visit with the crew we were told that our ride had arrived to take us back. What ride? I don't know what Buga was thinking, but I certainly wasn't ready to go back to the *Lincoln*. There was nothing good that was waiting for us back on our ship, and I wasn't in a hurry to get back there.

Our escorts had us practically running up to the aft flight deck, where an SH-60 was waiting with its engines running and its rotors turning. We were heading back to the floating gray prison we called home, and there was no way to get out of it. At least we were going to be able to get into some dry clothes.

During the twenty-minute transit back to the *Lincoln* our SH-60 pilots kept looking back at us with an odd glance, as if we were aliens from another planet. I'm not sure what they were thinking, except that maybe they were pissed we were dripping corrosive salt water on the deck of their clean passenger compartment floor. Or, maybe they were memorizing our faces so that they would be sure that we would find them in their next port so that we would buy them drinks. It is naval tradition to buy your rescue crew some kind of liquor after they pick you up, although I was not certain that this ride back to the gray behemoth qualified as a bona fide rescue. It would have been fun to have been hoisted out of the water by the helicopter crew, but someone else beat them to it and pulled us out first.

We arrived at the *Lincoln*, and the air boss directed our SH-60 Seahawk into starboard holding on the right side of the ship. Buga and I watched out the window while all the aircraft we had launched with landed. It felt odd to be the only guys in our group to come home without an airplane. As a consolation, at least we made it back on time. The military thrives on punctuality, and we returned promptly at our recovery time, even if we neglected to bring back our $36M fighter. It wasn't much, but it was all I had.

After the fixed wing aircraft recovered the air boss cleared our helicopter to land. We touched down, the doors flew open, and there were a dozen guys waiting for us. I saw two stretchers sitting on the flight deck, and I quickly made up my mind that I was going to walk down to the *Lincoln* sick bay on my own two legs, no matter what. A short argument with my commanding officer, Cdr. "Killer" Killian, ensued, and I embarrassingly loaded myself aboard one of the stretchers after he ordered me onto it for the third time. I tried not to notice as four relatively small guys struggled to carry me over to the bomb elevator, almost dropping the stretcher twice. In hindsight, riding the stretcher to the sick bay was the second most dangerous thing I did that day.

For the next two hours Buga and I were poked, prodded, X-rayed, checked out, and treated for our burns. About an hour into our medical check I got tired of smelling burnt hair, so I borrowed a pair of scissors from one of the corpsmen. I then snuck off to a nearby bathroom where it took less than two minutes to cut off what remained of my crispy moustache. The fire had also taken most of my eyelashes and eyebrows, but I didn't want to look any funnier than I already did so I left them intact.

In between medical tests my skipper led me to a side room where he handed me a phone. My wife Susie was on the other end. It was 3:00 A.M. in San Diego, and she had received "the call." I always told her that if she got the call it was good news, but if they showed up in an official Navy vehicle wearing their dress blue uniform it was bad. She was a seasoned Navy wife, and she was glad to get woken by phone. I downplayed my injuries, and we had a great conversation. Later she told me that she didn't sleep a wink the rest of the night.

As soon as the doctors finished their tests Buga and I were turned over to the Mishap Board, where the real fun began. Six officers had been assembled to serve on a board that would investigate every conceivable detail related to the loss of our fighter. A white-hot spotlight was firmly focused on our noggins, and there was nothing we could do but patiently work with them to get through a lengthy question-and-answer period.

One at a time Buga and I sat down at the far end of the long table and were grilled with countless questions about our flight, our personal lives, our families, our training, and just about everything you could think of. When you sign for your jet, take it out, and then neglect to bring home your multimillion-dollar government asset, there tend to be a lot of questions.

The day of the mishap the questioning went well past midnight, and it started back up again promptly at 0800 the next morning. The board was repetitive in their query. What did you see? Did you notice anything out of the ordinary? Was there anything strange about how the engines were running? How about the flight controls? Did you have any electrical issues? No matter how they rephrased them, the inquisition boiled down to the same set of questions that were asked over and over again. Personally, I didn't have a story to tell. One second we were flying along fat, dumb, and happy, and the next second we were tumbling out of control at more than 600 knots surrounded by fire. No matter how many times or ways they asked their questions, the answers were always the same. I didn't know what happened or why.

By the afternoon of the second day Buga was making friends with a few of the allegedly beautiful nurses at the Air Force Hospital in Guam. In contrast I was stuck on the ship getting a first-degree grilling from the Mishap Board. Considering Buga's burn injuries I definitely would not have elected to trade places with him.

By the afternoon of the third day the board decided that they had gotten everything out of me that they could. One of the board members, Lt. "Chuck" Norris took me to a room where a videotape of our crash was cued up and ready to watch. The tape had been recorded from the bow of the *John Paul Jones* by one of the *JPJ* crew members.

I never met the gent who recorded our crash, but I will be forever grateful for his excellent work with a camera. The video he took told a far more complete story about our mishap than either Buga or I could ever tell—even better, the video exonerated us from all responsibility for the unfortunate event. When Chuck played the tape for me, I was shocked by what I saw.

The videotape showed our fighter cruising along at the speed of sound, with a vapor cloud intermittently covering the back half of our aircraft. Just after we passed the *JPJ* our jet did a space shuttle *Challenger* imitation and exploded into a gigantic fireball. On the TV screen the fireball was about twenty times the size of the aircraft.

Less than a second after the detonation two distinct pieces of wreckage emerged out of the fireball, both engulfed in flames. In hindsight I believe that the larger piece was the main part of the aircraft and the smaller piece was the cockpit section that Buga and I were riding in.

After I viewed the videotape there were no more questions. Just like that, it was all over.

Two weeks later my burns had healed sufficiently enough for me to start flying again. A couple of months later Buga was back up in the air too.

FIVE months after the crash our squadron was in El Centro, CA, flying missions over the training ranges in California and Arizona. On one of the flights my new RIO and I were east of Yuma, turning eastbound in a right-hand turn at around 15,000 feet and 450 knots. As soon as I initiated the turn the nose of the aircraft dropped unexpectedly. I pulled back on the stick to counter the sudden movement, but the stick would not budge. I tried easing it slightly forward, but that only made things worse.

I quickly rolled wings level and started working to sort out the problem. Something was blocking the controls, and the stick would not move back past a certain point. Trim didn't help, and there were no other options with the flight controls. Nothing on the instrument panel indicated that there was anything wrong.

While watching the ground slowly get closer, I touched the lower ejection handle and felt the comfort of the black and yellow loop in my hand. I thought it was likely that I was going to have to eject again, but before I did that I decided that I would try pulling the stick back as hard as I could to see what would happen. At the limits of my strength something gave way, and the stick pulled through whatever obstruction had kept it from moving aft. It still felt stuck, but it rested slightly aft of where it was previously located, and we were no longer in a descent.

Using trim only, I flew our Tomcat back to El Centro, declared an emergency, and landed on the long runway. During a maintenance inspection of the flight controls a piece of rubber was found wedged in a pulley, right where a control cable was routed through one of the firewalls. That was close. I couldn't believe we nearly lost a jet thanks to a small piece of rubber.

A couple of months later I was mercifully assigned to NAS Lemoore to fly F/A-18 Hornets, where I served for ten years as a Strike-Fighter pilot. The Hornet is a beautiful jet with great flight systems and outstanding avionics. I never had a mission, in training or otherwise, where the F/A-18 gave me a reason to doubt that it would get me home.

During twenty years of flying fighters I stopped counting the number of jets that crashed and friends that died. By the time I finished my flying career I had personally watched three jets hit the ground, had been an On Scene Commander once, and had served on five mishap boards.

In the case of our Tomcat crash there was no definitive explanation as to what caused our jet to explode. The board blamed a faulty component in the engine oil system, but with the wreckage submerged in seventeen thousand feet of water, they never knew for certain. Personally I am at a loss to explain the event, but I am thankful that we made it back. I can't explain how we survived tumbling out of control at 600 knots in a fighter that broke apart, except to say that God was looking out for us that day.

23

LT. **MATTHEW P. KLEMISH–1994**

My name appeared in every major newspaper across the country in what was perhaps the most scrutinized mishap in naval aviation history. Yet, you may not know me. I was the RIO of Lion 103, the F-14 that lost its port engine on short final coming on board USS *Abraham Lincoln* in October 1994.

I don't want to rehash the ramifications or political fallout of that day. Instead, I want to recap the events to show why I am alive and to help someone else survive a similar situation.

We launched from NAS Miramar at 1400 and headed to W-291 for CQs. After we checked in and held in marshal for a half hour, it was time to push. The jet was operating perfectly, and we called in aircraft codes for up and up. We descended through an overcast layer at two thousand feet and pressed for the break as the wingman. We rolled out wide downwind and corrected with a cut toward the ship, which drove us to a slightly tight (1.0 nm) abeam position at 570 feet, 30 feet low. We agreed to extend off the 180, and I anticipated being a little wrapped up at the start.

We hit the 90 at 450 feet, 300 fpm VSI (Vertical Speed Indicator), and 147 KIAS, with a corresponding yellow donut for a Tomcat in a 30-degree bank, on-speed being 139 knots for our 54,000-pound fighter.

Approaching the 45, I glanced out at the barren flight deck and picked up a cresting high ball. I told my pilot, Lt. Kara Spears Hult-green, "We're a little low, eight knots fast."

We held VSI to 400 fpm as we crossed the wake. With approximately 30 degrees to go, I heard a single, barely audible pop behind me. I called the ball as we rolled into the groove with a centered ball.

Over the ICS, I reported "Five hundred (fpm), five (knots) fast." I scanned the ball, 500 fpm VSI, 140 KIAS, and said, "You're on speed."

A second later, I noticed we were 5 knots slow and told my pilot. My next scan revealed the ball centered, 10 knots slow. I urgently called, "We're 10 knots slow. Let's get some power on the jet."

The aircraft yawed aggressively and rolled left as we added power. Our descent rate increased dramatically as the bottoms of our seats dropped out. The carrier appeared at our one o'clock as we leveled our wings and the LSOs (Landing Signal Officers) called for the wave-off. Our descent continued, and I could tell that our flight path would carry us left and slightly below the flight deck. The LSOs called again for the wave-off, followed by several power calls.

The F-14 continued to yaw farther left as the right afterburner staged. The carrier had now drifted to the two o'clock position on the canopy, and our descent slowed. It felt like we would fly away. We were still descending, however, and as I looked at the ship—now at three o'clock—I decided that if we went below the deck, I would eject. At that moment, I felt an aggressive rolloff. I reached for the lower handle with my right hand and pulled.

At the time of the ejection, the aircraft was approximately 1 to 15 degrees nose up, in a 10-degree left bank. I was pulled back into my seat and watched as the canopy rails lit up. The canopy seemed to lift off very slowly and float away. I could see water on both sides of the canopy bow as the nose fell through 40 degrees, and we went through a 70-degree bank.

At 90 degrees angle of bank, my seat fired, and I felt a rapid forward-tumbling sensation. I heard the roar of the jet as I left the cockpit. With my head pinned forward, I looked between my legs as I tumbled over and over. The seat separated and drifted away, hitting me on the back of my right leg. A stream of gray material appeared between my legs and an instant later, it blossomed into a parachute. I snapped around and splashed into the water.

When I surfaced, my chute was dragging me by the right Koch fitting. The SEWARS (sea water activated release system) had failed to detonate. I released the Koch by hand and sank back underwater. My helmet, visor, and oxygen mask remained in place throughout the sequence, and my emergency oxygen worked. I tried to fully inflate my LPU by squeezing the lower lobes, but it didn't. (It turned out the LPU's spine had pinched, which kept air from getting to the upper lobes.)

The whole sequence seemed like a bad dream as I turned around and watched the carrier driving away. I saw a light blue area in the water where my F-14 had gone in. The drop tanks also marked the spot, having ripped off on impact. Two other Tomcats circled overhead for a couple of minutes before heading off into the distance.

I was slapped back to reality by a sharp jerk on my right leg. I reached down and felt the spaghetti of parachute line around my leg. Thoughts of water survival filled my head. I freed my right leg and began to scull away. I could see the chute's canopy in front of me. It was filling with water and starting its descent to the bottom. I felt sure I would not be accompanying it until another sharp jerk reminded me I had two legs.

This entanglement was more complicated than the first because several lines had become caught in my leg-restraint fitting. I was filled with urgency as I unwrapped the lines and threw them out in front of me. I sculled away until I couldn't see the chute, then I checked for more lines.

I looked back at the ship, wondering what would happen next, and reached for my raft release. Thoughts of opening my raft faded as the ship's SH-60 appeared. Minutes later, the helo was overhead and hoisted me out of the water. I was never so happy to fly in a helicopter.

It didn't occur to me that Lt. Hultgreen hadn't survived until I was in the helicopter, looking down at the water where our plane hit. A second helo hovered over the area searching in vain for her.

It's hard to decide to jettison an aircraft. No one wants to eject from a perfectly good plane. On the other hand, flight parameters change quickly, and the envelope for safe ejection can disappear in an instant.

Overconfidence can cause mishaps, but we had thoroughly briefed with the squadron LSOs and were anxiously anticipating the CQ. We thought we had covered all possible emergencies.

The Tomcat community talks a lot about single-engine procedures off the catapult, but rarely about losing an engine on final. The same rules apply: set 10-degrees pitch attitude not to exceed 14 units AOA. In the landing pattern, you are already above 14 units. Off the abeam, your descent rate may increase rapidly depending on how quickly you recognize the situation and add power. Use 17 units if you must, but no more.

It may seem unnatural to lower your nose toward the water, but you must keep the AOA and airspeed under control if you want to live.

24

LT. NEIL P. JENNINGS: KLEMISH/HULTGREEN INCIDENT—1994

Shortly after checking into VF-124 Gunfighters I joined a class that was in the process of completing their initial training in the F-14. The class consisted mostly of pilots who were new to the Tomcat. Interestingly, two of my classmates were the first two female pilots in the F-14. It was the post-Tailhook era, and the Navy had recently removed the barriers preventing women from being assigned to combat aircraft. The two ladies in this class went by the nicknames of "Flipper" and "Spock." Flipper was Lt. Kara Spears Hultgreen.

I took an immediate liking to Flipper. She was the better pilot of the two, but more important than that, she loved to fly, and she loved being a part of naval aviation. In spite of being saddled with the unenviable role of being the first female fighter pilot in the Navy, Flipper had that unmistakable fire in her eye and bounce in her step that marked her as one who would achieve great success. As I came to know her I recognized that Flipper was indistinguishable from any other aviator who wore a flight suit. She had talent, she had enthusiasm, and she fit in. Spock, however, was entirely another matter.

In July 1994 we completed carrier qualifications aboard the USS *Constellation*. Shortly after that the three of us checked into the VF-213 Black Lions. VF-213 had some of the best pilots and RIOs at Miramar, and they had the worst accident record in the history of the F-14. During my two-year tour with VF-213 that record would be sustained and lengthened. In two years we lost four aircraft and three aviators. It was a hideous tour, and our losses were devastating, both personally and professionally.

In October 1994 Flipper was assigned as my wingman, and I was excited to be in charge of a portion of her training. She was crewed with a young RIO that went by the name of "Shaggy"—Lt. Matthew Klemish. In my backseat I had a gent named "Bone." Shaggy and Bone were both in the middle of their first F-14 tour, and they were each stellar guys. They had great personalities and were very popular with their squadronmates.

On October 25 I led Flipper out to the USS *Lincoln* as our air wing began a four-week period at sea. We left Miramar early in the afternoon and proceeded to a holding point several dozen miles south of San Diego, where the *Lincoln* was stationed awaiting the arrival of its aircraft. Over the next two days more than forty aircraft would fly aboard the *Lincoln*, as we prepared for planned training exercises. Flipper and I were among the first aircraft scheduled to arrive.

We were assigned to hold twenty-two miles aft of the ship, as they prepared the flight deck to receive us. After a fifteen-minute delay we were signaled to turn inbound, commence our descent, and prepare to enter the landing pattern. A low overcast layer extended from eight hundred feet above the water to around two thousand feet. During our approach to the *Lincoln* Flipper and I entered the overcast and descended through it to get below the clouds. Flipper was on my right wing, flying close formation, and I was leading us through the required checkpoints for the type of approach we were assigned. This was going to be Flipper's first carrier landing in more than a month, and she was excited about the opportunity to hone her skills as a carrier pilot.

Ten miles aft of the ship we broke out beneath the ragged edge of the gray clouds that we had just descended through. They obscured the sky above us. It was early afternoon, and the sun provided occasional rays of light, peeking through a few holes in the clouds. Otherwise everything underneath was a shade of monochromatic gray. These were typical conditions for that time of year.

I brought Flipper into the "break" at 380 knots. The break is a 360-degree turning pattern, where you fly over the ship in the same direction that you land, then you initiate a hard left turn to reverse course back toward the landing area. As you are on "downwind," traveling the opposite direction of the ship, you lower the landing gear and flaps and slow the aircraft to landing speed. The ship passes off your left side, and you immediately commence a 180-degree descending turn to final. The last eighteen seconds of the approach are the most critical. During this phase you must work hard to ensure the aircraft is on glide path, on airspeed, and that line-up is squared away.

Carrier pilots aim for a spot in space that is around two feet high and plus or minus five feet wide. They are allowed less than two knots' deviation from target airspeed. They aim for this point in space while traveling more than 140 mph. As if this were not challenging enough, the ship is a constantly moving target. It turns, it speeds up, it slows down, and in rough seas it pitches, heaves, and rolls.

As we approached the break, Flipper and I continued a mile past the ship before I broke off and initiated a hard left turn toward the downwind. Flipper continued "upwind," delaying her turn for the seventeen seconds required to separate our aircraft for landing. This put her a mile and a half behind me on downwind and opened up a forty-five-second interval between our aircraft in the landing pattern. Forty-five seconds is the amount of time it takes the flight deck to clear an aircraft out of the landing area and reset the arresting gear.

I lost sight of Flipper behind me, as I commenced my break turn. I lowered the gear and flaps and completed a landing checklist. As I looked down at the *Lincoln*, I noted that the flight deck was empty, devoid of aircraft. Bone and I were going to be the first Tomcat to land aboard the *Lincoln* that day. We had our hook down and were ready for landing as we turned final and prepared for those critical final eighteen seconds.

Approximately ten seconds prior to touching down the landing signals officers (LSOs) turned on the flashing red lights and radioed for us to wave-off. The flight deck was not ready, and I pushed the throttles all the way forward and initiated a go-around. It was just as well with me. Flying is freedom and being stuck on the ship is like being on a floating gray prison. Our freedom had just been extended a few more precious minutes.

Landing signals officers are a necessary evil of carrier aviation. They stand on a small platform located near the aft end of the ship, and they closely watch and grade every single carrier landing. They are so critical to the process that if they are not back there on the platform, you are not allowed to land.

The best grade you can normally receive from an LSO is "OK." Everything else is a deviation of some sort and is a lesser grade. The LSOs will reward you with a "fair" or "no grade" if your approach is not nearly perfect. The grades the LSOs give out are displayed on a board in each of the ship's eight ready rooms. This board is called the "greenie board." Colored dots are lined up next to each pilot's name, allowing all to see how well they are doing in their landings, or not. There's tremendous pressure to do well in carrier landings, and the difference between the best pilot and the fifth-best pilot is often determined by a very thin margin. Comparisons between individuals and between squadrons are made daily, and everyone knows how well everyone else is doing.

When you're making your final approach to the ship the LSOs don't talk much on the radio. In some cases you radio to them your aircraft side number and your fuel state, to which they reply, "Roger ball." Otherwise, if and when the LSOs have to push the button on their mic and say something to you, it's only because you have deviated from a safe or smooth approach. When an LSO talks to you on the radio, it virtually guarantees you won't get an "OK" for that approach.

As I was directed to wave-off I continued upwind, spotted Flipper, looked to ensure there were no other aircraft nearby, and fell in behind Flipper and followed through the landing pattern. I passed directly abeam the ship and initiated a turn to final. That's when I heard the LSOs start talking to Flipper. It was a continuous stream of communication, and their voices were emphatic.

Bone and I focused solely on Flipper's jet as we watched it descend toward the water in a shallow left turn. It was not apparent she and Shaggy had lost their left engine and were rapidly running out of airspeed. Significantly, their aircraft did not appear to be leveling off. In an instant, and at an altitude of around fifty feet, their Tomcat rolled dramatically to the left. In slow motion I watched as the canopy explosively jettisoned. One ejection seat came out, rocketing away from the aircraft at an angle that was nearly parallel to the surface of the water. Less than half a second later the second seat fired at a 45-degree angle, directly down toward into the sea. At a terminal velocity of nearly 200 mph, the second seat skipped once off the water's surface and then disappeared beneath a wave. Simultaneously a parachute momentarily opened, and a small figure hit the water feet first with a full parachute canopy above them.

There's no training in the world that can prepare you for the emotional turmoil of losing a squadronmate. Even now, more than fifteen years later, it brings on a queasy, sickening feeling just to think about it. I admired Flipper as a person and liked her as a friend, and it was awful to lose her. Thank God for Shaggy's quick reaction. His life was spared by the thinnest of margins.

A week later I found myself assigned to an Aircraft Mishap Board whose purpose was to investigate the facts leading to the loss of an aircraft and a pilot, and to make recommendations to prevent similar events from ocurring in the future. It was difficult to relive the experience hundreds of times over and over again, as we played and replayed videotaped footage of the crash. As I watched the tape of the crash a thought kept coming back to me: "What was Flipper thinking in her final moments?" I wanted to know. I had to know. Was she scared? Optimistic? Resigned? Was she afraid? There was only one thing I knew for certain, and that was that Flipper was doing her darn best to fly that jet, all the way up until the point where she was ejected from the cockpit. She was no quitter, and I was sure she didn't give up, even to the end.

25

COL. RANDY LOVELACE—1943

As the war progressed, the special problems of military pilots facing the necessity of bailout at high altitudes received increasing attention. The dangers inherent in that endeavor—most obviously oxygen deprivation in the upper layers of the atmosphere—urgently demanded the attention of aeromedical researchers. Colonel Randy Lovelace, himself an outstanding physician, and his team at Wright Field soon designed prototype equipment that they thought would handle the problem.

However, their experimental gear—basically a small bailout cylinder containing an approximately twelve-minute supply of oxygen—clearly needed to be tested in the field. Though Dr. Lovelace had extensive experience in flying, he had never taken a parachute jump in his life. Nevertheless, he decided to take the first high-altitude leap himself, rather than assign the dubious honor to one of his subordinates.

On June 24 1943, he made his historic parachute leap, a jump which received extensive national press coverage, including pictures in *Life* and *Look* magazines. To demonstrate the dependability of the portable oxygen system developed by his laboratory, he dropped through the bomb bay of a B-17 laboring to hold 40,200 feet of altitude above the wheat fields of central Washington State. Garbed in a suit specially rigged by team members in Ohio, he wore a back-type parachute, which was attached to a static line in the aircraft, as well as a chest-type, fail-safe parachute.

The test protocol had been structured on the premise that there would be less shock if the chute were opened in thin, high air than if it were opened at a lower altitude. However, the opposite proved to be true. It was later estimated that Col. Lovelace experienced a force of 30 to 40 G's of pressure when the chute opened, with the jolt knocking him unconscious. As the chase plane watched in horror, he dangled like a pendulum bob, describing giant arcs through the air. After more than fifteen minutes of descent, during which he showed no signs of life, he roused at 8,000 feet, waved feebly to the chase plane, and finally landed hard in a field of wheat stubble.

Too weak to handle the chute properly, he tumbled and was dragged along the ground. For his landmark parachute jump, Col. Lovelace received the Distinguished Flying Cross from General Hap Arnold, and was then appointed chief of the Aero Medical Laboratory at Wright Field, a position he held for nearly three years.

26

MAJ. RAOUL LUFBERRY—1918

When the United States declared war, its armed services had fewer than four hundred aircraft. With a few thousand machines on order, the Air Service needed pilots to fly them and many times more mechanics to work on them. The famous race car driver Eddie Rickenbacker knew this, and talked to the Army about forming a pursuit squadron of racing drivers. Who else would be as comfortable under the stress of speed and as knowledgeable about mechanics? The Army turned him down.

"We don't believe that it would be wise for a pilot to have any knowledge of engines and mechanics," an officer told him. "Airplane engines are always breaking down, and a man who knew a great deal about engines would know if his engine wasn't functioning correctly and be hesitant about going into combat."

Rickenbacker joined up anyway. Of course he knew a lot about engines and was uneducated except in the school of hard knocks, so he was assigned to be a staff driver with the rank of sergeant and made it over to France in the same boat with Black Jack Pershing. Though the newspapers thought it made a good story to say he was Pershing's chauffeur, Rickenbacker made himself the favorite driver of Colonel Billy Mitchell, the head of the air service, who saw to it that Rick was transferred to work at the French flying school at Tours.

Seventeen days and twenty-five hours later, Rickenbacker became a pilot and a lieutenant, and was placed in charge of organizing the mechanical end of the advanced American flying school at Issoudun. There, on the sly, he learned to fly the French-built and American-bought Nieuports and trained himself to fly the more complex combat maneuvers like the tailspin.

"It was a good stunt to know, as in combat a plane in a tailspin is hard to hit," he said, and by constant practice he mastered it and the other important maneuvers originated by Pégoud. He had himself transferred to the gunnery school, where they rowed him out onto a lake and handed him a 30-caliber rifle and told him to shoot, standing, at a target in another boat. Once he got used to that they let him take up a Nieuport equipped with a machine gun and let him fire at a ten-foot-long sock towed behind a Caudron, and after he could hit that too, he was officially a combat pilot, so they had no choice but to assign him to the 94th Aero Pursuit Squadron, the first all-American squadron of the AEF. It was now March 1918.

The 94th was equipped with some twenty ratty old unarmed French Nieuports; on the side of each the men painted a hat tossed in a ring—the traditional symbol for accepting a challenge—only the hat was Uncle Sam's stovepipe. The squadron was led by Major John Huffer, formerly of the Lafayette Escadrille. Other seasoned Lafayette veterans fleshed out the staff, including Major Raoul Lufberry, who, with seventeen kills, was America's Ace of Aces. Like his German predecessor, Oswald Boeckle, Luf led the raw pilots into combat, showed them how to fly formation in a corkscrew path, and taught how to scan the skies for the enemy systematically.

Of all the new American pilots, Luf chose to initiate Rickenbacker to combat first. "All the boys tried to look as though they were not half mad with envy over my chance to get my head blown off first," Rick said. Then like Boeckle, Lufbury died in a freakish accident: with his ship going down in flames, he chose to jump instead of being roasted to death.

Of course, he had no parachute. No one except balloon observers and a few Germans were equipped with parachutes; the Allied commanders believed that having a parachute would only encourage pilots to abandon their machines when things got a little warm in battle.

27

RADM JOHN LYNCH—1937

Naval Air Station
San Diego, Cal.
8 Feb 1937

Dear Ma and Pa:

Despite the rain and floods they have had in California, I am still safe. From the papers one would imagine that conditions are pretty bad out here but outside of a few puddles around the streets I haven't noticed anything different. Of course Coronado and North Island wouldn't be affected by floods though good old San Diego was pretty wet last week. Some of the boys who went to San Diego on Saturday evening were stranded over there all night. Luckily I had gone to a cocktail party here in Coronado and was able to get back for a good night's sleep.

To get back to my career since I last wrote to you, I have quite a bit to tell. When I first got into aviation I said I would send back word of anything that happened to me and that is why I am telling you this story. Enclosed you will find a clipping that will give you a general outline of what happened, but to go into detail the story is somewhat as follows:

Thursday morning I was on a homing drill. This consists of making believe you are lost and trying to get back to your ship or station. To simulate this they have a truck go off into the hills someplace and send out radio signals. The purpose is to follow these signals and find where the truck is located. I did this without any trouble and, having a little time to waste, I started to put the plane through its paces. I had a great time for myself, doing all the stunts and got into some funny positions, and finally when trying to do two rolls at the top of a loop, the plane went into an outside spin. This had happened to me before but I always managed to get it out before it got wound up. This time it started spinning and despite all my efforts it wouldn't come out so when the ground loomed up pretty close, I released my safety belt and was catapulted out of the plane. In an inverted spin the plane is on its back and keeps twisting around with wings horizontal to the ground, so that when I opened the belt the force of gravity dropped me from the plane.

There was a quiet, peaceful sensation for a few seconds after I was pitched out; it was such a relief to be out of that twisting plane. Instead of having a sensation of falling, the impression I gained was that I was floating around in the air. This lasted until the jerk of my opening parachute took me out of my reverie. Dimly I remember reaching for the rip cord and throwing it far away. The ride in the chute was very nice though my only complaint was that just as I reached the stage where I was daring enough to start looking around to get my bearings, the ground rose up to meet me. I made an unusually gentle landing for a person of my size in a wild patch of sagebrush on the top of a huge knoll.

One of the fellows in my squadron, who had seen me jump, circled around where I landed and directed me to the nearest habitation. I never did see the plane again until the wrecking crew brought it back to the station. It was completely demolished. I gathered up my parachute and in my heavily fur-lined flying suit, I tramped about a mile and a half through the brush and some ploughed fields before I met a farmer who was coming out to investigate the accident. He had seen the jump and telephoned North Island before coming out. He informed me that there was an ambulance on the way to pick me up for they didn't know whether or not I was hurt. By the time we reached his house, there was an ambulance waiting for me so I rode home in style.

The accident happened about fifteen miles north of the Air Station. Of course there was quite a bit of excitement connected with the affair and the big question around the situation was to the effect "Why should a pilot have to bail out while on a homing drill?" I had to pay a visit to Captain Towers, chief of the Aircraft Battle Force, and explain all about it, but outside of a few words of caution nothing else was mentioned.

Now I am a member of the famous Caterpillar Club composed of those pilots whose lives have been saved by jumping in a parachute. They have an insignia which they give to all members. I expect to get mine in about a month or so. It is a small gold caterpillar with a ruby for an eye. I'll wear mine with pride.

Now after telling you all this I expect you to take the viewpoint that as long as I am willing to tell you of what happens don't have any undue fears and let your imaginations run wild.

Outside of that little adventure life has been pretty quiet. I went to a cocktail party at Captain Calhoun's house on Saturday evening and from there we went to the usual dance at the Coronado Hotel. I enjoyed myself very much so much so that I think I'll start my social life anew.

This week we go out to the *Saratoga*. Because of the shortage of airships I won't be flying aboard but I ought to get in a couple of hops. We will be in Coronado xxx over the weekend, go to sea again on Sunday night. Come in again on Friday and go out again late in the following week.

Well that's about all there is to say. I am still alive and kicking and getting plenty to eat. Don't do any worrying for I'll stay in my plane after this and take no chances on getting into a spot like that again.

Your loving son,
John

28

LT. LINDA MALONEY—1991

I was flying in the A-6 Intruder for about seven months when on a warm February 1991 day I was scheduled to fly an electronic attack aggressor flight with a senior pilot in the squadron. We were flying up to Jacksonville, FL, with another A-6. The flight would be a training exercise for the USS *Forrestal*, about 100 miles off the Florida coast. The pilot of my aircraft, who was the mission commander, briefed the flight for the two A-6s and all the emergency procedures, as is normal to do. After the mission brief, I walked down to the PR (parachute rigger) shop to inspect and put on my gear. The division that I led in the squadron included the PRs and after I said hello to them, I walked over to my locker to check out my flight gear. I *always* checked my radio and ensured it was working; that day, however, I was in a bit of a hurry and didn't preflight my radio as usual. The flight would actually take all day since we would do a couple of "runs" on the USS *Forrestal* and then fly into an Air Force base up near Tampa, FL to refuel.

We flew up the east coast along Florida's coastline and radioed the ship that we were ready to begin our simulated electronic attack. It was about 12:30 P.M. and we conducted the mission, then started to climb and head to the Air Force base to refuel. As we started our climb, the plane acted a little sluggish and the pilot looked a little concerned as he adjusted the controls. One of the hydraulic lights came on, indicating a hydraulic failure. I pulled out my PCL (pocket

checklist) and we started going through the emergency procedures. I radioed our wingman that we had an emergency and
needed to fly into Naval Air Station (NAS) Cecil Field to make an
arrested landing. The Air Force base did not have arrested landing
gear and NAS Cecil Field was just a short distance away. (Note:
Many Navy jet aircraft had a tailhook which can be lowered and
used to stop with arresting gear at the beginning of military air-
fields.) My pilot told the other aircraft to continue on, get fuel and
go out to make the afternoon mission. I radioed the air traffic controller that we were declaring an emergency and needed clearance
to Cecil Field for an arrested landing. We were flying at 15,000 feet
and 270 km when the aircraft started to slowly roll to the right.
More hydraulic lights illuminated as the pilot tried to steady the
airplane, but it was apparent that we had no control over the plane.
The pilot said, "I don't have control, Eject." I looked at him somewhat surprised and he repeated, "Eject!"

At that point I pulled the lower ejection handle and my seat
exploded through the canopy glass. My pilot ejected seconds
later. I lost consciousness briefly and when I came to, I was hanging in my parachute heading toward the ocean. I usually would
wear my contacts but that day I decided to wear the glasses I had
just bought. My helmet visor had ripped off during the force of
the ejection and my glasses were gone also. All I could see was the
ocean below me and the shoreline far in the distance. As I went
through my ejection IROK procedures (Inflate Life Preserver Unit,
Release raft, Options, release parachute Koch fittings upon water
entry), I was rapidly contemplating water entry and climbing into
the raft. Although it was February and Florida is generally warmer
than the rest of the country, the water was approximately 50 degrees. It was a sunny and very windy day and we ejected a little after
1 P.M. I did not see my pilot and wondered if he made it out of the
A-6. After I hit the water, I quickly climbed into my raft, inspected
my gear, lit off a few flares, and also released an orange dye marker
into the water. A P-3 Orion was enroute to Bermuda and the air
traffic controllers directed them on scene to try to find survivors.

I knew that they saw me because they were flying in a figure-eight and rocking their wings. It was within the same hour that I saw numerous helicopters in the air; one hovered above me and a Search and Rescue (SAR) swimmer was hoisted down into the water near my raft. The SAR swimmer, AW2 Steven Wishoff, approached my raft and asked if I was OK and when I said "Yes, I am" and gave a thumbs-up he was very surprised that I was a woman. Once I was hoisted up into the helicopter the SAR swimmer and I traded name tags, and I still have his name tag in my Navy scrapbook. Another helicopter picked up the pilot and we both were transported to the naval hospital at Naval Air Station Jacksonville, FL. We went through a battery of tests and X-rays. Neither of us had any serious injuries other than some minor cuts and very sore muscles. All of the knuckles on my hands were cut due to my not wearing my gloves. I had gotten into the habit of taking my gloves off once I got airborne and unfortunately my hands got cut and bruised up during the ejection. They were a bit swollen and sore for the next two weeks.

We spent the afternoon in the hospital and before we left we had to tape record the ejection events. It was determined, based on this interview and another one the next day, we were not responsible for the accident due to the aircraft having suffered a catastrophic hydraulic failure. The pilot and I both had minor injuries and were up flying again in a few weeks.

Unbeknownst to me I was the first woman to eject from the Martin-Baker ejection seat. Typically when guys eject from a Martin-Baker seat, they are presented with a tie. A company representative called me to let me know I would be presented with a Martin-Baker Pewter Pin designed just for me to commemorate the ejection. I also received a letter a few months later from the Martin-Baker Company inviting me to England to receive the pin during a visit from the Princess of Wales, Princess Diana. I was very excited to travel to England for this event but the Navy rejected the invitation because (I was told) they did not want to present any favoritism toward a company. My own opinion is that the ejection occurred during the ongoing debate regarding the combat exclusion law, which prohibited women from flying in combat, and that the Navy deemed it too sensitive of any issue to garner additional press about women aviators. Several months later I attended a gala event in Washington, DC that commemorated Martin-Baker ejection seats saving six thousand lives including the first woman.

29

CDR. NEIL MAY—1985

The seat rockets propelled him at a 60-degree angle-of-bank, blasting him over parked aircraft and into the blackness . . .

The memories from that night are the most vivid and frightening of my career. It was a cold, rainy night, dark as a sack of coal. The sea state was whatever number is bad on board USS *John F. Kennedy.* It was my first cruise. I was a fledgling LSO who had just relinquished the pickle when a Tomcat showed up, in the chute. He called the ball, and even though I was a novice, I could tell he was way high and lined up left. Calls were coming from the LSO. The aircraft passed the ramp coming down smoothly but with a tremendous left-to-right drift. Every LSO on the platform slowly turned in unison as the Tomcat passed.

We watched it land long, past the wires, in the glare of the waveoff lights. A KA-6 tanker was spotted on the crotch with a plane captain standing in the cockpit, wiping down the windscreen. The plane captain saw the Tomcat coming right for him and jumped to the flight deck as the tanker took the full impact of the Tomcat's right wing. Time stood still, and then progressed in super slow motion. Immediately I felt intense heat from a massive fireball and watched the plane captain outrun the leading edge of the inferno inches behind him. (I later learned he had broken both heels from the fall.)

I saw the RIO's seat fire at the end of the angle as the burning plane left the flight deck. The seat rockets propelled him at a sixty-degree angle of bank, blasting him over parked aircraft and into the blackness off the starboard side. The flaming Tomcat snap-rolled right off the angle and plummeted into the sea. I never saw the same brilliant flames from the pilot's ejection seat, so figured he was a goner. It was the first time I had ever seen someone apparently die.

At that moment, time seemed to take another turn, this time into fast motion. The OOD (officer on deck) on the bridge immediately turned the ship to use the relative wind to direct the flames away from the flight deck and marked the plane's crash site by ordering strobe lights into the water. The plane-guard helo began looking for the aircrew and reported that its hoist wasn't working, so the OOD radioed a plane-guard ship into position 500 yards on a relative bearing 180 from the strobes. The crash crew attacked the fireball, extinguishing the flames in less than thirty seconds—it was amazing to see them work so efficiently, dousing the huge flames. The 5MC loudly transmitted instructions to the flight deck personnel and the crash alarms were blaring. We got busy preparing to recover the remaining aircraft.

I looked down into the ocean, which should have been pitch black but instead was twinkling with strobe lights. I wondered if we had suffered mass casualties on the bow and if the strobe lights were from people who had been blown overboard from the explosions. I pulled out the spotlight stowed in the platform and scanned the huge swells. After a few cycles, I spotted a man waving at me—it was the RIO. I trained the spotlight on him, but he soon drifted out of range, waving at me as he faded to black. I radioed the helo and they began a hover over the general area.

The radios were alive with commands from the LSOs and tower while CATCC (Carrier Air Traffic Control Center) gave the "max conserve" call to the remaining airborne aircraft. Suddenly, the calls were interrupted by a faint voice over Guard, something like, "I'm cold, I'm cold. I'm OK, but I'm cold!" It was the voice of the Tomcat pilot! I was elated that he had survived, but given the water temperature, we knew he wouldn't last long. The folks on the bridge kept him talking on the radio in hopes of preventing him from giving up or blacking out. We had no idea where he could be in the multitude of strobe lights. The helo hovered over each light to find survivors. Once the fire was extinguished, the air boss ordered a quick, combat-FOD walk down while the crash-and-salvage crew cleared the big pieces of debris. Soon we were landing Tomcats, Prowlers, and Corsairs that were all low on gas. A remaining Tomcat had been sent to the tanker while the helo continued to look feverishly in the icy waters for the aircrew and others. After several minutes, the Boss reported the RIO had been plucked from the ocean by the plane-guard ship. He had drifted into its cargo nets. Soon, the helo crew found the pilot. The sea was so rough the SAR swimmer dared not jump in after the pilot, lest he become a victim himself. Instead, he elected to stay attached to the winch cable and try to snatch the pilot. We later learned each time the swimmer was dipped into the sea trying to reach the pilot, he absorbed thousands of volts of static electricity. The amperage was low enough not to be fatal, but the jolts were strong enough to make him convulse and lose control of his bowels.

Nevertheless, he pressed on to save the pilot. Finally, after several attempts and the helo well into its red-light fuel, the swimmer connected the pilot and began their ascent. Halfway up, the cable snapped, sending swimmer and pilot into the frigid waters below. The helo pilot, all the while lacking auto-hover trim, skillfully kept the helo overhead while his crew quickly made an emergency splice on the cable. It would be their last chance.

The helo pilot radioed that he had less than ten minutes of fuel remaining, and the frigid waters continued their deadly assault on the pilot. While the remaining aircraft finished landing, it became evident the pilot of the airborne Tomcat was having major problems getting into the refueling basket. After several more attempts, the word "uncle" was sounded, and the Boss called, "Rig the barricade!" on the 5MC. We gazed at one another, with mouths agape. We rigged the barricade, looked up the recovery numbers, and completed the nine-line brief. In the meantime, the helo finally snatched the swimmer and pilot to safety and hustled back to the carrier, landing on fumes. (The other plane-guard helo had gone down in the chocks.)

In preparation for landing, the Tomcat pilot pickled a bomb, and all was ready. We sensed we were getting the upper hand on the situation, and our confidence soared after the Tomcat pilot flew a flawless pass into the barricade—the first night Tomcat barricade in history. As the engines wound down on the entangled F-14, the flight deck became relatively quiet. The roar of cheers from below decks slowly replaced the roar from the jet engines. It was as if someone had scored the last second, game-winning Super Bowl touchdown (everyone had been watching the melee on the PLAT). The 19MC sounded once again with the friendly voice of the Boss. He warned us to standby to re-rig the barricade because the remaining aircraft, the tanker, was really low on gas (he had given his comfort fuel to his buds). CAG paddles recommended and received permission to lip-lock the Intruder pilot for one pass—a much safer proposition than flying into the barricade.

He flew a beautiful pass into an OK one-wire, and the recovery was over. The plane captain was being treated at medical; the RIO was drinking hot coffee on the small-boy; the fires had been extinguished; and the Tomcat pilot was in the infirmary getting better acquainted with Jesus. There had been no mass casualties on the flight deck, thanks to the quick reaction by the crash crewmen. The strobe lights I'd seen in the water were a result of wellmeaning attempts to mark the position of the aircrew. The pilot apparently ejected just forward of the bow and below flight-deck level at approximately 85 degrees angle of bank. A drag chute may have slowed him before he hit the water, but we never figured out how he had survived after ejecting so far out of the envelope. In just one recovery, we had executed procedures to handle a crash on the flight deck, mass casualties, fire on the flight deck, men overboard, search and rescues, and a barricade. I learned some major lessons about my chosen vocation that night:

The downed Tomcat crew nearly froze to death because they had opted not to wear exposure suits, which were extremely uncomfortable and cumbersome.

Given the pilot's performance on the pass that produced the crash, perhaps the wave-off lights should have come on at the start or in the middle. Throwing extra strobes into the water slowed the SAR helo's ability to quickly find the downed aircrew. SOP, a great job by the guys on the bridge and in the plane-guard ship, and the unwavering efforts of the helo crew helped save lives that night.

The only real injuries were the plane captain's heels and a hairline fracture to the Tomcat pilot's leg. A Tomcat and a tanker were destroyed, the cost of learning to do business better. That night, I went belowdecks feeling extremely proud of my shipmates and air wing for having done so well. Today, I smile and recollect that night every time I hear a shipmate bellyache about being nabbed to man a fire hose, parade to the ready room for man-overboard muster, suck rubber during GQ, or help rig the barricade.

Drills, drills, drills. Maybe no one on their death bed ever wished they'd spent more time at the office. But I guarantee that no aviator who has ever had an emergency ever wished they had done fewer drills.

30

GEN. MERRILL ANTHONY MCPEAK—1967

Fright is only the percussion cap of fear. It snaps rather than rumbles and its explosion is instantaneous . . . It hits, explodes, and may be gone as quickly, if it does not have time to ignite the keg of fear.

—Ernest K. Gann, *Fate Is the Hunter*

Del Rio could be the movie set of a West Texas border town. It's windy, here. The weather tends to extremes in winter and summer. The base, located six miles east of town, is named after 1st Lt. Jack Thomas Laughlin, a B-17 pilot and Del Rio native killed over Java within a few weeks of the Japanese attack on Pearl Harbor. Land is cheap, so the acreage is extensive. It's fairly level ground, desert sage, scrub brush. Elevation 1,082. It's a pilot training base, like the one I attended at Enid, Oklahoma. The Team flies in on October 20, 1967, for an air show the next day, honoring sixty or so lieutenants who are graduating.

We go through the standard pre-show routine. Lead and Five do their show line survey. The rest of us make the usual round of hospital and school visits, radio or print media interviews. We pick up rental cars and head to a motel off base. There's a dinner the night before. Lead cracks the same jokes about each of us and the audience chuckles, while we pretend the lines are not so stale. Next day, proud parents watch as new pilots pin on wings.

We brief at noon in the Flight Safety Conference Room at Base Operations. As usual, an "Inspection Team" comprised of base and local dignitaries join us for a photo session before we step to the jets. The film *Bandolero!* is in production at a location near the base. Its stars, Jimmy Stewart and Raquel Welch, show up in the Inspection Team and catch the crowd's attention. Jimmy Stewart is a reserve brigadier general, a founder of the Air Force Association, a big hero to all of us. Raquel Welch is—well, she's Raquel Welch.

Engine start is at 1420. We're wearing white show suits for this one. Lead can choose from among gray, blue, black or white, my least favorite. We look like Good Humor Men. In addition, I work hard during the demonstration and sweat soaks my collar circumference. This wouldn't matter much, except we do a lot of taxiing in trail. With only six feet spacing between the end of my pitot boom and Bobby Beckel's afterburner eyelids, I take a load of engine exhaust in my cockpit. Wearing the mask and using 100 percent oxygen keeps me comfortable, but soot clings to the dampness, leaving a very noticeable "ring around the collar" when I wear white. At Del Rio, I follow my usual practice and roll the collar under, once we have taxied out of sight. After the show, as we deplane, I'll roll it back out again, the chimney black still there, but now underneath, out of sight.

We taxi short of the runway for a "quick check." A couple of our NCOs do a pre-takeoff inspection, checking everything they can see. My aircraft, F-100D, serial number 55-3520, good old Number 6, is inspected and cleared for flight. We take the runway, the Diamond in fingertip and Bobby and I in element, 500 feet back.

The Diamond releases brakes at precisely 1430. Bobby and I run up engines, my stomach tightening against the surge of isolation and exhilaration that comes before every takeoff. Weather is clear and 25, temperature 73, wind 140 at 12, gusting 17.

By this time in the season, the Team is really clicking. We have a lot of shows under our belt and know what we are doing. Today is a super day, the show line a nice long runway with uncluttered approaches. Maybe the wind is not perfect. We would like about 5 knots, please, enough to blow smoke off the show line and not so much as to require adjustment in the maneuvers or make the air bumpy.

Twenty-one minutes into the show, it's going great, has a good cadence and rhythm, the script on automatic, most of the important information packed into silences between radio calls. We approach the climax of the demonstration, the signature Bomb Burst. I'm by now very experienced at putting on pigtails. I can judge the timing pretty well and get the rolls truly vertical. I'm doing lots of rolls, getting closer to Bobby's claimed all-time record 13 (yeah, right!). My crew chief, C. D. James, keeps count. If I ever get near 13, he'll make sure we got the credit.

Doing even a few vertical rolls requires that you establish a perfect vertical up line; doing more than a few means you must, in addition, begin the rolls with a ton of airspeed. I grab for altitude while Beckel entertains the crowd with his Wing Walk. I want to put at least seventeen thousand feet in the bank, more if I can get it. But I'm out in front of the audience, lagging the Diamond, and don't want to be noticed until I pop through their smoke. I sort of tiptoe up to altitude, using military power. The Narrator helps by drawing the crowd's attention to the Diamond as it pirouettes into the entry for the Bomb Burst.

At what I judge to be just the right moment, I hustle after them, roughly following their track over the ground, but keeping their smoke between me and the crowd. Airspeed builds rapidly. One thing I have to be mindful of is the rule that you don't go supersonic during an air show. The Thunderbirds transitioned to the F-100 in 1956, making us the world's first supersonic flying team. The next year, 1957, the FAA got even by banning public demonstrations involving supersonic flight. No booming the crowd. So, I want to be subsonic, but just barely—say, .99 Mach. Approaching the pull, I light the burner and activate the smoke switch, holding airspeed just at the edge of the Mach. At the bottom of the entry, I start up into the vertical. We don't have a Solo Pilot's Handbook, but if we did it would say this is a 6½-G pull.

The biggest mistake I can make is to be early. The Diamond is about to break in all four directions so if I misjudge and get there too soon, there's really nowhere for me to go. (In a pinch, I'll call the break, rather than wait for Lead to do it.) If I get it right, I'll hit the apex of the Bomb Burst five seconds after the Diamond separates, snap the throttle out of burner so as to make smoke, be perfectly vertical, and be going very fast. As the Diamond pilots track away from one another to four compass points, I'll put on those lazy, lovely pigtails, after which I better get the smoke off and figure out how to do a slow-speed vertical recovery. Nominally, I should stop rolling at 150 knots indicated so as to have at least a little control authority with which to point the nose, but just recently, as my confidence has blossomed, I'm staying in the maneuver and getting the last ounce of roll out of the airplane, making for some interesting recoveries. Oh, well, no guts, no glory.

But this one does not turn out right. On the afternoon of October 21, 1967, at Del Rio, Texas, I start an aggressive pull into the vertical . . . and the aircraft explodes.

F-100 pilots are accustomed to loud noises. Even in the best of circumstances, the afterburner can bang pretty hard when it lights off. Engine compressor stall is fairly common, usually moderate and of short duration, but sometimes more severe. Especially when the aircraft is loaded up during maneuvering, a violent cough of rejected air can be forced back up the intake. Flame belches out the nose, which will wake you up at night. The shock can kick your feet off the rudder pedals. Any F-100 pilot who hears a real loud "BANG!" automatically thinks, "compressor stall," and unloads the jet to get air traveling back down the intake as smoothly as possible.

So, I instinctively relax stick pressure to unload the airplane. I am by now fully into one of those fast-forward exercises where seasons compress into seconds, the leaves changing color while you watch. I move the stick forward lethargically; even have time to think, "That's no compressor stall."

In retrospect, the airplane has already unloaded itself, making my home remedy superfluous, but there is some antique pilot lore at work here: *No matter what else happens, fly the airplane.* Forget all that stuff about lift and drag and thrust and gravity, just fly the damn

Rick Hauck stands beside his battered ejection seat.
(Courtesy U.S. Navy)

Pete Purvis's
F-14 missile goes
lethally astray.
(Courtesy U.S. Navy)

Jim Hall ground
tests a rocket-fired
seat. *(Courtesy Weber
Aircraft)*

Dick Rutan and the Misty pilots celebrate.
(Courtesy Dick Rutan)

Scott Thomas (top row, second from left) and rescue crew.
(Courtesy Scott Thomas)

Keith Gallagher partial ejection 1. *(Courtesy U.S. Navy)*

Keith Gallagher partial ejection 2. *(Courtesy U.S. Navy)*

Linda Maloney before the incident. *(Courtesy Linda Heid Maloney)*

A bruised Linda Maloney describes her ejection.
(Courtesy Linda Heid Maloney)

Jon Kryway ejection sequence.
(Courtesy U.S. Navy)

1.

2.

3.

4.

5.

RAF safety warning poster. *(Courtesy Royal Air Force, United Kingdom)*

A Navy pilot test-fires an ejection-seat dummy. *(Courtesy U.S. Navy)*

Thunderbirds solo Chris Stricklin.
(Courtesy U.S. Air Force)

A Navy warning sign.
(Courtesy Kevin Coyne, The Ejection Site/U.S. Navy)

airplane until impact, then fly the pieces as deep as you can into the wreckage. Old 55-3520 has quit flying but I haven't, just yet.

But it doesn't matter much because now flames fill the cockpit. Alone among animals we have mastered fire, but it's an uneasy conquest. No decision to make—have to get out. Grab the seat handles; tug them up, jettisoning the canopy and exposing ejection triggers on each side of the armrest. Yank the triggers and immediately feel the seat catapult into the slipstream. Seat separation is automatic and too fast to track, explosive squibs firing to unlock the seat belt and shoulder harness. The seat disappears. Quickly curl into the semi-fetal posture used to absorb opening shock. Jump school helps here; I congratulate myself on perfect body position. For one elongated moment, I imagine how proud they'd be at Ft. Benning.

Then the chute snaps open much too quickly, jolting me back to real time and short-circuiting the transition from stark terror to giddy elation, the evil Siamese twins of parachute jumping. My helmet is missing. Now, where did *that* go? Look up. A couple of panels torn loose, several shroud lines broken, one large rip in the crown of the canopy. I'll come down a bit quicker than necessary. Not much altitude anyway. Going to land in the infield, near show center. Have to figure out the wind, get the chute collapsed fast so as not to be dragged. Heck! On the ground and being dragged already. Get the damn chute collapsed! OK. I sort of stand up. Maybe I'm in one piece. And here comes a blue van with some of our guys in it.

It begins to sink in. In fourteen years and a thousand-plus air shows, the Team has been clever enough to do all its metal bending in training, out of sight. This is our first accident in front of a crowd and the honor is mine. And maybe I'll never get the record for vertical rolls. I gather up my gear and climb into the van just as the Diamond bottoms out, low, right on top of us. Give me a break. At least they don't have the smoke on.

Somebody wants to take me immediately to the Base Hospital, but I say, "Let's go over to tell the ground crew I'm OK." So we stop by, I get out of the van, shake hands with C.D., toss the other crew chiefs an insincere thumbs-up. Jimmy Stewart is still there and comes over to say nice things, but Raquel hasn't stayed for the show, so no air kiss. I'd given Mike Miller some ad-libbing to do in the middle of his narration and he stops by to say maybe we should leave that thing, whatever it was, out of the show sequence. That's when I learn I've pulled the wings off the airplane.

On modern fighters, the wings are positioned well behind the pilot. You can see them in the rearview mirror or if you look back, but they're otherwise not in normal view. Of course, I was watching the Diamond, ahead and well above me, as I concentrated on getting up to them quick, but not too quick. I didn't see the wings come off. All I knew, the airplane blew up.

The F-100 has a large fuel tank in the fuselage, located behind the cockpit, forward of the engine and on top of the wing center section. When the wings folded, a large quantity of raw fuel from this tank dumped into the engine, which exploded. The shock wave from the blast propagated up the air intake and blew the nose off, removing the first six feet of the airplane, right back to the bulkhead forming the front of the cockpit pressure vessel. The tail end of the jet was also badly damaged, one semi-comical result being that the drag chute used for braking after landing was liberated from the aircraft. As it came fluttering down, some in the crowd thought my personal parachute had failed.

After it exploded, the engine began pumping flame through the cockpit pressurization lines. Conditioned air enters the cockpit at the pilot's feet and behind his head. My flying boots, ordinarily pretty shiny for an ROTC guy, were charred beyond repair; I never wore them again. Where I had rolled my collar underneath to protect show suit appearance, my neck got toasted.

I have no idea how fast I was traveling at ejection. I was certainly barely subsonic when the wings failed but with the nose blown off, the F-100 is a fairly blunt object and would have slowed quickly. On the other hand, I remained with the aircraft no more than a second or two after it exploded, so there wasn't time to decelerate much. When I came out of the jet, windblast caught my helmet, rotated it 90 degrees and ripped it off my head. It was found on the ground with the visor down, oxygen mask hooked up and chinstrap still fastened. There is also a neck strap at the back of the helmet that helps secure it to the pilot's head. As my helmet was rotated by windblast, this strap rubbed the burned part of my neck, causing some bleeding.

The Team wears an Air Force standard backpack parachute suitable for ejection at either high or low altitude. Opening is automatic and will occur even if the pilot is rendered unconscious during ejection. At altitudes below fourteen thousand feet, the parachute begins to open one second after man-seat separation. This one-second delay lets the human body, a draggy design, slow down a little and also gets some separation from the seat, which is even draggier. For flight at very low altitude, the parachute can be set to deploy without delay. In this configuration, a lanyard attached to the seat pulls the parachute open as the seat falls away. Ordinarily, this option is selected only for takeoff and landing, when you are relatively slow, close to the ground, and if you need the parachute, you need it now. Otherwise, you unhook the lanyard. At cruising speed, even at low altitude, the combination of your flight path vector and the upward thrust of the seat as it rockets out of the aircraft will give you the altitude you need and it's a better trade to have the one-second deceleration before chute deployment starts.

However, the Team does so much work at low altitude we just leave the lanyard hooked up for the air show. That explains why my chute opens so fast. Too fast, as it turns out. I don't get enough separation from the seat and it somehow makes contact with my parachute canopy after it is deployed. The damage to my canopy is probably the result of entanglement with the seat, although some of it could have been caused by the shock of high-speed opening. The opening shock is certainly harsher than normal and as my torso is whipped around to align with the parachute risers, these heavy straps do further damage to the back of my neck, the body part apparently singled out for retribution.

Walking into the Base Hospital I'm pulled up short by my image in a full-length mirror. Above the mirror a sign says: CHECK YOUR

MILITARY APPEARANCE. Mine looks like I've crawled into a gunnysack with a mountain lion. The white show suit is a goner, cockpit fire having given it a base coat of charcoal gray, to which has been added several tablespoons of blood and a final dressing of dirt, grass, and sagebrush stain. I can account for the camouflage, which came from being dragged along the ground. But I hadn't realized my neck was bleeding quite so much. I now doubted my judgment in stopping to visit with ground crew. *Bandolero!* turns into a slasher movie, *The Solo Pilot From Hell.*

They keep me in the hospital overnight. The Team visits. Mike Miller smuggles in a dry martini in a half-pint milk carton. They're leaving for Nellis the next morning. I tell the hospital staff I'm leaving too and ask Dickey to pack my stuff out of the motel. I ride the C-130 with the ground crew, arriving back at Nellis a few hours after the rest of the Team. I walk off the airplane and am sore for a couple of days, but we are about to take a break anyway. The 1967 show season is over.

My aircraft continued on a ballistic trajectory after I jumped out, scattering parts and equipment along the extended flight path. Most of the engine and the main fuselage section impact about two miles down range from my initial pull up. All the bits and pieces land on government soil. There is no injury or property damage. The aircraft is destroyed at a listed cost of $696,989, but if there is a good kind of accident, this is it. Nobody's hurt and all the scrap metal can be collected for post-game analysis.

The wings of the F-100 mate into a box at the center of the fuselage, the strongest part of the airplane, or so it is believed. When what is left of my wing center box is inspected, it is found to have failed. North American Rockwell, the airplane manufacturer, tests the box on a bend-and-stretch machine and it breaks again at a pressure rating that translates to a load of 6½ G's for my flight conditions when the wings departed. This should not have happened, since the F-100's positive load limit is 7.33. But it turns out my wing center box broke along a fatigue crack. There are about thirty more cracks in the vicinity of the one that broke.

THE static strength of an aircraft is its ability to take a simple load, without consideration for repetition or cyclic variation. For instance, the F-100 is designed to encounter a *limit* load of plus 7.33 and minus 3.0 G's, in the accomplishment of its mission. Of course, the aircraft will often be subjected to positive loads below 7.33 and negative loads less than 3.0, but these are the normally anticipated maximum loads and the aircraft must withstand them with no ill effects. Specifically, the primary load-bearing structures of the aircraft should experience no objectionable deformation when subjected to a limit load and should return to their original unstressed shape when the load is removed.

To provide for the (hopefully) rare instances when a load greater than the limit is required to avert disaster, the manufacturer designs in a safety factor, usually an extra 50 percent. The primary structure of the aircraft must also be able to withstand this so-called *ultimate* load—for the F-100, about 11 plus and 4.5 minus G's—without failure. Such a load will "overstress" the aircraft and permanent metal deformation may be expected, but no actual failure of major load carrying components should occur. During the construction of a new design, ground static tests, including destructive tests, are used to verify ultimate strength. If the aircraft is subjected to a load greater than ultimate, structural failure is imminent.

In service, aircraft accumulate structural damage that, while related to static strength, is more in the wear-and-tear category. If repeatedly flexed over time, metals develop *fatigue,* usually in the form of minute cracks that can enlarge and propagate into the cross section of aircraft structures. When a crack progresses sufficiently, the remaining cross section is incapable of withstanding imposed stress and a sudden, final rupture occurs. In this way, failure can occur at stresses much lower than ultimate static strength.

Interestingly, fatigue damage is cumulative. Just as it is said that all men will get prostate cancer if they live long enough, all aircraft structures will fail at some point because of metal fatigue. This is why even the most ruggedly built airframes have a service life. It is also why load-bearing structures of an aircraft are inspected regularly: to insure against the stored-up effects of metal fatigue.

Unlike nearly all aircraft load-bearing structures, however, the wing center box of the F-100 is not regularly inspected. First of all, it's hard to get at; more important, it's overengineered, at least in theory. That is, designers of the F-100 projected the spectrum and frequency of loads that could be expected in service and *other* primary structures were engineered to sustain these loads through anticipated service life without fatigue failure. Then the wing center box was made even stronger than that. It might fail, but it wouldn't matter because other load bearing structures would fail first, in the same way that most men die of something else before they get prostate cancer.

It should not have happened, but my wing center box failed, well inside the normal operating limits of the aircraft, from accrued metal fatigue. When the Air Force looked around, some other recent F-100 losses seemed suspiciously similar. These were cases of aircraft lost while bombing jungle targets in Vietnam. The recovery from a dive bomb pass is a lot like the high speed, high-G pull-up into the Bomb Burst. In the Vietnam cases, the pieces were not recovered and the aircraft were written off as combat losses.

After analysis of my wreckage, specialists are brought in to look at the other Thunderbird aircraft and a lot more fatigue damage is discovered in wing centerboxes. The Air Force puts a 4-G limit on the F-100 and initiates a program to run all the jets back through depot modification to beef up the wing center box. Thus, my accident almost certainly saves lives by revealing a serious problem in the F-100 fleet that could be and was fixed.

But it also means the Team is grounded for the rest of the year. Our red, white, and blue jets are scheduled first through the mod line, set up at Palmdale. With luck, we'll get them back by January to start training for the '68 season.

31

LCDR. JOHN A. MORRISON—2000

"Man, it sure is peaceful up here." That was the first thought I had upon waking up in my chute after ejecting from my trusty Intruder. My second thought was, "I sure hope the skipper's not sitting in a perfectly good jet wondering where I had gotten off to." Finally, I was wondering how hard it would be to change my designator to Intel. But seriously folks, I had just ejected on a dark moonless night from a high-speed, out-of-control A-6. The force of the ejection had rendered me momentarily unconscious; the last thing I remembered was pulling the low handle, and I awoke swinging in the chute. I had ejected at approximately ten thousand feet so I had plenty of time to enjoy the peacefulness of the autumn night—that was until I realized I was soon going to land in cold, shark-infested waters. Matter of fact, the previous day while I had been up in the tower on a tower-flower watch, the Boss had been commenting on the large concentration of great white sharks in this operating area!

Anyhow, being slightly dazed from the ejection and from getting hit in the side of the head with the metal connector at the end of my G-suit hose (actually, it had played cookie cutter on my ear and had cut out a crescent-shaped piece of flesh the doctor was able to sew back on), I could remember IROK, but for the life of me I couldn't figure out what those letters stood for. To back up a step, my helmet had blown off during the ejection and both of my contact lenses had been blown from my eyes. I couldn't see a lick. (No wonder, I was a BN!) I had a broken right shoulder, two hyperextended elbows, and various small cuts on my hands from going through the Plexiglas canopy. The doctor later surmised that I had broken my shoulder playing helicopter with my right arm in a 500-knot wind stream.

To continue, I finally figured out what IROK stood for and inspected my canopy (kind of hard to do in the dark when you're blind), inflated my LPA, released my raft, went through the options, and located my Koch fittings. I was careful not to lift the covers on my Koches—I had heard stories of dudes dropping hundreds, if not thousands of feet because they released too early. I waited patiently, swinging back and forth, for my feet to hit the water. I hit the water unexpectedly and I remember it closing over my head. I must have gone to sleep again because the next thing I know, I'm sitting in my raft. The thought of sharks must have really gotten my adrenaline going, not only had I climbed in my little innertube raft with a broken shoulder, I had accomplished it without removing my seat pan. Of course I didn't figure this out until later, when it got uncomfortable to sit on. All I know is that there must have been a lot of water flying around for a few minutes!

I was safe; I had survived an overwater ejection and was nice and cozy in my little raft. Soon, my air wing buddies would be coming to pluck me out. Not! I had punched out after I had checked out with strike and prior to getting clearance from L.A. Center. The ship thought I was merrily on my way home and L.A. thought we had gone NORDO (NO RaDiO) and landed at some military field. The SAR wasn't started until the fuel starvation time had expired and the SDO at home base couldn't find us at any airfield on the West Coast.

So, sitting in my raft I started to go through what I could remember from water survival. I drank my can of water, found my strobe and tried to put it on my helmet, but that was kind of difficult seeing as how my helmet was gone. No matter, it wouldn't have done any good because my strobe died after ten minutes anyhow. I pulled out my PRC-90 and tried to talk to somebody, but no one would answer, even though I heard plenty of aircraft flying overhead into L.A. International. Never did figure out how come it didn't work—it made the good hissing sound when you turned it on. I pulled out my pencil flares and prepped them; I prepped my smoke flare (three bumps for night end) and waited to be rescued. And waited. And waited.

Approximately four hours after I had fallen into the water, the SAR effort was started. It consisted of an S-3 from the ship and a Coast Guard Falcon jet. The S-3 homed right in on my beacon and located me in no time. I shot a multitude of pencil flares at it, but the aircrew stated they never saw any of them. The S-3 vectored a Navy SH-3 to my position but a Coast Guard SH-3, launched out of L.A., beat them to me. I heard the helo wandering around looking for me so when I thought it was close enough to see my smoke, I torched it off. What happened next scared the heck out of me: all these burning embers started dropping into my lap before I could get the situation under control and the flare held out over the side. I had had to hold the flare between my knees because my right arm was becoming unusable. I'm just glad I didn't try to hold it in my teeth.

Both helos saw my flare and proceeded to my position. The Navy helo hovered over me, and I waited in my raft for the rescue swimmer to jump down and square me away. While I was waiting I was trying to think of something cool to say to the swimmer when he showed up. I must admit, it was getting kind of tangled up in my raft. If you remember, every piece of gear in your survival vest is tied onto you with a length of parachute cord. So I had a veritable spiderweb in my raft that I wasn't going to be able to extricate myself from without some assistance.

I had lost SA on the Coast Guard helo until I heard something behind me—those Coasties had landed in the water and were water taxiing right up to me! They came up and the crewman in the door grabbed my feet and slid me, raft and all, right into the back. Much easier than going up in the sling! They lit out for the hospital right away where I was treated for mild hypothermia, had a sample of every bodily fluid taken, and was subjected to about a million X-rays (my next child was a girl).

Moral of the story: All that water survival training works. Even though I was dazed and injured, I managed to put all that training to use helping to ensure I survived. If, heaven forbid, you ever find yourself in a situation like this, you can rest assured all the training you have undergone and forgotten about will quickly come back to you. Moral #2: If you wear contact lenses, keep a pair of glasses in your pocket when you go flying.

32

COMMANDANT JOHN R. "DICK" MUEHLBERG—1944

I realized my dream, back when I was ten years of age, when I requested (years later) and was assigned to the Flight Test Division at Wright Field in June of 1944. Before, I had been flying combat in B-24s with the 98th Bomb Group in the desert against Rommel.

Col. Warburton was the Chief of Flight Test and was a wonderful person and pilot. He continually kept his finger on the pulse of the organization and really pushed those of us who demonstrated a real interest. Our primary job was to run tests on aircraft assigned to the Flight Test Division. Secondly, he wanted us to learn aeronautics and obtain flying experience on as many aircraft as possible. He was particularly adamant when he wanted me to attend the RAF Empire Test Pilots' School in England.

The P-39 was a rather small airplane for a person who was six foot four, but I had never flown it. Ours was being used for a hot-oil engine test. I was, fortunately for me, one of those people who read everything available on the airplane before I flew it. Also, I sought out a pilot in Flight Test who had as much experience as possible in the aircraft, and Capt. M. L. "Smitty" Smith was my man.

Together we went out to the flight line and looked the P-39 over. He could not have been more helpful until I asked, "How do you get out of this damn thing if the engine quits?" I was particularly concerned because the only exit was through two small doors on either side of the cockpit rather than, as in other fighters, a top canopy that could be jettisoned. Smitty was helpful up to a point; we got through the drill on the right-hand door, but he began to object when I asked, "How do you get out of the left door, if the right one doesn't work?" But he gave me the drill on that one too.

I flew the airplane for over an hour the first day—lovely airplane. Next day I took off again and went through the prescribed test program. I came back to land, and was at 2,500 feet preparing to enter the pattern, when all of a sudden the aircraft began to vibrate violently as though something had broken in the engine. I reduced power to prepare for a forced landing, but the engine stopped and the cockpit filled with smoke. I thought to myself, here I am at low altitude in an unfamiliar airplane and the engine's on fire behind me, not in front of me. Let's get out of here!

I went through the drill to open the right-hand door, to no avail. Thank God Smitty had told me how to get out of the left door. Then another problem started. As I maneuvered my long body to get through the door, the plane banked over to the left and started a shallow dive when my legs got involved with the stick. The next thing I knew, I seemed to be caught up in the throttle quadrant. By this time, as I continued the struggle, I clenched my teeth and waited to hit the ground with one big bang.

That's all I remember until I found myself running across Grobey's Peach Orchard to tell Mr. Grobey, who was running toward me, that I was OK. Obviously, the Lord had reached down and pulled me out of that airplane. Witnesses said I left the cockpit at 200 feet, a record jump as far as I know.

One must assume two things: the rush of wind must have opened my chute instantaneously, and the shroud lines must have been at full stretch and pulling up, just as my feet touched the ground. The P-39 and the big hole in the ground were only 150 feet from where I lit.

I was very pleased to see the face of Maj. Bob Ruegg a short time later at the scene of the accident, and I had logged two takeoffs and only one landing in the P-39!

Col. Warburton had me up in the air again within two days, and then off to the Empire Test Pilots' School by the end of the month. There I flew everything, from Spitfires to Lancasters to Sunderland Flying Boats. I continued to love fighters, but I had developed a fondness for airplanes with more than one engine.

At Wright, or rather its new name, Wright-Patterson Air Force Base, I wound up as commandant of the Test Pilot School.

33

FLT. LT. S. A. E. "TED" NEWTON—1953

Herewith a descriptive piece from Ted Newton about an ill-spent Friday afternoon.

DETAILS AS FOLLOWS:

Date:	27 February 1953
Time:	1500 hrs GMT (Zulu time)
Location:	Bottesdale, Suffolk
Base:	RAF Wattisham, Ipswich, Suffolk
Aircraft:	Meteor Mk. 8 (WH477)
Sqdn:	No. 257 (Burma) Squadron
Seat:	Martin-Baker Mk. 1

PREAMBLE:

Martin-Baker showed interest and informed me that I was the ninth successful ejectee in the RAF (twenty-fifth overall). They sent me a nice tie.

I subsequently met James (later Sir James) Martin at Denham, whilst on a remedial outing from the medical rehabilitation unit at RAF Headley Court (recovering from back injuries). He was concerned enough to drop his trousers and show me that he too had scars.

The accident was due to a midair collision. The tip of the starboard tail plane struck the weight on the bottom of the flag spreader bar, about two inches from the tip. The impact caused the whole tail section, including the rear section of fuselage, to break away. Thereafter the flying qualities of my machine left much to be desired.

HERE'S THE FULL STORY:

It was a beautiful day late in February 1953. Broken cumulus cloud accentuated the azure blue of the sky and framed the Norfolk countryside, five thousand feet below, to splendid effect. Visibility was superb. It was possible to see the coastline thirty miles away to the east and, beyond that, the sea basking and glinting in the afternoon sun.

I was flying one of a pair of Meteor aircraft detailed to carry out cine practice against a flag target towed by another Meteor aircraft. The exercise was both simple and enjoyable. While the target-towing aircraft flew north and south along a patrol line over central East Anglia, we simulated high quarter attacks alternatively from the port, and then from the starboard, side of the target. When the distance between the attacking aircraft and the target had been reduced to normal gun-firing range, the cine camera, mounted on top of the gun sight, was triggered to provide a pictorial assessment of the accuracy of the attack which, afterwards, could be analyzed, assessed and discussed. This sortie was one of a series being flown by the squadron in readiness for a week of live gun-firing practice which, for obvious reasons, would be carried out in a prescribed range area well out over the North Sea.

The attack which, for me, was to be the last of the day, started normally from a position about one thousand feet above and two thousand yards out on the starboard side of the target. The tug pilot gave clearance for the run to begin; I pulled the aircraft around to port, aimed the nose down toward a point ahead of the leading edge of the target, and then rolled to starboard to start tracking in from a range of about one thousand yards. My natural tendency to tighten up and overcontrol the aircraft as I closed the target was a fault I was trying hard to correct. Close attention was needed and I was deeply absorbed in the business of keeping the sight centered on the target, all the while ranging down by use of the twist grip on the throttle lever, and operating the cine camera with the normal gun-firing button. My intention was to get as close in as possible, but suddenly I realized I was too close to the target, slightly below it, and very definitely on a collision course. If I attempted to pull away above it, as was the normal practice, collision would be inevitable. The alternative was to make a hard break down and under the flag, a procedure not normally to be recommended. I tried to go under.

The aircraft bounced slightly as if in turbulence. Simultaneously there was a distinct thud, a momentary pause taut with suspense, and then a vicious, head-slamming flick to starboard. I was immediately and acutely conscious of being heavily buffeted in my seat. The motion and vibration were so severe that I could not think coherently, and it was impossible to focus my eyes on any instrument, or object, inside or outside the cockpit.

The noise was incessant and deafening.

Momentarily, the aircraft steadied and held a diving attitude of about 20 degrees below the horizon. A quick instrument check showed about 350 knots indicated airspeed and a height of about 3,500 feet but winding down rapidly. I tried to regain control but found the control column jammed fully forward and hard over to the left. In contrast the rudder pedals were free and easy, a certain indication that something was very wrong in the tail plane. Abruptly the aircraft resumed a peculiar tumbling, cartwheeling spin to starboard. The once beautiful landscape, alternating now with the blurred blue and white of the sky, had taken on an equally blurred but distinctly menacing appearance. It was clearly time to leave.

The difficulty in focusing my eyes made it necessary to grope for the cockpit canopy jettison handle. It seemed a long time before I found it tucked away to the right of the instrument panel. I snatched it to its fullest extent. Nothing happened. All the while the motion of the aircraft was violent and irregular, and the increasing range of my body movements told me that the seat harness was losing the unequal struggle to hold me in place. Suddenly I could see the leading edge of the cockpit canopy. It lifted an inch or two and then dropped back into place. A pause. An interminable pause. It lifted again, hovered for a moment, and was gone. With it went the dust and dirt of ages from the cockpit floor, maps, pencils, and sundry bits of personal kit. The feeling of relief was intense.

Consciously making an effort to put my feet in or near the foot trays of the Martin-Baker Mk. I ejector seat, I reached for the handle of the integral face blind and seat-firing mechanism above and behind my head. Initially it was difficult to reach because of the effects of varying 6-loads. Eventually I found it and pulled it, if not in the prescribed fashion at least with immediate and satisfying effect. At the instant of firing I was hunched above the seat pan. I sensed a movement below me, vaguely heard a muffled report above the general uproar and felt a painful moment of impact. Fleetingly I saw a pair of overall-clad knees from which dangled, seemingly far in the distance, a small pair of shoes set against the black and receding background of the cockpit interior. And, suddenly, there was silence.

The seat stabilized quickly and I was able to move on to the next stage of the proceedings without delay. I looked down to find and positively identify the seat harness release mechanism. Previously I had always been concerned that, in these circumstances, I might mistakenly operate the parachute release box. Once the seat harness was released and the thigh straps clear, it was an easy matter to role forward out of the seat. I made an effort to straighten my body and located the parachute rip cord. I paused long enough to double-check that the seat was clear and not likely to foul my deploying parachute, and then pulled the rip cord.

The parachute deployed normally and with it a notable feeling of well-being became apparent. So far as I could judge no serious damage appeared to have been done and all that remained now was the relatively simple matter, so I thought, of making a landing. I looked down and could see the wreckage of what had been a perfectly good aeroplane framed between my feet. There was no sign of the tail section. I judged my height to be something less than 1,000 feet but found it difficult to make an accurate assessment. There was barely time to make sure that I would not land in the hole made by the aircraft, and then the ground was rushing up to meet me.

It was not a good landing. I simply dropped on my backside in a wet and muddy field with pieces of aircraft littered around me. Once down I stayed down, determined to regain my breath, take stock of the situation and, at least for a few minutes, do absolutely nothing. In conditions of little wind the parachute canopy collapsed gently around me. I was covered in mud and my flying overalls were torn and ripped in several places. Blood flowed copiously from my mouth, nose and ears and splattered over the front of the yellow lifesaving jacket. Somehow or other, my helmet had managed to rotate some 90 degrees around my head and the oxygen mask was wedged near my left ear. Broken goggles obscured the right side of my face. All was quiet and still except for the crackle of burning wreckage scattered around behind me. I was content to sit, gently feeling, probing, and twitching in the hope that nothing was broken.

My attention was attracted to the hedgerow about fifty feet in front of me. A movement, and the figure of a man rose out of the ditch. A pause, and a second figure appeared. A longer pause while both men stood looking down into the ditch. From it rose a third man, covered in mud and water from head to foot. One could guess that this man, seeing the aircraft heading toward him in its final dive, had been quick to take cover in the ditch. His companions had followed in on top of him. Now they came toward me. They stood five or six feet away and looked down at me. I sat, not moving, and looked up. Nothing was said. A minute, perhaps, passed in complete silence and seemed like an age. Then, as if in the far distance, I heard my own voice say: "Good afternoon."

They didn't reply. Without a word, and as one man, they turned and walked away. I never saw them again.

CDR. RUSS PEARSON—1969

Probably the rarest form of ejection, ejecting while submerged. As odd as it may sound, it is feasible and has been done successfully. Once submerged, it is virtually impossible to open an aircraft canopy against the pressure differential between the water and the air in the cockpit. Once the cockpit is full of water, it might be possible to slowly push the canopy open and exit the craft, but the amount of time necessary for the cockpit to fill would allow the plane to sink below the depth a pilot could survive. The pilot's oxygen mask is optimized for use in thin-atmosphere conditions, and cannot be counted on to provide breathable oxygen under any depth of water.

The above factors mean that there is only one significant option available to a pilot once the craft becomes submerged: eject through the canopy. The same forces that prevent a pilot from opening the canopy manually would prevent the jettison charges from pushing the canopy safely out of the way of the ejection seat. The seat does not usually exit the water, it merely crashes through the canopy and then initiates seat separation. The pilot must then separate from the parachute that would usually partially deploy, and swim to the surface, not necessarily in that order. The following article describes one such incident:

SHORTLY after midnight, in the "zero-dark-thirty" hours of 10 June 1969, I was the pilot of a single-engine, single-seat A-7 Corsair II light-attack aircraft that departed the flight deck of the aircraft carrier USS *Constellation* (CVA-64) and plunged into the Pacific Ocean some sixty miles off the coast of Southern California.

The mishap occurred at the end of a marathon twenty-three-hour day that culminated with the first of six scheduled night carrier landings. The event was to have marked my final night of initial carrier qualification (carqual) training as a fleet replacement pilot with VA-122 at NAS Lemoore, California.

THE LANDING

The voice of *Connie*'s final approach controller came through the headset loud and clear, "Corsair 202 is on course, on glide slope at three-quarters of a mile. Call the ball." It was my cue to get off the instruments and fly the final few seconds of the approach visually. A light drizzle was falling from the low hanging overcast just above the landing pattern, but the visibility was good underneath and the sea state calm. The A-7 Corsair II aircraft strapped around my waist was the Navy's newest light-attack carrier jet and I was proud to be in one of the initial classes of first-tour pilots selected to fly it. "Two-Zero-Two, Corsair, ball, fuel state four-point-zero," I replied as my scan shifted outside the cockpit to the "meatball" of amber light beaming aft from the optical landing mirror on *Constellation*'s four-acre flight deck. The seat of my pants told me the plane was too high, but the ball was centered on the mirror to confirm I was on glide slope. My four thousand pounds of fuel was a comfortable reserve, ample to make it around the landing pattern a couple more times and still have enough fuel to "bingo" to the primary divert field at NAS Miramar if I didn't get aboard.

"Roger, ball. Keep it coming," the landing signal officer (LSO) acknowledged from his platform on the port side of the flight deck. The voice was not as relaxed as the LSO who had "waved" the class every night for the past month at Lemoore.

More than two years of flight training at five bases in four states were riding on this event. Tonight was the long-awaited "graduation exercise" from the training environment into the fleet, the final rite of passage into the Navy's elite fraternity of tailhook carrier pilots. In a few short months, I'd be flying combat missions in Southeast Asia from an aircraft carrier in the Gulf of Tonkin.

Scheduling such a significant event at the trailing edge of a grueling sixteen-hour day should have raised caution flags somewhere, but not with me. The instructor pilots had primed the class for months with sea stories about night carrier landings separating the "men from the boys"—now it was my time to prove I could fly with the eagles. The adrenaline was pumping.

The nonstop day that began with a 0330 wake-up call back home in Lemoore had been a test of endurance, but long days are part of the normal routine aboard carriers at sea. Besides, we were training for combat, and "hacking the program" was part of that training—this was the Navy, not the airlines. The squadron's mission was to pump out combat replacement pilots for NavAirPac's light-attack Corsair squadrons, and pilot output was running behind schedule. The pressure was on from the top down to catch up. In the light-attack community, "death before dishonor" was the unwritten code. Begging off the flight schedule, especially with a flimsy excuse like fatigue, was a sure way to be branded a "nonhacker" for the rest of your career.

The final half mile to the ship was over in a matter of seconds—it happened so fast that the tricky "burble" of turbulent air at the fantail passed practically unnoticed. But the bone-jarring jolt of the 25,000-lb. Corsair coming down at 650 feet per minute to collide with the ship's steel deck didn't go unnoticed. I knew it was coming but it still got my attention. The harness straps dug deeply into my shoulders as the plane decelerated from 135 knots to a screeching halt in three seconds flat. The first night "trap" had lived up to its billing: it was a cross between ecstasy and a head-on collision with a freight train.

"Piece of cake," I thought. "Five more and you're on your way to the fleet."

The landing was on speed and on glide slope, and the tailhook had engaged the targeted No. 3 wire. All was not well, however, as the plane was drifting fast toward the port catwalk. On this, the fifth man-up, third launch and eighth trap of the extended day, fatigue had finally overpowered my adrenaline. I had become so focused on flying the ball that the landing centerline had momentarily dropped out of my scan. A late lineup correction had set up a right-to-left roll-out as the plane decelerated down the angled deck.

OVER THE SIDE

The plane skirted the port deck edge like a tightrope walker on a high wire before stopping painfully close to the catwalk. I couldn't believe this was happening to me; could already hear the lineup lecture from the LSO back at the ready room debrief.

The cockpit was jolted hard as the plane's port main landing gear dropped off the deck edge. As luck would have it, the protective steel scupper plate guarding the deck edge had been removed during the ship's recent trip to the shipyard and had not been replaced. In less than a heartbeat, the plane was precariously perched on the edge of the flight deck.

It was hard to tell the plane's exact attitude with no visible horizon, but the fuselage was turned at least 60 degrees left-wing-down. To eject now would be suicidal—the trajectory of the ejection seat's rocket motor would send the seat skipping across the water like a flat rock on a farm pond. If the hook remained engaged with the arresting gear cable, the situation might still be salvageable.

As the magnitude of the moment settled in, my mind suddenly shifted into slow motion. Strangely enough, there was no panic—at least not yet. My thoughts were surprisingly calm and clear as I instinctively pulled the throttle aft and "around the horn" to shut down the engine. If the hook should release from the cable and the aircraft went over the side, the prospect of cold sea water combining with the Corsair's hot power plant was a recipe for an even more explosive situation. The engine was of no use now anyway.

As the engine spooled down through 65 percent RPM, the generator dropped off the line and cut off all electrical power; as the radio and interior lights went out, total darkness instantly enveloped the cockpit. All contact with the world outside was lost. I had been alone in a crowd before, but never like this. Except for the pounding in my chest, there was only dead silence and it had a deafening sound. If this was a dream, it was a nightmare! Unfortunately, I wasn't dreaming.

The momentary stillness was soon shattered as the aircraft lunged forward. The worst had happened—the tailhook had "spit out" the arresting cable. I was in deep, serious trouble and knew it. The plane tumbled off the flight deck and plunged downward some sixty feet prior to impacting the Pacific—the sensation was like falling into a black hole.

We had learned in survival training that a ditched aircraft normally sinks at about ten feet per second, and after one hundred feet, crew survival is highly unlikely. I figured I had about ten seconds if I were going to get out of this mess alive. It appeared that only a miracle could save me now. I had just run out of altitude and airspeed, and was about out of ideas too.

The ejection seat seemed the only chance, albeit a slim one. In the history of naval aviation, only a handful of pilots had ever attempted, much less survived, an underwater ejection. It was theoretically possible in the A-7, but no one had yet tested it.

There was also the chance I might eject directly into the *Connie*'s passing steel hull—or, even worse, into one of her massive propellers. The odds for survival were grim and getting worse each second.

EJECTION

I intentionally delayed the inevitable for a split second for the ship to pass clear. Then, like a death-row prisoner condemned to throw a switch and end his own life, I reached down between my knees for the seat's alternate ejection handle, the one we'd been trained to use when time is the most critical factor. Images of my wife Theresa waiting at home with Steve, our nine-month-old son, flashed through my mind. How would she react when the black Navy sedan pulled into the driveway and the skipper and chaplain came to the door? Realizing this might be my last conscious thought, I grasped the ejection handle, closed my eyes and, expecting the worst, pulled straight up . . . Nothing happened. Time seemed to stand still.

The delay was only a millisecond, but it seemed much longer. I had already decided that the ejection seat was not going to work and saw myself slowly sinking, to drown or be crushed to death by the depths. The Corsair's tiny cockpit seemed destined to be my coffin.

A sudden blast of brilliant light blinded me—the seat's rocket motor had fired following a built-in sequencing delay. In an instant, I was out of the cockpit and clear of the seat, though still submersed in the cold, dark water of the Pacific.

FOCUS ON SURVIVAL

I couldn't breathe. The water had forced the oxygen mask down around my chin and the emergency oxygen bottle in the seat pan was useless. For the first time, panic set in and I became totally disorientated—I couldn't tell up from down. It was as if I had been shot out of a high-powered cannon into a pool of jet-black ink, a far cry from the Dilbert Dunker simulator in the crystal-clear water of the training tank back at the Water Survival School in Pensacola. In less than a minute, I had gone from being a cocky, self-assured carrier pilot to a desperate young twenty-five-year-old Navy Lt. JG fighting for his life.

I had to do something fast or it was all over but the memorial service. Just then, a cluster of lights flickering on the surface caught my eye. As an 80,000-ton aircraft carrier cutting through the water at 30 knots doesn't stop and turn around on a dime, the flight-deck directors had tossed their watertight flashlight wands over the side to mark my plane's location for the plane-guard destroyer and the search and rescue (SAR) helo. Though I was still underwater, the lights reoriented me and I instinctively swam toward them.

I gasped for air as my helmet broke the surface—it felt great to be alive. But that lungful of fresh sea air was accompanied by an excruciating pain as if a butcher knife had been plunged between my shoulder blades and twisted. Something was seriously wrong, but there was an even more pressing problem.

The altitude-sensing device that automatically deploys the parachute had activated and the chute had partially opened. The canopy and its nylon shroudlines were streaming behind me, overpowering my frantic efforts to keep my head above water. I had to stay clear of those shroudlines and get rid of that chute, now.

I grabbed for the nylon toggles that inflate the lobes on the Mk-3C survival vest, but they weren't where they should have been. Panic began to set in again and time was running out. I was fast losing the struggle to keep my head above water—it took all the strength I could muster just to stay afloat. The parachute was winning and I was on the verge of being dragged under.

My body suddenly went numb as something below the surface brushed against my feet. During the ejection through the Plexiglas canopy, my left forearm had been sliced and was bleeding profusely. The gash on my arm was even more reason to be alarmed. The survival vest contained several packets of shark repellent but I was too busy trying to keep my head above water to get to them. When the object brushed against me again, I realized that it was the plane. It had impacted the water with minimal force and was virtually intact. With its wing fuel bladders and over half of the fuselage fuel cells filled only with air, Corsair 202 was floating upside down just beneath the surface, still bobbing from *Connie*'s passing wake. I had surfaced alongside the aircraft and my legs had brushed against the tail. Hanging onto the horizontal stabilator for support, I finally located the life vest's inflation toggles, which had wrenched around to my side during the ejection. Grasping a lanyard in each hand, I pulled down and away and *whoosh*, the flotation lobes inflated instantly.

But I wasn't out of harm's way yet—the parachute still streamed out like a huge sea anchor. Should it fill with water and sink, even the inflated vest wouldn't help. I glanced around just in time to see *Connie*'s plane-guard destroyer bearing down on me. From my water-level perspective, the "small boy" looked anything but small, and if she didn't change course, the rescue part of the mission would be over and recovery and salvage operations would begin.

Using techniques learned in water-survival training, I rolled over on my back and reached upward along the parachute risers until I located the Koch fittings, the small metal latches that connect the harness to the parachute. I lifted up on the cover and pulled down on the latch. In an instant, the chute was gone.

SAR HELO TO THE RESCUE

Moments later, I was floating center stage in a large beam of bright, white light shining down from the ship's SAR helicopter that hovered noisily overhead. Like most jet jocks, I had never fully appreciated helicopters except when they brought the mail—they had always been high on my list of low-priority aircraft. Never again! Just now, that homely, wind-blowing, water-churning contraption looked like an angel of mercy—nothing could have been more beautiful. Fortunately, the destroyer had veered off to starboard and yielded to the helicopter.

Minutes later, a rescue swimmer from the helicopter was in the water next to me.

"You okay, sir?" he yelled over the din of the thrashing rotor blades.

"I'm okay," I yelled back, "but it hurts to breathe." I didn't tell him that it also hurt to yell.

"Hang on, sir. All we've got is a horse collar, but it'll get you out of here," he shouted as he guided my arms through the opening in the pear-shaped rescue sling that nestled under my armpits.

As the hoist began lifting us slowly out of the water, my body dangled helplessly from the horse collar like a wet dishrag. Weighed down by soaking flight gear and steel-toed flight boots, and whipped about by the helo's downdraft, the pain became unbearable. The next thing I remember was sprawling on the deck of the helo's cargo cabin, heaving salt water.

Moments later, the helo recovered aboard the carrier and I was transported to sick bay on a stretcher. The alternate ejection handle may have expedited my exit from the cockpit, but at a painful price. Reaching down between my knees to grasp the secondary handle in an inverted, submerged cockpit had placed my upper body in a vulnerable, dangerously curved position. The brutal G-force of the seat firing had broken my back.

THE MIRACLES CONTINUE

Three days after the mishap, the ship's senior medical officer, a newly selected Navy captain, arranged to accompany me ashore on a medevac flight to Balboa Naval Hospital in nearby San Diego. By coincidence, the flight was scheduled with the same crew and aboard the same helo that had rescued me earlier.

Just prior to boarding the flight, a casualty on the flight deck created an unexpected dilemma—the medevac helo was configured to carry only one patient. The doctor had an instant decision to make. Needless to say, I was not happy to learn my name had been scratched from the manifest only moments before launch.

About an hour later, a young corpsman came running into the ward. He was out of breath. From the look on his face, I knew something terrible had happened.

"You're either living right or somebody's looking after you, Lieutenant," he blurted out. "Word just came down from Air Ops that the medevac flight had engine problems and went down in the water about halfway to the beach. The crew got off a Mayday and another SAR helo found the wreckage right away, but there were no survivors. Not even the doc."

I respectfully declined a second chance to medevac ashore, electing instead to ride the ship back into port a few days later. Shortly after *Constellation* moored at the carrier pier at North Island, the corpsmen carried me ashore on a stretcher to be transported by ambulance the short distance to Balboa Naval Hospital.

NAVAL aviation had turned out to be as dangerous as it was glamorous. In three short days I had cheated death twice and, in the process, learned firsthand that the thrill of flying high-performance jet aircraft off the decks of aircraft carriers sometimes demands a hefty personal price. I now understood why guys get paid for a job most of us would gladly pay for the privilege of doing.

Whether my survival was fate or just sheer good luck is debatable. Maybe the corpsman was right—maybe someone was looking after me. But one thing is for certain: without the first-class water-survival training all tailhookers receive as they earn their Naval Wings of Gold, I would have been remembered by friends and family at a 1969 memorial service rather than honored by them at a 1992 Navy retirement ceremony. Every day since 10 June 1969 has been a gift of life for which I am thankful.

35

CÉLESTINE-ADOLPHE PÉGOUD—1913

When, some years ago, during my rambles in Morocco I read of the then wonderful flights of my elders, the first pupils of the pioneers, there came to me a desire to fly, which, in time, developed into a vocation. To qualify for this vocation it required courage, cold blood, skill, mastery of oneself, a certain amount of disregard for one's life . . . yes, all that. . . . Was I adapted for it? Often times I asked myself that, and I confessed to myself that I believed I had all these qualities.

My experience at the Camp of Satory, where I had the honor of learning the ABC of aviation from the lips of Captain Carlin, decided my future. I felt an imperative desire to do big things, great things, to accomplish feats of utility, to do something to advance aviation or develop greater progress.

Dream of youth, may be. . . . As soon as I was in possession of a Bleriot monoplane I defined what I could do to accomplish something worthwhile. Before long I became what they call an acrobat of the air. I had had experiences for five years as a cavalier on land—that made the task of becoming a cavalier of the air really easy.

At this time my dream began to become a reality. To prove that a naval aeroplane does not need floats to be a part of a battleship Mr. Bleriot proposed that I would demonstrate how the aeroplane could be hooked to a cable by means of his landing and receiving apparatus. I made this demonstration before the Minister of the Navy.

Then it seemed to me that with my aeroplane I could do almost anything, and, having the assurance of self-mastery and physical strength, I asked Mr. Bleriot to allow me to loop the loop in the air, to demonstrate how the aeroplane that I was flying could fly upside down and regain its normal position by a simple exercise of control. In accordance to what I consider my vocation, I wanted to demonstrate to pilots that it is possible to fly with the aeroplane turned upside down; that no matter what happens, the aeroplane does not necessarily have to drop; no matter what position the aeroplane assumes it does not constitute danger; that, given mastery of oneself, a simple maneuver will make the aeroplane reassume its normal position.

Mr. Bleriot had confidence in me. After hesitation, which I understood quite well, he made me an aeroplane of the ordinary army type with reinforced trussing.

Meantime, I had the pleasure of demonstrating the Bonnet parachute, letting the aeroplane drop to earth while I was borne down by the parachute, showing the apparatus is as practical as I had thought. Following this demonstration I had the pleasure to fly upside down, and everything came out as I had expected it would and I had told Mr. Bleriot.

Their experiments are not ended. I want to be able to say to aviators, "You can upset, you can drop perpendicular, you can turn sidewise, you can slide on your wings or on your tail . . . all that is of little importance; your apparatus does not need to lose control— you can make it reassume its normal position by a simple maneuver."

I further want to be able to say: "Even if your life is entirely in danger, here you can have a lifesaving device, the parachute, with which you can save yourself, letting your aeroplane drop down. You can come to earth without hurt, the parachute breaking your fall."

I shall, maybe, have the satisfaction of having many tell me, as several officer aviators have said to me: "My dear Pégoud, now I don't fear anything."

If my demonstrations show—and I am certain they will—that the security in aeroplanes is a fact, I shall be satisfied. It will seem to me that I will have worked for the good of aviation and for national defense.

36

FLT. LT. CRAIG PENRICE—1985

A good pilot is defined as one who has the same number of take-offs as landings. Well I guess the events of 19th September 1985 between myself and XS921 contrived to make sure that I will never be able to lay claim to the title of being a good pilot. The trouble is that once you have managed to accumulate one more takeoff than landing in your log book it is nigh on impossible to redress the balance. Try as I might, I have been unable to come up with a foolproof plan of achieving it.

This article comes, long overdue, in response to a request for Lightning stories for this Lightning Flying Club publication. This is not the normal Lightning story of "There I was . . . short of fuel . . . etc."

Or "There I was . . . gunning the brains out of a blind Phantom crew." This article is about one of the times when things did not go quite as planned, but thanks to the wonderful invention of Sir James Martin I am at least in a position to tell the story of how I became one of the nearly 5,000 people he has cast into the realms of "not-good" pilots.

THE day started all very normally. This was my second day back at work following a wonderful ten days of leave spent in a cottage on the west coast of Scotland opposite Skye. Well-deserved leave, I might add, having just returned from our annual six-week detachment to Akrotiri, Cyprus for the squadron's APC (Armament Practice Camp).

It was just before 5 P.M. when I took off as number two of a pair of F-6s on our way to undertake our normal bread-and-butter training sortie of medium-level PIs (practice intercepts). We would each take it in turn to act as Target (bad guy) and Fighter (good guy). The fighter controller on the ground at RAF Boulmer would vector us apart by about forty miles, then turn us toward each other. The fighter would then have to use his AI-23 radar to first detect the bad guy and then, through some nifty mental gymnastics, work out the target heading and altitude before making corrections to his own course to achieve the correct point in space from which to start a turn to end up in a missile-firing cone behind the target.

The sortie all went as we had planned it. We were almost down to recovery fuel and I was acting as the target. Once the flight leader had completed his turn to end up behind me and was closing to finish his attack I started a gentle turn to the left so that we were heading back more directly to Binbrook.

Things went downhill from here.

Having moved the control column to the left to roll the aircraft into the turn, the aircraft thought it would be a jolly good wheeze if it kept moving the stick of its own accord. Despite my best efforts the stick continued to move all the way to full deflection left and the aircraft duly did as it was told and kept rolling left. As the aircraft passed the inverted position the nose started to drop and very quickly I found myself in a near vertical spiral dive (not a spin). The ailerons had gone to full deflection (normally they were limited to half deflection with the gear up) so the aircraft was rotating very quickly and as I was going downhill the speed was also increasing rapidly.

At this point I did a number of things. The first was to make a call on the radio in which I said, "I've got a very bad control restriction." At the same time I swapped hands on trying to move the stick and used my right hand to switch off the auto-stabs in the hope that they were the source of my problems. (The auto-stabs effectively had the job of smoothing out the ride for the pilot at high speed around the transonic region, where, if it were not for the auto-stabs, the aircraft would exhibit a pronounced nodding tendency.)

After what seemed like an eternity, but was actually in the order of three seconds, the flight leader came on the radio and asked "Is it better now?" I answered "No"—about four octaves higher than my normal voice. Immediately after that I ejected. There was no thinking about it or time to prepare, the situation was obvious, the aircraft was rotating rapidly, and going downhill like a train.

I was now in cloud, speed was increasing, my one action that I could think of to make it better had done nothing and the answer to the question "Is it better?" was quite definitely NO! So I ejected.

I can remember pulling the lower ejection handle with my left hand while simultaneously throwing my head and shoulders back against the seat with as much force as I could manage and trying to grab my left wrist with my right hand in order to secure it against the windblast. As you will see subsequently, this latter action proved somewhat futile. The next proper recollection that I have is sitting facing backward on the cabin floor of the Wessex just as the side door was being closed and feeling very very cold—nothing else, just very cold. This was about fifty minutes later. I wish I could fully describe how cold I felt, but in all the times I have recounted this story I have never been able to satisfactorily describe the intense, all-encompassing cold that I felt then.

Some interesting things are worth a mention at this point. This was a Thursday; on the Monday of the same week the entire fleet of Binbrook Lightnings had had a modification embodied to the ejection seat such that the PLB (personal locator beacon) would be activated during the normal ejection sequence at the point when man-seat separation occurs, rather than having to be manually operated. This was considered to be a great improvement—if the pilot were incapacitated the beacon would still be operative. In addition, with the beacon transmitting from ten thousand feet its range could be increased and transmission was more immediate than previously. The PLB was stowed in a pocket in the life jacket we wore all the time and auto-activation was achieved by means of a sticker strap incorporated into the existing lanyard, which attached the dinghy pack to the life jacket. As man separated from the seat the lanyard pulled taught and a cam rotated the power switch of the beacon to ON.

The only drawback of this arrangement comes under the heading of "old dogs and new tricks." Previously there had been no big deal when getting out of the aircraft if you stood up having not disconnected the dinghy lanyard; you simply felt a tug (and a bit of a fool), which reminded you to undo it. The same was not now the case—all the above was true except in addition the PLB was set off and a transmission was going out on the distress frequency, until you scrabbled around and managed to extricate the beacon from its pocket and switch it off. This in turn resulted in three things: some work for the safety equipment fitters who had to rebuild the jacket; the rescue system initiating a scramble for the nearest helicopter unit until they had obtained confirmation through the ATC network that the beacon they had observed near Binbrook was in fact an inadvertent activation; and much embarrassment for the individual pilot concerned.

In my case, the rescue helicopter unit at Leconfield was in the process of walking out to their aircraft for the umpteenth time in the week, cursing those idiots at Binbrook who were incapable of extracting themselves from an aircraft without alerting the safety coordination system. However, it soon became apparent that the signal from this PLB was much stronger than previously experienced, and by the time the rescue crew was in the aircraft and in radio contact with their control center they were getting the message that this was a real scramble; this probably saved me about five to seven minutes, time that would become invaluable.

I mentioned earlier that this was my second day back at work following some family leave, which I had booked following the squadron's annual detachment to Cyprus. It was mid-September and pleasantly mild. The average temperature in the North Sea was around 13°C; this was about as warm as it ever gets. Our rule book stipulated that when the sea temperature over the area of operation was less than 10°C we were to wear an immersion suit—in practice this meant that about eight months of the year all the air defense squadrons in the UK were flying in bulky immersion suits. This temperature cut-off was not just an arbitrary figure; it was based on medical study and experiment to measure body core temperature decay over time in different ambient conditions. This was then compared with expected rescue times and a realistic figure for survivability versus cockpit comfort was established. This figure of 10°C was based on a reasonably healthy individual having been ejected from an aircraft, immersed in water before climbing into his dinghy, and waiting for about an hour for rescue. Sure, he would be cold, but nowhere near " life threateningly" cold hypothermic.

So here was I, flying around on this lovely autumnal afternoon in my flying suit, under which I was wearing thin cotton long johns, a T-shirt, and green roll-neck shirt. I was a reasonably healthy individual who had been ejected from an aircraft and immersed in water and that was about as far as it went, and that was why I was feeling so incredibly cold sitting on the floor of the helicopter. I had been in the water without an immersion suit for almost an hour.

Another interesting thing had happened in addition to the PLB implementation that had contributed to speed up my rescue. A Nimrod was on its way back from the Baltic en route to Kinloss and on hearing my beacon going off diverted to the scene of the search. With their more powerful and sensitive homing equipment and their speed they were able to locate me before the Wessex was halfway to me. The Nimrod then dropped a large beacon in the water beside me that allowed the Wessex to come directly to me instead of having to enter its normal search pattern based on homing to locate by PLB. Again, this probably saved another very valuable five to ten minutes.

In addition to this, my flight leader added his part to the search in a little amusing way. After our conversation just prior to my ejection, having had no reply to his subsequent transmissions and on hearing my PLB going off, he immediately dived down to below the cloud to a height of about two thousand feet. As he broke out of the cloud he saw what he described as a huge water eruption. He then spent the rest of his fuel orbiting around this area looking in the water for me. However, what he failed to realize was that I was still above him floating down on my parachute. The parachute is set to deploy automatically as the seat descends through ten thousand feet, and it takes about fifteen minutes to float the rest of the way down to the surface. I often wonder what would have happened if we had passed close to each other or even if he had impaled me during his search for me—which would have made interesting reading in the accident report.

When I was found in the water there was evidence that I had done a number of things despite having no memory from pulling the handle to sitting looking out the door of the rescue helicopter. I had inflated my life jacket, undone the parachute harness, removed my oxygen mask, and for some reason taken off my gloves. I had partially managed to separate myself from the dinghy pack that forms the seat portion while in the aircraft—this is normally dropped on a lanyard during the parachute descent by undoing two clips, one on each side, that rest around the small of the back when you are hanging in the chute. Because of my injuries (more about them later) I was not able to undo one of the clips. This meant that I was still connected to the parachute through my lanyard to my dinghy pack and in turn to the harness—effectively I had the biggest sea anchor you have ever seen. With the exception of removing the gloves all the things I had done were part of the taught descent drills, which we were required to practice on a regular basis.

The medical theory is that despite having no memory of these events I was actually conscious at least for the initial part after leaving the aircraft, but as I got colder and colder the brain is very clever and it blacks out the bits it does not like to save you the nasty memories. During my recovery the doctors offered the suggestion that hypnosis would probably be able to rekindle these memories for me—I declined their offer!

Meanwhile, back in the helicopter, apart from feeling very, very cold I felt that my arm was a bit sore and my leg was a bit achy too, nothing agonizing, just a bit uncomfortable. I had an overwhelming sensation that this was a very bad dream, one you know you are sure to wake up from soon but until then it was still very realistic. The trouble was that no matter how much I wanted to, I simply could not wake up from this dream.

My injuries were quite significant and almost entirely due to the high speed at which I ejected. I had started the turn at 27,000 feet doing Mach 0.8 (eight-tenths of the local speed of sound, which at that height equates to about 350 mph of real wind). Post-crash simulation showed that by the time I left the aircraft I was doing about 0.95 at 18,000 feet, or more importantly in excess of 500 mph of wind blast.

My right arm had flailed and been broken against the elbow joint as it smashed against the ejection seat. Similarly my left knee had been pushed outward by the control column as the seat left the aircraft, this allowed it also to be flailed and broken against the joint outward rather than forward. I received some significant grazing burns to my neck from being thrown around as the parachute harness deployed. My face looked like I was the Michelin Man, all puffed up and swollen; the whites of my eyes were totally red. Finally, I had dislocated my left index finger—the theory is that I just would not let go of the ejection seat handle, but its three hundred lbs. finally won.

When Binbrook got the message that I had ejected, the Boss and his wife went around to break the news to my wife. They waited until they had received a message from the helicopter that I was on board, cold but alive, no word of how alive I was. My wife knew as soon as she saw the Boss and his wife climbing out of the car that I had had an accident. She spent the next hour until I got carried off the helicopter remembering the incident of a wife in a similar position who went to meet her "injured" husband only to find out shortly afterward that he was in fact dead. Needless to say she appreciated my wink to her as I was carried off the chopper.

Once I was in the medical center at Binbrook they started to determine the extent of my injuries and started the process of warming me up again. They soon realized that the broken elbow and knee would require orthopedic surgery, but the acute hypothermia needed arresting before I would be stable and able to be moved. Later that evening I was airlifted to the RAF Hospital at Ely, Cambridgeshire. The Sea King helicopter that flew me, my wife, and a medical team to Ely had been scrambled just after the Wessex from Leconfield. The Wessex does not have the capability to perform a night hover rescue with no lighting on the surface; the Sea King does. The Rescue Coordination Center had scrambled the Sea King as a precaution in case the Wessex had been unable to locate me before darkness fell. Thankfully the Wessex and Nimrod combination got to me in time.

TO conclude this tale, the accident investigation was never able to locate the exact component that would prove their theory of what caused the control column to move on its own to full left. In fact they found no more than a couple of skips' worth of bits. They were able to reproduce the symptoms I had experienced with an aircraft in the hangar. Two hydraulic jacks mounted on the ailerons themselves power each aileron; each jack has a port to each side of the aileron that is to move it up or down. When a control is demanded in one direction, there is an open circuit that slowly drives the jack assembly back to a neutral, closed position. In this way any demand from the pilot in the opposite direction to that originally demanded will immediately result in a jack force being available to move the aileron. However, if in the short period when the open circuit is catching up something falls into the gap the system sees that as a continuing demand for more aileron to roll the aircraft. What baffled the engineers before they tried it in the hangar was how could one jack overpower the three other unaffected jacks. The answer comes from the fact that the one affected jack is in the process of supplying a demand whereas the others are merely in a follow-up mode.

This was not a new accident cause that had just been discovered— similar accidents had happened on a Jaguar and a Buccaneer and possibly others. It was just an accident cause that was quite well forgotten. The only way to prevent it would have been to encase the aileron PFCUs (powered flying control units) in some form of shroud to prevent any loose articles from getting into them. So what was this loose article and where had it come from? The answer is nobody knows. The last recorded work on the PFCUs themselves was quite some time before the accident and they were able to identify many migration routes from all over the aircraft to the PFCUs, so it proved impossible to positively determine the direct cause.

An interesting precursor to this story occurred when we were in the line hut checking the aircraft Form 700, when the flight leader asked if I would mind if we swapped aircraft. We had been allocated aircraft with tail codes BL and BA. BA (XS921) was the Boss's allocated aircraft but BL was his aircraft, and as this was his last week on the squadron—before being posted to RAF Valley, and subsequently the Red Arrows—he wanted to fly "his" jet as much as possible. I had no objection to swapping, so we made a quick call to the ops desk so that they could note the change in authorization sheets that we had signed to record the proposed details of the sortie. It was not until weeks after the accident as some physiotherapist was torturing me that I suddenly remembered this event. I quickly asked for a telephone and tracked my illustrious leader down at RAF Valley. When I told him what I had just remembered there was a very sheepish silence and shuffling of feet at the other end and "Err, urn, well I had hoped you wouldn't remember that." I wasn't fussed, but whenever I get the chance I make sure I tell everyone about his embarrassment. There have been several instances since then when I have been asked to swap aircraft. My answer since that day has always been an unequivocal NO!

MY return to flying took the best part of a year; I needed ten nuts, bolts, and screws to fix my knee and thirteen to fix my elbow. That operation took seven hours to complete. I was not operated on until a week after the crash, as I was so cold and weakened from the hypothermia. In that time, despite happily eating all the hospital food they brought me I lost twenty-six pounds in weight; such was the drain on my metabolism warming me up again. The medical verdict after this was that had it happened ten years earlier I would almost certainly have had to lose my arm, the damage was so severe to the elbow joint. Sadly, I was not out of the woods just yet. I had not been able to raise my wrist or stretch my fingers since the accident; the doctors hoped that this was due to pressure on the responsible nerve from the broken bones that would recover once the bones had been arranged back into their correct positions. It turned out that the nerve had in fact been severed and would never recover on its own. I had to have a nerve transplant to fix the damaged one. Some nerve fiber responsible for the sensation in my inner arm was removed and inserted to replace the damaged portion of the radial nerve. Recovery from this type of damage is a slow process, with the nerve having to regrow down its sheath and reconnect with the muscles that have been unused and atrophied for some time.

It was a long battle to get back into the cockpit—many hurdles had to be jumped through to prove that I was safe and able to operate one of Her Majesty's Aircraft once again. Some of my determination to do this came through overhearing two doctors discussing my condition and saying something to the effect of ". . . he'll never fly again . . ." In addition to a great deal of physical support and encouragement from everyone on the squadron, I would have been at a complete loss if it were not for the love, devotion, and attention that my wife expended during my recovery and beyond. For this I will be forever grateful.

37

FLT. LT. CRAIG PENRICE—2003

On the afternoon of Sunday the first of June 2003 I had reason to part company with Hunter Mk. 6 G-BVVC before I had otherwise intended to.

Previously I had said that a good pilot is defined as one having the same number of takeoffs in his log book as landings, that was on recounting the story of my ejection from Lightning XS921 on September 19, 1985. Now that I have two more takeoffs than landings in my log book, I can add some more wisdom to the tale; having ejected once does not make you exempt from further intervention by the fickle finger of fate.

THE flight in question was supposed to be the end of a fine weekend's flying displays at the Portrush Air Show in Northern Ireland. The jet had been operating out of Blackpool to assist in the overall logistics. Following the display the intention on this day was to fly directly back to Exeter, where the jet was normally based, before driving back to my home near Warton in Lancashire.

The aircraft had been troubled with some electrical problems, but these were suitably mitigated—it was thought. Nothing in this mitigation, however, could cope with the fact that at 25,000 feet over the middle of Wales the engine flamed out. Prior to the flameout the electrical system had packed in completely and the battery had become exhausted, leaving me without communications. In anticipation of this happening, ATC had been warned that I might lose the radio, and as a result I was following my flight-planned route with the intention of a landing at Exeter without radio, using visual signals only.

Out of the blue there was a slight shudder felt through the airframe, not too dissimilar from the normal IGV (intake guide vane) chatter familiar to all "big engine" Hunter operators. I thought this to be somewhat strange as this shudder was not at the normal RPM where one would expect it; indeed the engine was in essentially steady-state cruise conditions. It took some time before the realization dawned that the engine had actually stopped. I guess I had always imagined that when the engine stops in a single engine aircraft it will all go very quiet (like it does on the ground after shutdown). However, the noise level in the cockpit was essentially unaltered. This was due to the fact that the engine was windmilling satisfactorily and predominate noise was from the pressurization system and external wind rush.

Anyway, on acceptance of the fact that the engine had quit and I was now in a brick, the following events unfolded. First off I set course for the general direction of Llanbedr (Airfield) in the hope of a dead-stick attempt onto the runway there. It quickly became apparent that I had insufficient altitude to glide that far. I discounted jettison of the external tanks primarily because I could see the banner headlines if they landed in someone's back garden or worse. I really didn't want to jeopardize future ex-military jet operations following an outcry about my tanks landing somewhere inappropriate. The same concern was true when it came to planning my exit from the jet—which was slowly beginning to dawn on me as inevitable.

My previous ejection from the Lightning had been a bit of a rushed affair, a control restriction had robbed me of the ability to control my destiny and in a very short time (less than ten second) I went from flying along happily to going for the handle. Since that experience I have said many times that I was thankful that I didn't have a long time to think about things, but here I now was with a long glide running up to an inevitable ejection.

There was very little thought involved with attempts to get the engine going again. I had no electrical power, therefore no way to get the flame lit again—it's kind of hard to get a jump start for a plummeting brick! My attentions were then focused on the best course of action for me, the jet, and the unsuspecting population below. Having determined that Llanbedr was out of the equation I set about making for the coastline in an effort to jump and dump into Cardigan Bay; it looked like this would be possible. I elected to stay with the jet below the recommended height for a premeditated ejection of nine thousand feet for the reasons of potential third-party damage I have already mentioned.

As the glide progressed it became clear that it was going to be a very close-run thing, but I had the consolation that there was an estuary running along my flight path, just prior to the coast. My personal preference has always been the water landing rather than smacking into the ground, or trees, or buildings. We get dropped into the water twice a year for practice, but we don't get the same exposure to the risky ground landing.

The time during the glide was taken up with tightening straps and going through in my head the drills, posture, and a lot of swearing. Why was this happening to me . . . again? I think I was really annoyed at the fact I had a lot of time to think about it, but the inevitable was fast becoming a reality.

In the end the final moment came a bit sooner than I expected. I quite suddenly spotted a village coming into view from behind a mountain spur.

The village was Borth and it was clear to me that my ejection point at or near the coast was going to leave a pilotless aircraft to make up its mind as to its final resting place in close proximity to the village. As I was currently over the estuary and could see some sparse marshland ahead, that was my subliminal message to go for it. I pulled the seat pan handle. I had descended from twenty-five thousand feet to two thousand feet during the preceding five or six minutes.

In comparison to my previous experience—where I have no recollection from the point of pulling the handle until the time I was sat in the helicopter—this one is in crystal clear Fujicolor. There was a huge, massive explosion and the most enormous force acting on my behind. There was a pain in my back like I had been hit by a plank of wood. I watched the cockpit disappear from around me and I watched from above as the jet flew on without me. I saw it pitch up steeply and I saw it start to wing over at the apex of its short climb. That was the last I saw of it.

During this time I was aware of the various seat mechanisms operating and being jerked around like a rag doll as the drogue and then the main chute left me hanging. This was accompanied with a feeling that my legs had swollen to enormous size and the pain in my back was now excruciating. I did what I could manage of my parachute descent drills and managed to reason that as I could still wiggle my toes the pain in my back could not be that serious. I was aware that the water below me was rushing up at quite an alarming rate. It was at about this time I realized that I was still attached to the seat; man-seat separation had not occurred. I was able to release the appropriate harness and the seat fell away. I could not have been at more than 300 feet when this happened. I will return to this fact a bit later.

Just prior to hitting the water I took a deep breath, closed my eyes, and placed my hands in position to release the parachute harness on water entry. I next recall being desperate to release my breath, but not being aware that I had floated back to the surface. I opened my eyes to find that I was in all of eight inches of water. I had hit the water as the tide was out and all my best intentions of a soft landing were gone in an instant. I was dragged for a short distance before I released the parachute harness.

It was a lovely warm afternoon. The pain in my back was awful, but if I lay still it was bearable. I could not move my legs, but I could once again wiggle my toes. I could therefore believe it was not a broken back—but it was. I was able to remove my helmet after some time and managed to get myself into a position that was "comfortable." I was now lying on a sandbank with the water receding. The sun was shining, my back was broken, and I was about a mile from the nearest shoreline. I got out my Oakleys and even got out my mobile phone. I had the intention of calling my wife to let her know I had banged out (again) but was alive—luckily the phone was soaked and did not work. I could do nothing but wait to be rescued. I could hear sirens from various directions around the shoreline. I had no worry that I would be rescued, I had no place to go and no way of getting there.

It was about forty-five minutes before the first person arrived on scene. A man out walking had seen the jet and my ejection and had waded, swam, and walked from the shore over to me. We established that he could do nothing on his own but he did have some water, which was gratefully received. Next on the scene was an off-duty policeman who had called the emergency services before he too had made his way to me. Shortly thereafter I could hear the sounds of a boat repeatedly getting grounded on the sandbanks as the estuary continued to drain—this was the RNLI from Borth making their way to me. Very soon the sky was filled with choppers and the RAF Valley and Chivenor aircraft arrived on scene closely followed by the North Wales Police helicopter. Quite soon there was a fairly large group of people on the sandbank to keep me company and get me to hospital. As you would expect the professionalism of this bunch and in particular the winchman was exceptional and I was strapped to a back board and winched into the helicopter and on my way.

WITHOUT going into vast reams of medical details about the days, weeks, and months that followed, the force of the ejection resulted in a burst fracture of one of my vertebrae. The fragments of bone embedded themselves into my spinal cord. The result of this was to effectively paralyze me from the waist down. The spine was fixed by the introduction of yet more metalwork in the form of a supporting cage around the burst vertebrae. I have been able to regain the use of my legs but am still devoid of feeling and function below the waist. My days of flying bang-seat-equipped aircraft are over, but I guess it was time to grow up and find a proper job. As those of us who fly know all too well, it could have been worse. I'm still here to tell the tale.

Returning to the fact that I found myself still attached to the seat at a late stage of the descent and the apparent failure to achieve man-seat separation, this was investigated. This appears to have been a result of my tightening of the lap straps possibly a little over-zealously. The mechanism worked as advertised and released the lugs in the seat pan, but the tension from the straps acting at ninety degrees to the release direction resulted in a geometric lock being set up. This was only released when I was able to activate the QRF and the seat dropped away.

The AAIB said this accident was a salient reminder to those operating old aircraft that any snags which are being carried must be carefully considered, and that my injuries may have been lessened if I had elected to use the face screen handle instead of the seat pan handle. This, they suppose, would have given me a better posture. An interesting observation—most modern seats have only a seat pan handle. I presume the move away from "bang" seats to "rocket" seats has resulted in a transition from good posture afforded by the face screen handle against the more rapid access of the seat pan handle. With gentler (relative term only) rides from rocket seats the importance of posture has diminished in favor of more rapid egress. I never even contemplated the face screen handle as an option. My routine training has always been to use the seat pan handle. I have many people to be thankful to in getting me from there to here. The rescue services, the surgeons, nurses and physiotherapists who helped to patch me together physically. My friends and work mates who helped keep my spirits up. But most of all to my wife and family who once again I am forever indebted to—without their love and support this would have been far, far worse than it already was.

38

S. M. "PETE" PURVIS—1973

"Hey, I'd like you to meet the guy who shot himself down." Quite often, that's how my friends have introduced me. This unique honor belongs to me and another Grumman test pilot, Tommy Attridge, who did it in an F-11F-1 fighter that he flew into a hail of 20mm rounds he had just fired during a supersonic gunnery test. Several years later, as a test pilot for Grumman Aerospace flying out of Point Mugu, California, I found a more modern way to do this using a Sparrow missile and the no. 6 F-14A Tomcat—at that time, the Navy's fighter of the future. Over thirty-five years later, that day—June 20, 1973—remains sharp in my memory.

This is how it's supposed to go: the missile drops down far enough to clear the airplane and then travels on its merry way. A photo from the actual misfiring sequence shows the severity of the flames from the initial firing; the failure of the missile to drop and properly clear the airframe; the missile dangerously close to the cockpit and the wayward Aim-7 about to tumble away from us.

It wasn't a dark and stormy night. The midday sun was bright in the clear blue southern California sky. The Channel Islands off Point Mugu stood out in blue/gray stark relief against the glistening ocean below as Bill "Tank" Sherman and I flew west toward the test area in the Pacific Missile Test Range. Tank and I had known each other since we were in the same class in the Navy's F-4 replacement air group training. He had a combat tour as a Navy radar intercept officer (RIO) and was good at his business: analytical, competent and cool—the kind of guy you wanted to have along when things got hectic. I had learned the real value of a good RIO over North Vietnam while flying combat missions in the F-4B Phantom from the USS *Coral Sea*.

One of the myriad development tests of a tactical airplane is weapons separation, whether those weapons are bombs or missiles. That day, we were testing a critical point in the Sparrow missile launch envelope. We weren't testing the missile's ability to kill airplanes, only its ability to clear our airplane safely when fired. The crucial test point took place at .95 Mach, at 5,000 feet altitude and at zero G, and it consisted of firing Raytheon AIM-7 Sparrow missiles from the farthest aft station (no. 4) in the "tunnel" that is under the F-14 between the two engines where most missiles and bombs are hung. On the F-14, the Sparrow missiles are mounted in semi-submerged launchers in the tunnel with two of its eight cruciform wings (four forward, four aft) inserted into slots in each launcher. These triangular fins are sixteen inches wide and, when the missile is attached to the launcher, stick into the bottom of the fuselage.

The test point for that day was in the heart of the low altitude transonic range where the high-dynamic pressure low fields close to the fuselage are mysterious. The zero-G launch parameter meant the missile would not get any help from gravity as it was pushed away from the airplane by the two semicircular feet embedded in the launcher mechanism. Each of these feet was attached to a cylinder that contained a small explosive charge that was set off by pulling the trigger on the stick.

This particular launch was not thought to be risky from a pure separation standpoint because preceding Sparrow launches from the F-14 wing pylon, forward and mid-fuselage positions in identical flight conditions had demonstrated favorable release dynamics and good clearance between the missile and the aircraft throughout the entire launch sequence. In fact, Raytheon—on the basis of its own aerodynamic analysis—was concerned that the missile would severely pitch nose down as it had on two of the three prior launches at this condition, and possibly be so far below the air-craft as it passed the F-14's nose radar that it could, in the real world for which it was designed, lose the rear antenna radar signal and compromise the target acquisition portion of the missile tra-jectory. Raytheon engineers had predicted a two-foot clearance. Independent Grumman wind tunnel tests confirmed the Raytheon analysis. Such, however, was not to be the case for this launch. Hal Farley—the other Grumman test pilot sharing the missile separa-tion program—and I had flown an extensive buildup series to get to this critical data point. Flight-test programs are very orderly evolutions.

Engineers and test pilots study historical and forecast data care-fully as test points progress from the mundane to the hazardous. This one was no different. Neither Hal nor I had flown missile sepa-ration tests before this series. And they didn't cover it at the Navy Test Pilot School, either. One of our Grumman colleagues, Don Evans—a former Edwards USAF test pilot and one of the most ex-perienced sticks in the outfit—had warned us during flight test "bonus" discussions that for other than first flights, high-airspeed tests and structural demos, weapons separations were the most perilous, primarily because of their unpredictable nature. Hal and I listened to Don, but his thoughts didn't sink in until we did a bit of on-the-job training. We soon learned that, once they departed the mother airplane, stores sometimes had minds of their own; they sailed away and were known to barrel roll over the top or, perhaps, disintegrate ahead of the airplane. Once you've seen that happen, you become wary of staying too close when chasing the test air-plane. We often had eager Navy pilots flying photo chase, and we had to warn them in no uncertain terms that this wasn't a Blue Angels' tryout.

During the preflight briefing, the engineers once again dis-played graphs that showed the predicted missile-to-fuselage clear-ance as a function of time after trigger pull. As expected, clearance was seen to be tight. But we had the utmost confidence in Grum-man's lead separation engineer, Tom Reilly, and his data. All previ-ous launch data used during buildups had come out on the money.

We were good to go. The test missile was a dummy AIM-7E-2, an obsolescent model of the Sparrow with the same form, fit, and function as the AIM-7F, the missile scheduled for the Fleet. The 7E-2's casing, however, was slightly thinner than the 7F's.

The missile launcher feet contained a smaller charge because Raytheon's engineers thought a larger charge might fire the feet with enough force to break the missile casing. The rest of the briefing was routine. As usual, F-14 no. 6's test coordinator, Bob Mottl, was facilitator and ensured that all the supporting cast had their moment. Tom gave us the usual five-inch stack of five-by-seven-inch index cards that detailed each step of the test. Jim Homer, Grumman's range coordinator, briefed us on the boundaries of the test area and an array of test frequencies and range procedures. Tank and I briefed our chase F-4 crew—Lt. Col. Fritz Menning, USMC, from the VX-4 tactics development squadron (who had chased many previous flights) and PH1 Bill Irving, the top aerial photographer at the Naval Missile Center, Point Mugu. After the routine ground checks, we took off and flew directly to our test location about eighty miles offshore between Santa Rosa and San Nicolas Islands, directly west of Los Angeles.

The test pilot—in this case, the test crew—has two primary jobs: first, to hit a specific data point (aircraft attitude, altitude, airspeed, G loading) in the most efficient manner, and then relate unusual phenomena and analysis to the folks back on the ground. On this day, the second part was covered by several million dollars' worth of test instrumentation. Very fortunate, because things were about to get exciting.

We hit our point in the sky (567 KIAS, 5,000 feet, 0G), and I pulled the trigger. *Ka-whumpf!!*—a much louder *kawhumpf* than we'd experienced before. The missile appeared in my peripheral vision as it passed from beneath the left nacelle. It was tumbling end over end, spewing fire. That's weird! My first thought was, "I'll bet stray pieces FOD'ed the left engine." My instant analysis seemed to be confirmed a few seconds later when the master caution light flashed in front of me. My eyes jumped to the caution panel, which had begun to light up like a pinball machine! HORIZONTAL TAIL and

RUDDER AUTHORITY, numerous lesser lights, then BLEED DUCT! That's the one that usually came on before fire warning lights. I disregarded all but the BLEED DUCT light and tried to punch it out by turning off the bleed air source. That didn't work! Now the chase told me I was venting fuel, and I had a "pretty good fire going." "How good is that?" I asked in my cool-guy, smart-ass best. There's the left fire warning light! He's right! Shut down the left engine. Well, that didn't work either.

As I reached for the left fuel shutoff handle, the nose pitched up violently; so sharply that the force of more than 10 G curled me into a fetal position. I couldn't reach either the face curtain or the alternate handle between my legs. It didn't take long for me to figure out that I was no longer in control of the situation. "Eject, Tank, eject!" And as the high G force (data said it peaked at 1.3 seconds) bled off to a point at which one of us could reach the face curtain, either Tank or I initiated the ejection sequence, and in just one second we went from raucous noise and confusion to almost complete peace and quiet. The ejection was smooth, and after my body completed about four somersaults, the chute opened. The opening shock was gentler than I had expected. In fact, I hardly noticed it. All the action from missile launch to our ejection took only 39 seconds! It seemed much longer. We had ejected at an estimated 350 knots, having bled off 150 to 200 knots in the pitch up, and at 7,000 feet—2,000 feet higher than we started. Post-accident analysis of the instrumentation showed the violent nose-up maneuver was caused by a full nose-up stabilator command, the result of a probable burn-through of the control rod that actuated nose-down commands. Had the stabilator command gone full nose-down, you wouldn't be reading this story.

As I reached for the left fuel shutoff handle, the nose pitched up violently; so sharply that the force of more than 10 G's curled me into a fetal position. I couldn't reach either the face curtain or the alternate handle between my legs. It didn't take long for me to figure out that I was no longer in control of the situation.

As I stopped swinging in the chute, I saw Tank about seventy-five yards away and one hundred feet below me. We waved at each other to indicate we were in good shape. We both waved at Fritz, who circled until he was low on fuel. We had hoped to wave at a helicopter, but to travel 80 miles in a helo flying at 120 knots takes a long time—even though it launched a few minutes after we ejected. Our airplane descended in a slow, shallow left spiral, burning fiercely in a long plume reaching from the trailing edge of the wing to well beyond the tail. It hit the water in the same altitude as it had descended—5 to 10 degrees nose down and in a 10-degree left bank. On impact, it broke up and scattered pieces in a 100-foot radius. The largest chunk was the left portion of the tail section that floated in a pool of pink hydraulic fluid. The parachute ride was calm, serene, and long. The only noise was the chase plane roaring by several times.

As I hung in the chute, my thoughts turned to the next phase: water survival. The sea below was calm. First thought: Did the airplane crash sound reveille to the sharks, who must be lurking hungrily below awaiting their next meal? Oddly, that was the last time I thought of sharks for the rest of the day because my mind soon became otherwise engaged. Sharks weren't something I could control, but water entry was, so I began to go through my water survival tactics. I pulled the right handle of the seat pan to release my life raft, which was supposed to remain attached to the pan on the end of a long yellow lanyard, or so I'd been told. I peered carefully below, but saw no raft or shadow on the water; pulled the left one. Still no sign. Sure hope there is one.

Bear in mind that the last time I had hung in a parachute harness was in preflight some sixteen years before, and then not for very long. I wasn't about to perform a creative search for my life raft using chute steering or other acrobatics best left to the 82nd Airborne. Nor did I care to enter the water in other than the prescribed manner, so I gingerly walked my fingers up the risers and found the parachute's quick-release fittings (they're parked a foot or so above your shoulders when you're hanging under a parachute) so I could actuate them when I hit the water to avoid becoming tangled in parachute and shrouds—yet another way to die.

After what seemed like a very long time hanging in the chute, the water suddenly rushed up at me, an event that according to survival school anecdotes signaled impending water entry. Water entry was like jumping off a ten-foot diving board—just like they said. I plummeted about ten feet under, and then bobbed to the top while trying to actuate my life vest all the way. In my state of diminished IQ—probably about 20—I had forgotten that very basic step on the way down. I flailed about the surface, kicking, treading water with one hand, and searching for the life-vest toggle with the other, then treading water with both. My addled brain realized that this maneuver wasn't going to be a long-term survival technique.

Epiphany! You'd better stick your head underwater, submerge if you must, open your eyes and find the damned toggles, or you're going to die. Doing so, I found the right one, pulled it, and once again ascended to the surface, this time from about eight feet down. Next, find the left toggle. Now that I was at least floating, I figured I didn't need to perform my immersion act again, so I somewhat calmly found the left toggle and inflated the rest of the life vest that contained most of the neck collar and thus, lots more comfort.

Now that the most basic water survival goal—floating—had been achieved, I turned my attention to getting rid of the chute, which I found still connected to my left quick-release fitting. Release was a bit difficult because no tension was on the riser. Small problem. A few shrouds plus the yellow raft lanyard were wrapped around my left ankle. The shrouds untangled easily, but not the lanyard. The life raft episode, which at times brought to mind thoughts of monkeys playing football, would roll an audience in the aisles if included in a water survival flick. Where was the raft? Because I hadn't seen either the raft or its shadow on the way down, I assumed it hadn't inflated but it must be on the water nearby. I couldn't turn around very well because of my stiff neck. I soon saw the raft about five yards away out of the corner of my eye. I remembered rafts being yellow, but this one was black and at first glance seemed partially inflated. Both illusions were caused by the protective cover draped over the raft's side. I began to swim toward it and after splashing through one yard of the five-yard gap in about ten seconds, the light turned on. I'll bet if I pulled on the yellow raft lanyard it would come to me. I did, and it did.

Now the fun began! I remembered the raft was attached to the seat pan, so there was no way I was about to get rid of the seat pan and see my new home headed toward Hawaii. I didn't recall that the raft had a lanyard to attach your harness to the raft. Now came the time to board the raft. I remembered the "method" from earlier days in water survival training: Face the low end of the raft, grab the sides, pull it toward you, do a snap roll, and you'll be in a nice, comfortable position on your back. Right! But this approach didn't consider that the idiot boarding the raft still had his seat pan strapped to his butt. The outcome of this trick was an inverted raft parked on top of my head. I flipped the raft and rested.

Let's try this a different way: hoist yourself into the raft on your stomach, rest, then try a sneaky slow-roll. After about 45 degrees of roll, I became hung up on something. My oxygen hose was still connected to my seat pan. I fumbled around and eventually freed the hose. Now, continuing my roll to 135 degrees, I was sort of faceup but still hung up. It must be the seat pan. I disconnected it, and very carefully pushed it to the foot of the raft—I certainly didn't need to puncture it now. Still hung up! OK; disconnect the mask from the harness. No luck.

About now, my tired and befuddled mind decided to take stock of the situation and sort out priorities. I am in my raft and floating nicely; it's pretty calm (a 5- to 7-knot wind and a 4-foot swell at about twice a minute), and I have better things to do now than flail about trying to get flat on my back in this raft. Where's Tank? I figured he was behind me because he yelled from that direction a few minutes ago. I had replied by waving my arms. I was too weak to do much else after flailing about, and I was nauseous from swallowing sea water. I turned on my Guard channel beeper— mainly to see if it would work. Half the world knew where we were, probably including the Soviets who regularly shadowed Pacific Missile Range operations with trawlers offshore. Planes had been flying around us when we ejected: two F-4s (Bloodhound 96, the chase, and Vandy 6 from VX-4) and Bloodhound 21, an S-2 used by PMR for range clearance. We also carried a PRC-90 survival radio, which is much better suited for talking to other humans, so I stowed the Guard beeper and pulled out the PRC, connected the earphone plug to the plug on my hardhat (this was probably the most coherent thing I'd done since jettisoning the airplane), turned to Guard transmit/receive and held a short confab with Tank.

We were both fine. We were the only people talking on Guard, so I attempted to raise someone on Plead Control, PMR's main-range control frequency. Another problem. After about a minute of turning the channel selector in both directions to select the channel, I realized one must push the button in the center of the selector to change channels. Another victory for the IQ-challenged! Bloodhound 21 flew low overhead, and we began conversing about our major concern. Where was the cavalry? It was about ten minutes away, in two helos. Super! Relieved, I tried to get comfortable. I first sighted the helo as he passed the foot of my raft several hundred yards away, headed for the wreckage. Almost in unison, both Bloodhound 21 and I let him know neither Tank nor I was at the wreckage. "I'm at your nine o'clock." (I was really at his three; another good argument for giving direction first, then clock code.) I vectored him to me over the radio. He quickly locked on. "Don't need a smoke." I was happy to hear that. If lighting off a smoke flare followed the trend of my misadventures of the past hour, I probably would have doused myself in orange smoke or opened the wrong end and burned myself. "Do you have any difficulty?" asked the helo pilot. "I'm hung up on something in the raft," I said. "I'll drop a swimmer," he said.

After about thirty seconds, he splashed down about five yards away, disconnected me from whatever had me hung up, and then guided me toward the horse collar being lowered by the second crewman. Using sign language, he told me to get out of the raft. Hesitant to leave the security of my newfound home, I somewhat reluctantly obeyed. Strange thoughts race through the mind at times. I got into the horse collar the right way on the first attempt.

(Getting in the wrong way is probably the most common mistake in rescues.) As I came abreast of the helo's door, the crewman grabbed me and pulled me in. I let him do everything his way.

At this point, I wasn't about to insert my own inputs, the wisdom of which I had begun to suspect not long after entering the water nearly an hour before. I saw the other helo getting close to Tank, who had a flare in his hand that was billowing immense clouds of orange smoke. I walked forward in the aircraft as far away from the door as I could get and watched as the crewman hoisted the swimmer aboard. Both helped me out of my flight gear. Then I strapped myself onto the canvas bench along the left bulkhead, looked out the open door at the welcome sight of the ocean now below me, and smoked one of several cigarettes offered by the crewmen as we flew to the beach some forty minutes away.

Naturally, a large welcoming committee had gathered on the ramp to meet us: Capt. Clyde Tuomela, the Navy's Mugu F-14 program manager; Cdr. "Smoke" Wilson, his deputy; Mike Bennett, Grumman's local flight test manager; Hal Farley, and a host of others. Tom Brancati, Grumman's manager at Point Mugu, happened at the time to be en route to Washington to brief the Navy on program progress. You don't lose a hand-built development airplane costing untold millions every day, so Tom, after being notified of the loss of the F-14 as he passed through Dulles airport, had to gather his data and thoughts quickly to explain this one. We had lost two airplanes previously: number 1 on the second-ever F-14 flight when the hydraulic system failed; and number 10, the carrier suitability demonstration airplane, which flew into the water during an air show practice at Patuxent River, killing the F-14 project pilot, Bill Miller, who had ejected earlier from no. 1 along with Bob Smyth, the director of Grumman's flight test.

One tenet of the fighter pilot's creed is: "I would rather die than look bad." You have got to look cool as you dismount—just as though nothing had happened, kind of John Wayne-like. Yeah, right! As I stepped down from the helicopter and my feet hit the ground, I began to shiver uncontrollably, and I had great difficulty talking. The thermal shock from flailing around in the 60-degree ocean for almost an hour had hit. This embarrassing state didn't wear off until later in sick bay, after I had belted down four raw brandies. Shooting myself down was merely a prelude to the water fiasco. It was apparent to Tank and me—and to our management—that we required some remedial survival training. And so we got ours in the middle of December in the outdoor, unheated pool at NAS Miramar. But that's another story.

That evening, Tank and I had our Grumman bowling league scheduled. We went. Luckily, neither of us dropped a ball on our foot.

39

LT. GEORGE B. QUISENBERRY—1950

While I was assigned as a test pilot in the Cargo, Trainer and Miscellaneous Section of Flight Test, several small aircraft manufacturers flew one of their aircraft to Wright Field to enter into a competition for a contract award to manufacture the Army L-19 aircraft. Cessna finally became the winner of the contract.

One of the competing aircraft was built by Fletcher Aviation Company and it was designated the Fletcher FL-23. Also, I believe, it was licensed only as experimental. I was designated to make the initial flight of this aircraft. To the best of my recollection the date was April 20, 1950. Mr. Richard Reed from Test Engineering accompanied me on this first—and only—flight.

The purpose of the flight was to do a check on the airplane's climb, and it was scheduled for early in the morning. The takeoff and climb proceeded routinely without incident until it was determined that the aircraft would not be able to reach to service ceiling claimed by the manufacturer. The climb was then discontinued and I reversed our heading to return to Wright Field.

After the beginning of our descent I decided to check some of the aircraft flight characteristics and started doing a series of stalls, first power off and no flaps, and progressing up to power approach configuration because decreasing airspeed made the aircraft tend to roll to the right. When I reached the point of having full left aileron applied and still had not stalled, I decided to discontinue any further tests and proceed directly back to base.

Small, fair weather cumulus clouds were beginning to form, and as I let down I started turning as necessary to avoid the clouds. I started dropping the nose with reduced power to increase the rate of descent and found that, as the airspeed began increasing, the aircraft began exhibiting diverse longitudinal stability; that is, it became nose heavy, and I brought the nose up to correct the situation.

I wanted Mr. Reed to see this for himself, so I asked him to place his stowed control stick in his control socket, explained to him what I had found, and told him to begin lowering the nose.

When he reached the same angle of descent I had used I told him to hold it there and note the nose heaviness. After a few seconds I asked him to bring the nose back up to level flight. The nose did not come back up so I took control of the aircraft and started pulling back on my stick. The stick had a soft and mushy feeling as I continued to pull it back with no change of the aircraft altitude. Suddenly there was a severe buffeting and the aircraft nosed over violently. The windshield and overhead Plexiglas were breaking apart and, when Mr. Reed and I released our seat belts to bail out, we fell through the top of the aircraft due to the high negative G loading.

My parachute harness caught on something and I put both hands against the outside upper structure and pushed myself free. Our parachutes functioned normally and I next heard a whishing sound and saw the aircraft spinning down, inverted, between Mr. Reed and me. I swear it was so close by we could see the rivets in the fuselage.

I breathed a sigh of relief and called to Mr. Reed to ask if he was all right, and he gave me the OK hand signal. The aircraft continued spinning downward until it crashed near a barnyard. I estimate our altitude at bailout at approximately six thousand feet. We landed near a farmhouse approximately forty miles north of Dayton, and I pulled my feet up just before landing to avoid hitting a fence and wound up spraining my left ankle.

The farmer came running out to Mr. Reed, and the two of them assisted me to his house. To this day I wonder who he was. I didn't have the presence of mind to get his name. He offered the use of his telephone and I called Wright Field and informed Captain "Ike" Northrup of what had happened. A short while later a CT & M helicopter, flown by Captain Tom Cecil, appeared and he continued to circle around to lead an ambulance to our location. Mr. Reed and I returned to base in the ambulance and were examined by the flight surgeon and released. Other than a sprained ankle, I had only a few scratches and abrasions on my face. I don't believe Mr. Reed had any injuries. Investigation revealed that the aircraft had lost a portion of the horizontal stabilizer and elevator system sufficient to cause it to be uncontrollable. Whether this structural failure was sudden or progressive is not known.

40

LT. RICHARD "DICK" RUTAN: STROBE 01 INCIDENT—1968

It happened in the summer of 1968, but remains as surreal as if it were a dream I had last night. When I first arrived in Vietnam, I was assigned to an F-100 fighter wing at Phu Cat, about halfway between Saigon and Da Nang. The primary mission was to provide close air support for the ground troops. A few of those missions were very rewarding—we could see immediate results of our efforts—but the majority of the missions were just busting trees. I figured that as long as I had to be in 'Nam, it might as well be in the middle of the action; and for this fighter pilot, that action was in North Vietnam.

Our base hosted a special unit called Misty. The Misty's flew the two-seat trainer version of the F-100—fighter pilot seated in front, forward air controller (FAC) in the back. We ranged low and fast over the lower panhandle of North Vietnam and Laos, and when we would find anything to do with the movement on war material down the Ho Chi Min Trail, we would direct air strikes on the target. These missions were long—often between four and six hours— they were exhausting, but they were also full of action.

On this day I was in the backseat with Captain Donald E. Harland. We had just completed our in-flight refuel from a KC-135 just off the coast over the Gulf of Tonkin, when we heard a Mayday call to Waterboy (GCI Site). The call was from Strobe 01, an RF-4C Phantom coming out of North Vietnam, just above the DMZ. He reported he had taken a hit and had smoke in the rear cockpit . . . that he was losing hydraulic pressure and was heading feet wet. Turning on our tape recorder, we listened for a while to the conversation and discovered we were almost head-on to Strobe 01. I jumped into the conversation and asked Waterboy to vector us for a rejoin so we could check him out. After a few vectors, we found ourselves in a stern tail chase with too much speed and overshot him. Idle, speed brakes, full left rudder, right aileron, we had skidded right by him. We slipped back on his left wing, and from what Harland and I could initially see, all looked normal; we didn't spot a gaping hole or see a stream of fluid. Strobe 01 stated they were losing hydraulic pressure and they were getting heat in the rear cockpit. We requested a "hold steady" so we could come in closer and do a visual battle damage check. We began our inspection just as Strobe 01 rolled wings level, a few miles feet wet and parallel to the coast. He radioed he would try to make Da Nang.

Harland was new to Misty, and I had been around awhile, so I took control. I slid close in underneath the ugly fighter. Harland noticed the fire first; it was near the nose through a small hole in the belly near the aft part of the camera bay. Soon I could see them, too; small flames flickering in the hole, but there wasn't a big fire. Harland also spotted a small amount of smoke burping out of the seams in the belly. I crossed back over to the left wing and we forwarded these tidbits of information to Strobe 01. During this entire check, we had no idea there was a general officer in front, and that we were not talking to the pilot, but rather to the "seeing-eye major" in the backseat. All along, I thought it was just a "poug" captain and his brown-bar navigator in the back. Generals, after all, were prohibited from flying up North.

Strobe 01 acknowledged the fire sighting and said, "Okay, we're going to go ahead and bail out." It should have been a very by-the-book ejection: ten thousand feet, straight and level, ideal speed, under control, leading to a routine water rescue . . . Up until this moment I had not witnessed an ejection sequence up close, and the notorious F-4 seat, known as the "back breaker" with its complicated system would be a neat ejection indeed.

I eased the F-100F out to route formation and waited what seemed an eternity, but nothing happened. Two minutes later, the rear seat fired. Later I asked the "seeing-eye major" what had taken so long, especially since they had been told they were on fire. He reported that the general did not want to eject, and they argued about the position of the command ejection handle in the rear cockpit. The major, upholding his duties, wanted it in the command position (the guy in back command ejects the front), but the general outranked him and ordered him to leave it in the off position, thereby making each seat a single initiated ejection. The major reluctantly pulled the D-ring on his seat, leaving his general to fend for himself.

From my vantage point this first ejection from the rear cockpit was absolute textbook. I can still remember it vividly, as if in slow motion. The aft canopy opened and separated cleanly, clearing the tail by a good twenty feet, then the seat started up the rails. Just as the bottom of the seat cleared the canopy seal, the rocket motor ignited, burned for 1.2 seconds and the seat went straight up, very stable. When the rocket stopped, the small, drogue chute came out and the seat rotated back 90 degrees, eyeballs straight up, the major flat on his back, as he cleared the tail. Now, looking back over my right shoulder, the main C-9 canopy came out and as it started to open, the seat separated and kept right on going. Now, with the canopy fully open, the pilot swung back underneath. The whole thing was neat as hell, I thought.

Then I looked back to the stricken aircraft, and could not believe the horror I saw. The front cockpit was totally engulfed in fire, with an occasional flash of a white dot of the pilot's helmet through the smoke and flames. The general was sitting straight up as before, but motionless, and seemed totally oblivious to what was happening. Huge flames, like two blowtorches, were streaming from the rudder pedal wells through the front cockpit around the pilot and out the now open rear cockpit. The fire painted the exterior of the Phantom, and turned into a dense black smoke trail that obscured the tail. The aircraft flew on undisturbed. For a moment

I thought he must not be aware of the fire, so I began hollering on the radio, "Strobe 01! Bail out! Bail out!"

I continued to call again and again, but the general took no action. The wings were level, but now the aircraft started a shallow descent. "My God!" I screamed. "Why doesn't he eject? How can he just sit there? What in the hell is wrong?" Then I figured it out; he couldn't hear me. I flew right up next to the burning cockpit and continued to demand, "Strobe 01! Bail out! Bail out!" Harland called, "Oh my God! Look at it burn!" We moved in closer—so close that the air pressure between the two aircraft caused the fiery ball to roll up in a right bank. As I pulled back, the burning Phantom rolled wings level, and was now pointed directly at the beach in a slightly steeper descent.

By this time, we could no longer see the pilot's white helmet, just a charred canopy. The paint was blistering, and then there were a couple of explosions that blew some of the panels loose and sent other pieces flying off the aircraft. The whole nose was a charcoal mess. The flames subsided, and dense, thick smoke streamed.

For some strange reason I just couldn't let go and continued to call Strobe 01, begging him to get out. At about five hundred feet AGL and still close on his wing, the old Phantom gave one last dying gasp, pitched up a little and then dove straight into the beach, one hundred yards feet dry. I still couldn't let go. Harland screamed, "Goddammit, Dick! Pull up!" I know Harland's stern direction and reality wake-up call saved us. I could have crashed right beside Strobe 01; I could have just followed him in. I pulled up left and told Waterboy, "Strobe 01 just impacted on the beach." Waterboy called and asked if there was any chance of survival. My sad reply was, "Negative survival, negative survival."

We turned back to find the major, and heard an unusual amount of radio chatter about securing the area. Such an intense amount of interest in this crash site seemed odd. Except for the interest level being way out of the ordinary, Harland and I still had no idea who was onboard, and we wouldn't find out until we returned to Phu Cat.

It was time to concentrate on locating the major. We quickly found him, still in his parachute about five thousand feet above an angry Gulf of Tonkin with a motorized Vietnamese vessel rapidly approaching. We could make out three or four people on board the boat flying the Republic of South Vietnam flag. Even if they were friendly, they could still kill the pilot if they did not know what they were doing. We decided to make a low pass across the boat's bow to encourage them to turn around. We pulled up, but the boat continued motoring toward the major, who was now drifting closer to the water. We decided to give the boat one final warning and Harland placed a long burst of 20mm right close across the boat's bow. As we pulled up and came around, just as the major hit the water, the threatening boat made a sharp 180-degree turn and beat feet back to the beach. Soon afterward, a Jolly Green helicopter arrived and picked up the downed airman.

Harland and I headed back and returned to Phu Cat where there was quite a welcoming committee of colonels as we taxied in. I told Harland, "I don't know what we've done, but it must have been a major screwup." The first colonel up the ladder said in an angry voice, "What are you doing here? You should have landed at Saigon!" Boy, were we confused.

I said, "Yeah, that was real bad and, uh, hey, I have a tape of the whole thing." The colonel's eyes got big and he literally grabbed the tape recorder from my hands. Harland and I climbed out of the aircraft totally bewildered until it finally dawned on the colonel that we had no idea who was on board Strobe 01.

"It was General Bob Worley." And not knowing what to do with the recorder, he handed it back to me and said, "Get in a Class B Uniform, pack a bag and a Scatback (T-39) will be here in thirty minutes to take you both to Saigon. MACV wants you guys to brief the generals."

"Oh, Goody," I thought.

On the ride to Saigon, I listened to the tape. Thank God I did, because there was one extremely bad thing said that needed to be edited. When we made Saigon, it seemed every damn general required his own private briefing and wanted to listen to the tape.

These hallowed halls brimming with stars were quite a change of pace for a couple of "up-country Poug Mistys."

The tragic crash of Strobe 01 killed General Bob Worley, who was a true, honest-to-goodness tactical fighter pilot. As it turns out, he was the only USAF general officer to die in combat during the Vietnam conflict. Worley was a strong and much-needed voice for the fighter pilot. What was doubly sad was that it was Worley's last mission. In Vietnam, one receives double credit toward an Air Medal for an out-of-country mission. The major said Worley really wanted that Air Medal and some special photos. You know "the grand finale."

Last-mission shoot downs are not uncommon, and are almost a disease. Often, commanders would not even share with the crew that they were on their final mission until after they had landed safely. Seems everyone wanted the big BDA and to fly their final mission in grand style. I remember one Misty's going-away party, where four of the five troops being honored got shot down soon after the party. When this dawned on someone, it was pointed out to the boss that, of the five, all but one had been shot down. The only remaining one was a good buddy of mine, who at that very moment was on his final mission in North Vietnam . . . but that's another story.

Reliving that day of Strobe 01's final adventure, I have often wondered why I kept calling for the general to bail out, and why we stuck so close all the way in, unable to let go when it was obvious Worley was dead mere moments following the major's ejection . . .

41

LT. RICHARD "DICK" RUTAN—1970

It was the summer of 1970, and I had just completed a combat tour in Vietnam. My new assignment was at Lakenheath Air Base in England, about sixty miles north of London. This was the same field that launched B-17 bombers during WWII. The primary mission of our 48th Tactical Fighter Wing was to provide close air support of the ground troops in Germany and a nuclear strike mission into the Soviet Union from forward alert bases in Turkey and Italy.

I was bored with the nuclear alert routine, and got checked out as a test pilot doing functional check flights (FCF) on newly overhauled F-100s before returning them to operational status. Due to a long period of typical lousy English weather, we had a large backlog of aircraft in need of FCFs and our wing was close to not being able to meet its nuclear operational commitment. This was a BIG no-no during those Cold War days. Before long, the wing's higher-ups, under the pressure of operational readiness, signed a weather waiver to launch me into the English murk to check out an F-100 that had just days before been in pieces all over the hangar floor.

Still soggy from the continuous downpour, I strapped into the sleek, single-seat, single-engine fighter, lit the afterburner and blasted off into ragged overcast. Seconds after liftoff, I was in cloud and did not see the sun until I broke out in the clear at about forty thousand feet. Now, over the North Sea, I pulled the "HUN" out of burner and started the long litany of checks to make sure all was well with the aircraft. One check was to fly inverted (negative G) to make certain nothing was loose and the engine would keep running. When I rolled over and pushed the stick forward, I heard and felt a huge shift of weight right behind me. When I rolled back to level flight, the weight crashed down, making a loud bang. Being curious, I had to check it again. I pulled the nose up and pushed the stick hard forward into negative G, and sure enough, the same shift of weight and huge noise happened again. I pulled back on the stick and returned to normal flight, only this time, simultaneous with the crunch, the oil pressure went from 42 psi (normal) to zero within the blink of an eye.

"Oh, my God!" I thought to myself, "I am at forty thousand over the North Sea with weather all the way to the deck and I have zero oil pressure!" The good news is jet engines will run a handful of minutes without oil if you don't move the throttle too much. So I set 83 percent RPM, about the power setting I needed for final approach, put out the speed brake, and headed home, straight into the English murk.

My first thought was that the whole engine was loose and as it shifted up and down, it must have pulled a wire off the oil pressure gauge sender, which wouldn't be a big problem. I was about ready to push the mic button to call for help, when I thought I had better make an ops check of my voice. Sure enough, the first attempt aloud in the cockpit was a broken, squeaky, and full of panic voice. So, with a couple of deep breaths and a few practice calls, I conjured up a fairly good "Yeager cool" voice and called "Pan-Pan-Pan" on the guard emergency frequency. The radar controllers did their magic to get me back ASAP. So far, all was fine. The engine seemed happy and as I intercepted the radar Ground Control Approach (GCA) glide path, I retracted the speed brake, extended the landing gear, and put down half flaps. With an engine problem, the procedure is to use half flaps to reduce drag, and 20 knots extra so if the engine fails there is enough speed to level off and eject. If you are not level, the chute simply won't open in time.

At about six hundred feet, and more than halfway down the glide path, I was beginning to break out of the ragged overcast.

Twelve and a half minutes had passed since the oil pressure had gone to zero. Suddenly, there was a slight vibration that grew rapidly into a horrible grinding noise. That was followed by a loud BANG! as the engine compressor disintegrated and stalled, and then fire shot out of both ends of the stricken HUN. The compressor stall was so violent it knocked my feet off the rudder pedals and blew dirt up in my face. Every light on the fault-warning panel lit up like a Christmas tree. I was coming back on the stick to get level and, looking ahead, I still could not see the runway, but did see the little village of Brandon directly in front of me.

The airspeed was bleeding off rapidly and I was at that small corner of time when the aircraft is just level before the stall, when one must eject. With no time to turn, I reached for the left ejection handle, and, with my right hand still on the stick, gave the aileron a couple shots of left-roll trim. I then squeezed the left-seat ejection trigger and an explosive charge blew the canopy off. I did not have enough time to get my head back against the headrest and as the engines seized beneath me, the rocket seat fired me up the rails, and out of the cockpit I went; my head slamming forward onto my chest.

The parachute opened immediately, and I swung twice, and just before going into the trees, I could see the runway and the doomed F-100 in a gradual left turn. It impacted the trees in a huge fireball, just to the left of the little village.

Meanwhile, the entire base was aware of the emergency, and all were listening to the radio. The mobile controller, located in a small windowed trailer next to the runway to check gear down and grade landings, had seen my aircraft come out of the clouds with its landing light on and watched it crash into the trees about two or three miles short of the runway. He did not see a parachute deploy. The mobile controller hollered, "No chute! No chute! Get out there quick!" It was no secret that if you didn't bail out, there was no chance of survival.

As I came crashing through the trees, my parachute snagged on the branches and slowed my descent. I landed literally at the feet of a typical English gentleman trimming trees in the Queen's forest. He had heard the explosion, he saw the rocket seat go out, and now here before him stood this man in a white helmet with a gold visor and oxygen mask on—an alien from outer space.

With adrenaline pumping through my veins, I ripped off my helmet and hollered, "My name is Major Rutan and I am alive!" Being fresh out of combat in SEA, my first sense was to escape and evade. Checking my parachute emergency radio beeper, I saw that, just like my bailout in Vietnam, the beeper had failed and I had to get to the other radio in the seat kit to call for rescue. Finding the kit, I pulled the release handle and there was a loud hissing noise as the life raft started to inflate. This added commotion had scared the English bloke so badly he had started to run away. I took off my parachute harness and went running after him. I said, "Come back, come back! Please! I need your help!" He stopped and very reluctantly came back and helped me get the parachute down out of the trees. I located the emergency survival radio and made the call: "This is Ring Dove Flight Test Two One. I'm down. Come and get me." From the time I squeezed the ejection trigger until I made the first radio call, a mere ninety seconds had passed.

At the time, I didn't know that my parachute had not been spotted, and since my radio beeper had failed, the consensus was that I had gone in with the aircraft. My good buddy, who flew the base helicopter rescue, knew I was coming home with a bad engine and he was airborne in an HH-43 Husky air base rescue chopper. Underneath his helicopter was a round, pressurized container that held the fire fighting suppressant. His job was to land that unit right next to the crash site, where the helicopter rotor would blow the flames away. The firefighter corpsman would don his fire resistant gear and, with the suppressant hose, fight his way through the fire into the cockpit, pull the pilot out, and drag him out of the flames. That was the standard procedure.

When the mobile controller started hollering, "No chute! No chute! Get out there quick!" my helicopter buddy, sensing the urgency, inadvertently jettisoned the fire suppression bottle to get to me ASAP. He knew his good buddy, Dick Rutan, whose wife was two weeks overdue with their second child, was inside that fireball and it was up to him to save his friend. As he orbited the burning wreckage, the thought that he had just lost a very good friend was overwhelming. And then he heard my radio call, "Hey, come out and get me!" With the mobile controller yelling, "No chute!" my copter buddy thought I was inside the fireball calling for him.

This was the kind of emergency he was trained for—to land, fight the fire, rescue the pilot—but he had dropped the fire suppressant containers three miles back at the base. He was heartsick, and all he could do was sit there circling the crash site and watch the fire burn. When he heard me call again, it began to dawn on him that no one could be in that fireball alive and be calling on the radio.

In disbelief, eyes still on the fire, he pleaded, "Dick, where are you?"

I heard his call on my survival radio and said, "I bailed out about two miles short. Get your tail out here and get me!"

Reluctant to believe I was still alive, he responded, "You bailed out? You're okay? You're not in the fireball?"

With a great sigh of relief, he flew over to a nearby soccer pitch (football field), landed, and I climbed in. While we flew back to the base, I was assessing my injuries. There were none sans a few scratches and a very sore neck.

Weeks later, the accident investigation team found that an oil sample bottle in the oil tank, dropped by an errant crew chief, had floated up during the negative G check and lodged in the oil pickup tube, ceasing the oil flow. The loud noise was the lead ballast in the ammunition bay that had not been secured properly. The noise and weight shift had nothing to do with the oil failure. But needless to say, the HUN did not pass its FCF and would never again pull nuclear alert.

42

LCDR. E. D. "SANDY" SANDBERG—1960

Sometime ago the editor of *Slipstream* asked me to write the story of the first night ejection from an aircraft in Australia. That incident occurred on 15 June 1960 at RAN Air Station Nowra, NSW when a Sea Venom FAW 53 of 724 Squadron struck a tree on the downwind leg of the landing pattern. The pilot and observer ejected safely.

As this happened in 1960, I obtained a copy of the Board of Inquiry report to refresh my memory. I wrote to the Navy Office, but as the documents were over thirty years old they had sent them to the Australian Archives. I obtained a copy from them. During this era naval pilots gained their wings with the RAAF and completed OFS at NAS Nowra in either fighter or antisubmarine specialization. 724 Squadron was equipped with Sea Venom and Vampire aircraft to carry out night fighter-pilot training.

The Sea Venom FAW 53 (FAW = Fighter All Weather) was a side-by-side two-seater aircraft built by De Haviland in the United Kingdom and shipped to Australia in HMAS *Melbourne* in 1956. The aircraft was fitted with a Ghost 104 engine and radar that enabled the observer to locate a target passing in the front sector of his aircraft. The observer's job was to verbally guide the pilot into a position where the pilot could see the target under all weather conditions, day and night. Although, when all went well, the radar was magic in its day, I understand that it is pretty basic compared to today's equipment whereby pilots pop off a missile at a blip. We only had 20mm cannon thus the pilot had to actually see the target before shooting. The Sea Venom was a good aircraft.

The characters in the story are mostly confined to Sub Lieutenant Brian A. Dutch and Lieutenant E. D. (Sandy) Sandberg because some of the other players are no longer with us. I would like to begin by thanking all the old 724 Squadron ground crew, the NAS Nowra Air Traffic Control staff and particularly all the Armourers and Safety Equipment Branch sailors, without whose skills, this tale would not be told by me.

Flying on the evening of 15th June 1960 began with a twilight takeoff for Air Interception (AI) instruction. It was the twentieth time I had flown with Brian, so we were pretty well used to one another. I had a lot of confidence in him and to my way of thinking in those days; he was the better pilot on this particular training course. As the senior observer of the squadron, I had the choice of pilots on a course and checked all their logbooks before selecting him. He was three years my junior in age; he had been flying for about eighteen months and I for just on nine years. I have flown with a lot of pilots, in a lot of aircraft, and I still rate Brian as a good pilot. This particular AI course was programmed to finish that night, so there was pressure on us to get the appropriate number of exercises in—I don't recall how many, but something like three or four night interceptions would satisfy the syllabus. In fact we flew three sorties that night to get the required runs in.

A Naval Board of Inquiry was convened to determine the cause of the accident and several people on duty that night gave their version of the event to the Board but it was the pilot who naturally underwent the most questioning and his version is the best account of what actually happened. He informed the Board that on returning from the first detail of the night the conditions in the circuit were slightly turbulent but didn't worry him at all. The detail as a whole was successful and the landing uneventful. After refueling we took off for the second detail in the same aircraft. But because the radar was unserviceable this time we returned to change aircraft. We experienced very severe wind gusts in the circuit area this time. On one occasion the weather sent us down two hundred feet and then up four hundred feet in a very short time. It was not a very nice night.

Within half an hour we had changed aircraft and were airborne again. Shortly after takeoff, Brian had trouble with his oxygen equipment. We stayed low until he sorted out the problem. Fortunately this was not long and we were soon chasing our target (a Vampire flown by Lieutenant Rolley Waddell-Wood) all over the sky for a successful mission. Now it was time to return to base and have a couple of beers to celebrate the completion of yet another night fighter course. Below three thousand feet near Nowra the turbulence started again. In the circuit area the pilot was doing those meaningful little things that a pilot does when coming into land. As I said earlier, I had considerable confidence in Brian's ability as a pilot and I was not concerned in the circuit—after all, there was nothing I could do: flying the aircraft was his part of the ship!

On the run upwind at 900 feet the turbulence was again quite severe. In fact we gained 100 feet on the turn downwind and this was not caused by bad flying. The airspeed at this time was around 250 knots decreasing to wheels-down speed of 210 knots. I did my usual prelanding checks; there weren't many but because of the turbulence my navigation bag down by my right leg was bouncing around. I bent down to secure it. While I was doing that I felt the bang . . . I bolted upright! The windscreen was opaque. My radar was on my lap—I pushed it back. Fortunately it stuck in its cradle otherwise it ejected with me or I left my legs behind at the kneecaps. I switched on my microphone and shouted, "Birdstrike, eject, eject!!"

Naturally in a situation like this nothing works as it should. Of course the intercom was U/S. It says volumes for my power of command that the pilot heard me and responded in the only way possible—by ejecting the canopy. Normally it was the observer's job to do that little chore but these were not "normal" times. I don't know where Brian got the extra hand from to release the canopy but he did it. After all at that time he had the control column back in his stomach getting height and the throttle full on getting power. I suppose it comes back to that old adage "If you want something done in a hurry, ask a busy man."

As soon as the canopy went, I went! No good hanging around at that time. In its normal flying position the observer's ejection seat is tilted slightly to the rear. When the canopy is ejected the seat springs forward to arm the ejection rocket. To fire the gun it is necessary to reach above the head and pull down the D-ring at the top of the ejection seat. Attached to the D-ring is a felt and canvas hood that covers the face to prevent injury to the head from windblast, flames, or other nasties one may meet on the way out.

I felt nothing of the bang one would expect to feel in that portion of the anatomy one would expect to feel it. My first recollection was being clear of the aircraft and a recognizable moment when movement seemingly stops. I was hanging in the air thinking, "Is this automatic thing going to work automatically?" Then the straps holding me to the seat fell away. It felt an eternity until that jolt that stopped the fall and the parachute straps uncomfortably tightened on my body. I was hanging there. But I couldn't see anything—it's all so black!

Most people that have been in a life-threatening situation will have experienced the adrenaline that races the mind. You think very fast indeed. I was thinking very fast indeed as I hung up there in the black but it wasn't black for long. *WHOOMPH!!!* The aircraft hits the ground, seemingly in front of me and explodes. Flames shoot into the air and again I realized that I was still airborne but this time without that comforting shell of the aircraft around me.

Night becomes day below me but in front things are still black. Hell, I'm blind! I feel for my eyes and instead feel my helmet—or more correctly, I feel the D-ring from the ejection seat is still over my head. I throw this off but it's still dark. The visor on my "bone dome" is down and the cloth cover is on it. I push this back and lo and behold there was light! Not any old light, though. Light that shows my partner dangling like me but between me and the flames from our downed aircraft. "Get out of there you bloody mug," I yell to him. I don't think he heard me but right now I have more problems of my own. I realize I must be getting close to the deck and I start to wonder about landing. Like a flash those periods of dummy parachute drill race out of my mind. I can't think of a bleeding thing to do. Do I put my feet to the left, to the right; cross them, spread them, or what? I look down again and see I'm going to land in a gully. What's more, that gully has steep sides and tree stumps! Oh hell, what the heck. I'll withdraw my feet altogether and stick them up around my neck somewhere out of the way. Thus I landed on my back somehow but at the time all I felt was the exit of some wind (from the mouth) and considerable jubilation at still seemingly being in one piece.

Now to find that stupid pilot. Like me he was approaching the deck fast but his immediate concern was his proximity to the burning aircraft. I need not have worried because he must have remembered his safety equipment drills for he was not hurt on landing. Before long we were reunited and became very happy indeed. We were alive! We would fly again!

Meanwhile, back at the station all hell was breaking loose. The Air Traffic Control Staff had watched the whole event, saw us eject and sounded the alarm. The Fire Tender boys responded and raced to the scene. An interesting side story here. I understand one of the drivers thought he was driving a tank and did all sorts of wonderful things on the way to the crash site but I'll leave that one to the crew to tell. We all know how dedicated these fellows were (and I'll bet, still are). The duty chopper was scrambled and the medics prepared for whatever remains they got. Generally everything worked as it should. A soon as the ambulance arrived they whipped us back to the sick bay (instead of the wardroom!), checked we were still whole, put us in bed, shot us full of morphine and left. Meanwhile, up in the wardroom a party was building up. We missed it but some kindly soul did slip us a little later on in the evening.

I am sure the reader will appreciate that most of the trees around NAS Nowra are not very big for obvious reasons. The one we lopped was thirty-three feet at our point of impact. Relax, Greenies, it was already dead before we hit it. The Martin-Baker ejection seat fitted to the Sea Venom were the best available at the time. The use-by label indicated that to work automatically the seat needed to be 200 feet from the ground and have a forward motion of 200 knots. That they worked in our situation I thank Mr. Martin and Mr. Baker and our squadron maintainers, especially the Armourers and Safety Equipment lads.

Now comes the Board of Inquiry:

Commander R. E. "Digger" Bourke Ran, being the specialist aged aviator, was the main inquisitor and a bloody thorough job he made of it too. He threw questions at Brian at a great rate of knots. He asked about his airspeed, his altimeter, his artificial horizon; his bank and turn indicator. He asked when he did this, when he did that. He asked about his power setting and his dive brakes. He was quizzed on stalling speeds in certain configurations, what "G" did he pull, how he was flying at the time—normal or pulling the aircraft in the turn, how the control surfaces were reacting. Then came the point of impact questioning.

"Around 210 knots."

"At that time were you turning or had you straightened up?"

"I was taking off bank, still turning."

"You were straightening up?"

"Yes. Slightly port wing down, slightly nose down."

The crunch questions.

"Could you find the undercarriage lever without searching for it?"

"Yes, sir."

"You were on instruments all the way (in the turn)?"

"Yes, sir."

"But yet you saw no increase or loss of height either on the altimeter or the vertical speed indicator?" asked Digger.

"To me," said Brian, "everything was in order as I selected undercarriage down, and it was almost at the same instant that we hit the gust and the windscreen shattered."

The score at this point was slightly in favor of the pilot. He had the answers. He answered truthfully.

The questioning returned to the instruments. Brian was asked about his instrument hours and then about the instruments' performance at the time of the turn downwind.

"What was your height at this point (again)?"

"Nine hundred feet."

"Did you see any alteration of the altimeter reading during the turn?"

"No."

"Did the artificial horizon indicate the aircraft was descending?"

"No."

"Was the altimeter reading steady or oscillating as the ASI was?"

"It was fairly steady."

"Was it steady during the turn?"

"Yes, sir."

"Was the needle of the VSI steady during the turn?"

"No, sir. Fluctuating quite a bit."

"Did you read the fall of speed pretty accurately between 250 and 210 knots?"

"It was impossible to get an accurate reading as it was fluctuating over 20 knots. It got to 210 and jumped to about 230 as I selected the undercarriage lever."

"What was the altimeter reading when you selected undercarriage down?"

"One thousand feet."

"After the first impact you applied power. Did you get any response from the engine and did your controls respond satisfactorily to any movement?"

"The sensation I had was of driving a car in mud and suddenly coming out onto good road. The controls seemed to be operating correctly but I was getting a lot of control changes as I was getting a lot of buffet."

"She was handling satisfactorily?"

"Yes. I was getting into the climb with wings level."

The pressure eased. The questions were answered satisfactorily and the crew is alive. How come? Was it an "exemplary" ejection because of the drill between pilot and observer? Was it because of briefings between the two, or was it squadron drills?

The pilot answered, "We carry out drills. On this occasion I couldn't contact my observer on the intercom so I jettisoned the canopy to let him know I had heard him shouting."

So ended the inquiry.

Now what did their Boardships in Navy Office think of this little lot? You may well ask the question.

Firstly FOICEA (RADM George Oldham) was not very amused and had a few harsh words to threaten our future with, but DA-WOT (Director of Air Warfare and Operational Training) in Navy Office had a more moderate view and, fortunately for Brian and me, his view prevailed. Naturally we both incurred the displeasure of the Naval Board.

Brian was informed that his actions were below the qualities expected and the Naval Board noted with concern the lack of knowledge in elementary parachute drill displayed by the observer. To that I say "Amen." I was required to carry out dog-watch instruction in elementary parachute drill for one week.

We were informed of these findings by a somewhat bemused captain of HMAS *Albatross* (Captain Tommy Morrison).

Hell's Bells! We were alive and our thanks still go to all those that made that possible. Brian learnt to fly better and I had dog-watch instruction in elementary parachute drill. Fortunately I have not had to use those skills again. What happened after a short spell of "survivor's leave"? Well, it was back to flying. Brian and I finished the course proper and we continued to fly together until the end of that month. I was posted (banished?) to 723 Squadron and Syca-more helicopters on 25 July 1960, then back to Venoms in 1961 while Brian went on to bigger and better things elsewhere.

But that, as they say, is another story for another day.

43

JACK L. "SUITCASE" SIMPSON—1955

I was a Lockheed experimental test pilot on the development of the F-104 Starfighter, the world's first jet fighter designed to fly more than twice the speed of sound. Lockheed Aircraft Company hired me because of my experience as an Air Force test pilot at North American Aviation, flying out of Los Angeles International Airport, on the development of the F-100 Super Sabre. The F-100 was the first supersonic fighter to move into mass production.

As a Lockheed experimental pilot, I felt I was part of the legacy of famous aircraft and intrepid men. Lockheed designed and built the P-38 Lightning for WW II. It became famous in the Pacific theater of operations. Lockheed also designed, in its renowned "Skunk Works," the F-80—the first operational jet fighter. I flew the Shooting Star, as it was named, both in gunnery training at Nellis AFB and in Korea in preparation for my first combat mission.

The F-104 was born in Kelly Johnson's famous Skunk Works; the design aim was to produce a supersonic fighter that would have a performance capability in excess of Mach 2 and combat altitude of over sixty thousand feet. So, although I was alone in the cockpit that day trying to figure out what went wrong at thirty thousand feet, I was in the company of esteemed designers, builders, and widely known experimental flight test pilots. I radioed the flight-test engineer in the control room at the Lockheed Flight Test Center and said, with more that a little trepidation, "Larry, I'm sure I followed the flight-test procedures you detailed me on the mission profile card, but as I reached the first test point on airspeed, angle-of-attack and yaw input, the plane went crazy; it snapped into an inverted nose-down roll. It really surprised me; it took me over nine thousand feet to recover. Remember yesterday; it didn't act like this at all."

Not like yesterday at all, as I stated earlier to Larry, meant that I had flown this specific stability and control test the day before and everything had gone according to the flight test plan. But the electronic mechanism designed to send signals from the test aircraft to the control room had malfunctioned; none of the data collected was usable for studying past performance before planning the next experimental flight. When you hear about aircraft accidents today, the familiar word is the importance of recovering the flight data recorder. Well, forty years ago, it wasn't as sophisticated; therefore, I was asked to do the experimental test over again. I agreed to do so.

I took off, climbed to thirty thousand feet, and started my experimental flight. I controlled the aircraft as precisely as called for on the flight test card. I was less than forty seconds into the test, when *wham*, the plane snapped into a pitch-up and inverted roll. It was then that I radioed Larry, after I got control of the plane and myself!

"OK," I said to Larry, "maybe I did something wrong. I'm going to try the test once again, but if it reacts the same, I'm coming home. I'll climb back to designated altitude, and I'll talk my way through. That way, we'll both be able to try to determine the unusual behavior of this lady with, it seems to me, an agitated composure."

"That's a good idea," said Larry, "but everything seemed to go so well yesterday. Hope nothing is wrong."

How soon we were to find out!

"Roger," I remarked, as I leveled off at the proper altitude. "I'm ready! I'll talk through each step! OK! Here goes! I'm at altitude, attaining—there I am—at the indicated airspeed as called for, angle of attack coming—coming—there it is—holding angle-of-attack-airspeed. OK, here comes the rudder—more—more—WOW! Why so much rudder? Damn it, Larry! Here I go again!" I yelled. "I have a vicious pitch-up! I have a huge roll input! Going crazy—I'm upside down—the plane's going crazy!"

The nose had yawed right with horrific violence. Everything became a blur as the plane tumbled out of control toward the ground. I said to myself, "This is crazy; this isn't me, this is terrifying!" For a nanosecond, my first combat mission flashed before my eyes, with the terror I experienced in seeing flak and tracers, and realizing for the first time that the enemy was trying to shoot me down with the intention of killing me!

Now this @#%*_?&# plane was trying to do the same thing!

I couldn't talk anymore. I had to get control; the airplane had stalled out. I was about 60 degrees upside down and yawing. I didn't even know which way, I was so disoriented, but I knew I was heading down fast. I didn't move the stick or push either rudder pedal. I didn't advance the throttle; I quickly checked the exhaust gas temperature and the RPM gauge; the engine had not flamed out.

"Take it easy," I said to myself. "Take it easy—don't fight the controls. You have altitude—let it go—let it go. OK now, roll it upright—little roll input—easy—easy—little rudder—whoops! The other way—easy on the stick—check the tuck—little more roll—little bit at a time—just a touch of rudder—just a touch damn it! Don't know what's wrong—little bit—little bit . . ." Slowly, ever so slowly, I started to lead and the lady was following me; we started our majestic waltz-gliding on thin air. I had talked her out of her determination to fatally test the law of gravity. I finally had number 55-2962, the eighth YF-104A manufactured, flying level. She had an eight ball tattooed to her right side. I had lost sixteen thousand feet. Yes, I had literally been "behind the eight ball."

I called Larry, gave him the particulars, and told him something was definitely wrong. I didn't know what it was, but I knew something was amiss; so much so that I instinctively started to climb and head for the dry lake at Edwards AFB. The dry lake had saved me many times during past test flights when things were not functioning properly, particularly with the new YJ79-GE-3 (General

Electric) engine; a beautifully designed, but, what turned out to be, an extremely vexatious—and deadly—engine.

In experimental flight tests, we were stretching the state of the art for an innovative fighter. Everything was new: new design of aircraft, new engine, new variable guide inlet guide vanes, new main fuel regulator, new type of afterburner, new altitudes never explored, and speeds never researched. It was the first time in any aircraft that the engine was combined with a fully variable duct system that could adapt itself to all contrasting conditions from takeoff to Mach 2.2; at least it was supposed to. The F-104's wings were also unique. Tailored purely to the supersonic regime—extraordinarily small span and area—the wings were without sweep. The next time you take a look at the new generation of fighters—the F-14, the F-15, the F-16—look at the leading edges of the wings. They look like Mt. Rushmore to the F-104's 15/100-inch-thick leading edges.

The Starfighter had a new radar and a new gun. A new pilot's handbook had to be written, meaning new operational and emergency procedures had to be written and tested.

Front line, air-to-air combat pilots convinced Kelly Johnson to go for performance at all costs. The result was one of the most startling airplanes ever built; the "missile with a man in it," as it was called. As far as moving at high speed in a straight line, it had few rivals.

But nothing worked as designed. More than a dozen times, I would be in the throes of an experimental test flight and the engine would flameout—just flat quit—for no apparent reason. I would get the engine started and gingerly head for home. Sometimes, no, many times, I couldn't get the engine started again, so I hurriedly took the option of the dry lake bed at Edwards (the same dry lake bed where the space shuttle first landed twenty-five years later) and landed the aircraft "dead stick." That five miles of lake bed gave us both lots of room.

Was the lake bed going to save me one more time? I headed toward Edwards for a couple of reasons. I was too far away from Palmdale in case of an emergency; experimental pilots aren't paid to eject out of every test vehicle that presents a sudden, unknown problem. Also, Edwards (named after an experimental test pilot who died in the crash of a flying wing) is a wide-open lake bed that would give me options for direction of landing and a high indicated airspeed on final approach. I planned to avoid any pitch-up, yaw, and roll situations. One Lockheed test pilot had recently been killed in a 104 during a flare-out at landing—the "eating an ice cream cone" maneuver used to decrease sink rate just prior to touchdown. It had pitched-up and catapulted while rolling to the right, spewing pieces of airplane and fire that tumbled and reacted explosively along the edge of the runway and into the adjacent field. I was there and saw the results to both pilot and plane. We still hadn't been able to confirm why it happened. We think the plane stalled and pitched up, yawed, and then rolled uncontrollably to the right. If I could help it, I wasn't going to let that happen to me.

I reached what I thought was a safe altitude, called Larry, and told him my plans. He told me to switch frequencies so Lockheed could monitor my approach to Edwards. I gave him a "Roger" on that and radioed Edwards.

"Edwards tower, this is Lockheed test 2962—over."

"Roger 2962; go ahead," came the instant reply.

"Edwards, 2962 is declaring an emergency although it is not a Mayday. Request landing on the lake bed at speeds above normal; not sure of my direction as yet; don't want to make too many turns; not sure when I'll drop my gear; would appreciate, however, fire truck following, over."

"Roger 2962. Wind is light, varying north to northwest at 5 knots, altimeter 30.01."

"OK, Edwards. I'll have to make a 90 toward the north—will call about three miles out on final straight-in toward north."

"Wind's not that bad and I don't want to move this thing around too much," I said to myself. "I feel like I'm encased in an eggshell."

"Edwards," I radioed, "I'm presently at three one thousand feet west of Barstow; parallel to 58 [highway 58]; have Harper Dry Lake at one o'clock. I'm on the letdown."

"Roger 2962," came the reply from Edwards. "Keep us informed.

I understand Lockheed is monitoring this frequency. The fire trucks are rolling." Fire trucks! That sent a chill though my spine.

I gingerly started to lose altitude, pulled the throttle back to about half quadrant, and cracked open the speed brakes. I had descended about 2,000 feet when I ran into a rumble of clear air turbulence. I inched back on the throttle and instinctively closed the speed brakes to reduce buffet. I told the tower I was in CAT; I knew Larry was listening. I then said to myself, "OK eight ball, take it easy; we've been through a lot of things together. We'll get through this. Take it easy."

But just as I looked down to check the airspeed indicator, the nose violently pitched almost straight down and continued to move through 90 degrees. I was starting to tumble. I called "Larry!" as I was pulling hard, real hard, back on the stick. "I've lost control! I have zero pitch input! I've got to get the hell out! Now!"

At that instant, I reached for the ejection ring between my legs with both hands and pulled as the aircraft continued to tumble. *Boom!* I was out, ejected upward, upside down at twenty-seven thousand feet.

I might explain. The F-104 was at first designed with a "downward" ejection seat because it flew extremely fast at low altitude where, of course, the air is dense. Any ejection, up or down, at high speed would be like hitting a brick wall—a thick brick wall—at 700 mph. No question: that's Excedrin headache number 1! The seat ejection systems at that time were not powerful enough to eject the pilot "upward" for fear of jamming him, due to high pressure, into the horizontal and vertical tails, each having a leading edge with a .01-inch radius. I wasn't ready for sliced "Suitcase"! Thus we ejected "downward."

It's a funny thing about life, or fate. Three of my test-pilot friends were killed in the F-104 when they were forced to eject close to the ground. The ejection system didn't function for them at low altitude, or they were too close to the ground when they made their decision to eject.

I can still remember the powerful, full force of rushing air—pinning me to my seat, like going downhill in the front seat of a mile-high roller coaster. Only this blast was instantaneous; it hit me at about 450 mph. One second after I ejected, the lap belt separation system worked; it blew the belt in half and freed me from the seat. For a few seconds, the seat and I were inches apart floating to a stop as we reached the apex of our arc. A lanyard, one end attached to half of my seat belt and the other end attached to a pin in my chute, seemed to be hanging around, slithering like an eel in water. Then the seat drifted, or fell, away. The eel became a frozen rope and pulled the pin that armed my parachute to open at fifteen thousand feet.

I started to roll and tumble and corkscrew for about ten thousand feet, like an oak leaf being blown from a tall oak tree in a vicious windstorm—sway and tumble, no control, no power over anything, no stability, just another body simply subjected, nakedly to the divine agency to which the order of things is prescribed. Would I be a favorite son, or a fatality? Would I be vicariously and rudely shoved back in time to Greek mythology and become Icarus and fall to my death by flying too close to the sun, or would I become the winged horse Pegasus carrying the thunderbolt of Zeus and be allowed to live and, like he, be captured by my Bellerophon (Lockheed) and continue to ride through many adventures?

Speaking of thunderbolts: what the hell happened? This isn't me, falling through space hoping my chute will open. Where's the ring for manual opening? Where are my hands? What happened to my airplane? Was "eight ball" angry with me? Did I step on the lady's toes too often?

My thinking was interrupted with an abrupt, cruel, and intense punch to my crotch and chest. My chute opened with a vicious snap, a whoosh, a big shaking, followed by a smaller one: it was extremely violent. I was a rag doll in the mouth of a giant killer lion, and then he dropped me—plop! And there I was! Hanging by two leg straps and a chest belt fifteen thousand feet in the air. I was stunned—this wasn't me. I'm having a nightmare!

I'm dreaming—Clark Gable and Spencer Tracy and a snazzy blond in *Test Pilot*. But then, a sudden reality; the wind came, wheezing through the shrouds rocking me back and forth, back and forth.

I was in a backyard swing, only I couldn't put my feet down to stop it. I was afraid to look down, but when I did, it was most frightening—oh my God!! Would those straps hold me? Will I fall out? I still had about twelve thousand feet to go. My first experience in a parachute. I will never forget it!

I looked around. I could see San Bernardino, Barstow, Edwards, Lancaster, Palmdale, and the Valley—all those places and hundreds of thousands of people; yet I was all alone. I looked at my legs and arms and hands. I moved them. My hands were holding on to the rigging with a tighter grip than snap-on pliers. I wasn't about to let go. Somewhere along the line I had lost my left glove and my watch; my flight suit looked like the remains of a flag flown at full mast during a hurricane. It was in shreds. But my helmet and oxygen mask stayed with me; I was sucking, rather readily I might add, emergency oxygen. My laced-up boots were still on my feet. I looked down and moved my head around. I didn't dare make a body turn, didn't want to disturb anything. The wind still had that eerie sound as it continued to pick its way through the shroud lines. It reminded me of *Inner Sanctum*, but that was a squeaky door. I really felt depressed. How could this happen to me? And I started to think, "You're in the big leagues now, Suitcase. This is serious stuff, ejecting out of an experimental aircraft. You're not a 'flyboy' anymore. You are dealing with a very profound, abstruse, difficult subject matter—this test-flying stuff. It's beyond the ordinary knowledge or understanding of almost everyone. Most people think of you in a leather jacket and a white scarf in the company of glamorous women. No glamour here. You better pray it wasn't your fault because of a dumb mistake."

I was looking for smoke from my crash—nothing! I remember thinking that I hoped a United Airlines DC-6 wouldn't run into me. Why United? Why a DC-6? I have no idea.

I looked down. "Wow!" I said to myself. "I'm coming down pretty darn fast. I better get ready for a sudden stop."

I don't know at what rate of descent I hit the ground; I went from so many feet per second to stop! Just like that! I do remember, as I neared the ground, seeing a small ranch house, or cabin, with clothes hanging on a washline. A blessing! The clothes gave me an indication of which way the wind was blowing so, when I hit the ground, I would be prepared to get up and run in the direction of my chute and grab the lower shroudlines and collapse it. Sounds good! That's what they do in movies. But everyday life is serious play, and you're never given any time to practice. This was my first ejection and parachute ride, and I was never given any in-depth lectures or practices in landing—in a harness, say, by jumping from a tower as you see in the training movies.

The clothesline was strung from the roofline of the cabin to a pole about thirty yards away. It was high enough to help me in my depth perception. When my eyes were even with the clothesline I closed them, tucked in my legs a bit, went limp, and waited. *Whomp!* I hit the ground—hard. The chute did not collapse; the wind was stronger than I anticipated. And let me tell you, there was none of this get-up-and-run stuff; I was being dragged. I managed to roll over onto my stomach, used my elbows for speed brakes—I still have the scar tissue—and slowly crawled forward to shorten the distance to the bottom of the chute. I finally managed to get it to collapse—then I did too!

In a few long minutes, I sat up and looked around. Nobody came from the cabin, but I was more concerned about what had happened to the aircraft. I kept thinking, "My God! What if I was responsible?! This really isn't happening! I'm going to lose my job! Is my experimental career over already?"

I also was looking for smoke from the wreckage, but there was nothing except a lot of dust and haze on the 360-degree horizon. The wind was getting stronger, blowing from the west. I pulled in more of the chute. I was alone in the middle of nowhere, sitting in a dusty, dried-up, brown, grasslike field and my back was killing me. I decided not to move. Lockheed would be looking for me by now anyhow. I unhitched one side of the parachute risers and let the chute flare out.

I heard a motor. It wasn't the sound of an airplane. I struggled to stand up and saw a truck driving toward me. It continued until it came right up beside me and stopped. It was driven by a farmer with eyes the size of an on-deck batter's circle. I had taken off my helmet, so at least he knew I wasn't from another planet—I think!

"I seen ya come down from way off," he said. "Took me a time to git here. What happened? Is you busted up? You one of them paratroopers from out yonder at Bicycle Lake? Where'd ya'll come from?"

I said, "I don't know what happened. I just got here myself." My try at dry humor went directly over his head. "I'm OK, but I would appreciate a ride to the nearest town. I'd like to make a phone call."

"Boy, ain't no towns 'round here. Ya'll in the middle of no-where. This used to be alfalfa—ain't nothin' now. No water. As I says, ain't no towns, but I kin take you to a country-like store. They got a phone outside. C'mon, git in."

He—his name was Gus—helped me gather my chute and helmet and off we went. I made the mistake of telling Gus my back hurt a little. From that time on, until Lockheed picked me up at the edge of a dry lake bed, Gus told me about his back troubles, his wife's lumbago troubles, his kids' troubles, and money troubles. On the way to the "country-like" he asked, "How much do you trouble-shooters make?"

"Not enough," I answered.

"You married?"

"No thanks."

"Hey, hey, hey! Yeah, marriage is like jumping into a hole in the ice in the midd'l winter; you do it once and you remember it the rest of your days! Yer smart! Got girlfriends?"

"Not enough! Although I am dating a blonde right now."

"What's 'er name? She pretty?"

"Her name is Jane and, yes, she is very pretty; she could make a bishop kick a hole in a stained-glass window just to see her pass by."

"Heh, heh, heh! Probably wanted to see mor'n that. Heh, heh! That's a good'n."

"How long have you been married, Gus?"

"Heck man, I've been in love with the same woman for thirty-eight years. If my wife ever finds out, she'll kill me. Heh, heh, heh! Naw! Just kiddin'," Gus said, "I'm married to mah third one. Nice lady. Took on two of her kids, and I guess she liked that. We ain't got much money, but we git along. You see, I drive a tractor for a big rancher near'n Ridgecrest and, when I work, pay's pretty good. Long hours, though."

We were now bouncing along a dirt trail in Gus's pickup truck headed toward the edge of Harper Dry Lake. I had called Lockheed, collect. Ellie Hawks, the chief of all flight tests, accepted the call. The conversation was surreal.

"Hi, Suitcase. Where are you calling from?"

"I'm out here at a crossroads gas station."

"Oh? Where?"

"I dunno, somewhere south of Harper Dry Lake, so I'm told." I was beginning to realize that, for some reason or other, Ellie didn't know I had lost an airplane. I found out later that the guys upstairs in engineering were in a panic and Ellie had just returned from the bank or something; no one had had the chance to call him.

"Did you have a breakdown or something?"

"Yeah, Ellie, your number eight airplane is broken way down— into a thousand pieces, is my guess. For God's sake, Ellie, I just ejected from number eight."

Dead silence for a long, long second!

"Wha! What! Ya, ya, ya, mean ya, bailed out? Wha-wha-where?? What happened? Are you OK? Where are you calling from?? Are you OK? Can we come get you? Ca-ca-can you walk?"

"Yeah, yeah, Ellie; I'm OK. I don't know what happened. I lost all pitch control. The airplane just pitched down and started to tumble on me, so I had to get the hell out. I had a nice guy pick me up; took me to this *Grapes of Wrath* junction."

"Gosh, I can't believe it. Wait a second! Larry just walked into my office. Just a minute." Mumble, mumble. "OK! Can you get to Harper Dry Lake?"

"Yes, I'm sure this man will take me. But I want to give him a tip: I didn't bring any cash with me."

"Heck, don't worry about that. We'll pick you up in the Bonanza, within the hour."

"OK! Great! Have Larry review the voice tapes with you. That's

all we have left anyhow. See you in about an hour. And Ellie, I'm
OK. Relax."

"Hey! Wait! Wait! What's the number there? I'll call you right
back."

So in a few minutes the phone rang and, after discussing what
happened in more detail and Ellie reaching his zenith of excitement and then calming down—plus knowing I was OK—Ellie told
me my boss, famous test pilot Tony LaVier, was on his way by
plane to pick me up. I suggested to Ellie to have Larry accompany
Tony so he could brief him on the way.

My conversations with Gus were vapid, passing the time as we
drove, but he turned out to be a very nice man. And it helped me
through my anxiety of being in the middle of nowhere, having
lost an experimental airplane worth tens of millions of dollars and
not knowing the reason why; that's what was haunting me.

Tony landed the twin Beech on Harper Dry Lake and taxied to
a stop, bringing a cloud of thick red dust with him. Larry, my
flight test engineer, was in the copilot seat. I introduced the two
men to Gus, and while Larry was helping with the chute and helmet, Tony took me aside and said, "Don't worry, Suitcase, we think
we know what went wrong. Larry and I could see the wreckage from
the air. We saw the hole the airplane made, then the ripped-off tail
section, and finally the mangled tip tank. It looks like the tip tank
was torn loose due to the clear air turbulence you reported. It probably wasn't installed correctly. It then, somehow, jammed into the
tail and cut through it like butter. It reminds me of the fatal accident
we had at Big Spring in a T-33; the tip tank came off and tore into
the tail. Only the instructor was at low altitude. Do you remember
that?"

"How could I forget? The pilot was one of my instructors."

"Anyhow, we think that's what caused your tumble; thank God
the ejection seat worked perfectly. We have some experts on the
way to the sites now; I radioed the coordinates."

I was relieved, but depressed. How could something like this
have happened? I asked Tony if he had a few bucks. He went over
to Gus and thanked him, and then we said our goodbyes. When

Tony shook Gus's hand, his palm had a one-hundred-dollar bill in it. Tony LeVier was that kind of man. When it was my turn I didn't say much, just shook Gus's hand, gave him a hug, turned, and climbed into the airplane.

When we arrived at Palmdale, I was given a big welcome, reported to the flight surgeon (my back was just a bruise and I was given a prescription for pain if it got worse), filed a tape recorded detailed report, and visited with Ellie, Tony, and Larry. Things were getting serious—we were losing too many aircraft. I didn't know it then, but my time would come again.

Tony flew me to Burbank. On the way, Tony told me my aircraft, the number 1 YF-104A Simpson's Appleknocker (my crew chief had painted a flying suitcase on the right side), which I had been test flying, was still down for maintenance and would not be ready for another week. The Appleknocker was the first YF-104A off the assembly line as a test aircraft. He said, "I don't want to even hear from you until a week from tomorrow."

I went to my apartment a few miles from Burbank. I did go to the plant a few days later, though. It took me a few days to recover any semblance of walking correctly because I had never hurt so much in my life: my neck, shoulders, chest, elbows, inner thighs, and even my rear end. I played tennis or worked out religiously every other day, and I thought I was in good shape. Tarzan probably could not have taken the abrupt tugs, pulls, and shakes on his body without hurting in the same way, and he had a Jane who worried about him too!

Anyway, I had our flight-test secretary type a letter for me thanking Gus. I wanted it on Lockheed stationery. I also packed a model of the F-104 and sent it to him—with the tail on!

Tony talked to me while I was there. His first premise turned out to be true. The tip tank had been installed improperly. The rest is history. He didn't offer to show me the pieces.

44

CAPT. JOHN SINCLAIR—1987

The 28th of December, 1987 seemed to begin quite normally for me, but it was to become the most horrific day of my life, and one which would affect my life considerably.

I was tasked, together with other colleagues from 3 Squadron, to plan and fly an individual low-level (250 feet) navigation training exercise in the Eastern Transvaal. The meteorological forecast en route was clear weather with good visibility. Seventeen minutes after takeoff I struck the top of a mountain peak near Lydenburg and rebounded back into the air. I ejected as the aircraft began breaking up in the air. In this article I would like to share this experience with other aircrew, should they ever have the misfortune of finding themselves in a similar predicament of having to make the split-second decision of whether or not to eject.

The start-up, taxi-out, takeoff and departure from controlled air space proceeded normally. I experienced slight technical problems shortly after leaving controlled air space, but these were not serious enough to have to abort the sortie at that stage. The pilot of the aircraft ten minutes ahead of me, who was flying the same route, warned me that the mountains just past the first turning point were covered in mist. I acknowledged his call and planned to make my decision whether to continue the sortie at the first turning point.

I was approximately two minutes from my first turning point, and was flying over a ridge of hills and into a valley which had a road and railway line running along it. This would lead me to my first turning point. During this time, I noticed that the weather was deteriorating to the east. I attempted to call the pilot in the aircraft ahead of me to establish whether he had continued to the next turning point, or whether he had returned to Waterkloof, but was unable to raise him. I was concerned for his safety at this stage.

I identified my turning point and noted that I was exactly on time. My speed was 505 knots. There was a high mountain on the starboard side and I planned to fly around it by executing a right-hand turn and then flying into a valley which ran roughly in the direction I was heading. I was at approximately 350 degrees AOL as I entered this turn and noticed that mist was covering the mountains about six kilometers ahead. I rolled out of the turn on my heading and began a shallow climb to clear the mist. There was another layer of altostratus type cloud at what I estimated to be between 8,000 and 10,000 feet AMSL (above mean sea level).

My decision either to continue between the cloud layers to the next turning point, or to return to Waterkloof, was going to be made once I had determined whether the next turning point was visible or covered in cloud. I looked into the cockpit to see which VHF radio I had selected, my intention being, once again, to attempt to contact the pilot ahead to ascertain the condition of the weather ahead. I looked up just in time to see a mountain no more than five hundred meters ahead of me and that the peak in front of me was about 15–20 degrees above the horizon. I immediately pulled back on the stick to what I roughly estimate to have been 5–6 G's. The nose of the aircraft cleared the mountain peak, and in that short period I still thought I was going to make it over the top. However, it was then that I felt the mush of the aircraft because it was still fairly heavy with fuel.

I felt the ground rushing toward me and from that moment the nightmare began. When I realized that I was definitely going to hit the mountain, my instinctive reaction was to eject. However, there was insufficient time for me to do this and I struck the mountain with a deafening crash. I think I passed out momentarily from the impact. I realized I was still alive when I saw fire all around the cockpit as it tumbled. I was subjected to positive and negative G as the aircraft rolled and tumbled in all directions. Through it all, I was wondering whether I was tumbling on the ground and was expecting to strike something solid which would kill me. I could hear the rush of air and the roar of something solid stalling through the air as the aircraft hurtled uncontrollably. The front instrument panel had small torch-like flames emitting from between the panel and the instruments. These flames were being fanned by the rush of air through the cockpit and were coming straight at my body and face.

From the moment I had decided to eject prior to hitting the mountain until now, I had been grasping frantically for the seat pan ejection handle with my right hand, and at the same time I was trying to stop myself from being tossed around the cockpit by pressing my left hand against the canopy above my head. My seat harness was in the locked position and my seat straps were tight against my body, restricting movement.

Until the moment I ejected, I felt as though I was living through a nightmare and I remember thinking *several* times, "Don't worry, you are just having a nightmare and will wake up soon and you will be safe." Yet at the same time, I felt that I had to find the ejection handle and pull it just in case it was not a nightmare. I had a false sense of security while I was in this extremely dangerous situation, and it took considerable willpower to convince myself that this was real, and that my only chance of survival was to eject— regardless.

My right hand located the seat pan handle, and I pulled. To my relief it extracted with extreme ease! When I felt the explosion of the ejection, I realized that this was no nightmare. My helmet was ripped from my head and I think I saw my seat falling away slightly to my left as I was being ejected from the cockpit. I noticed that my height was approximately 200–300 feet AGL (above ground level) as I felt my drogue chute and main parachute stabilizing me. I could see and hear large pieces of flaming aircraft striking the ground all around me. There was a fairly strong easterly wind blowing (I estimate between 10-20 knots) I as drifted over the ravine towards the western side of a fairly steep incline. I completely misjudged my rate of descent and the last fifty feet seemed to flash past, barely allowing me time to prepare for landing. At the last moment I had to swing myself clear of a large jagged rock, and landed against the mountain rolling onto my left side. It seemed as though I had been stabilized in my parachute for 4–5 seconds before I landed.

During this whole nightmare I experienced an incredible feeling that time had slowed down, when in actual fact things happened rather quickly.

My thought processes were very clear, and my first concern was for my back, which had taken the brunt of the ejection and landing. I therefore lay quite still on my back with my lumbar pack still in position behind me and my seat pan survival pack lying just to my right. My next reaction was to check my body for injury. It was a relief to realize I could move my whole body and there appeared to be no broken bones or major hemorrhaging. A C-160 Transall was flying just to the north of me from the direction of Hoedspruit and Waterkloof. I took out my Pelba survival radio and my 50' pencil flares and tested both. By this time, the C-160 Transall was out of range. My Pelba was serviceable, but when I tested one of my flares it flared on its upward flight path, but burnt out by the time it started its descent. I unpacked all the necessary survival equipment and laid it out next to me.

My next concern: shock. We had been taught to drink as much water as possible to counteract this, so I immediately drank 400 ml of dextrose while waiting for the pilot, who was to follow me, to fly over my position. Approximately 20–26 minutes later I heard him fly past on the far side of the mountain. There was no time for me to fire a flare or call him on the radio. It was then that I noticed people on the other side of the ravine surveying the wreckage. After I had fired a day/night flare to draw their attention, they sprinted down the ravine and up the other side toward me. By the time the farmer had reached me, I was uncertain of whose condition was worse, his or mine. All he could do was to rest his arms on his knees, stare at me, and pant as though he was about to take his last breath.

After I had instructed my rescuers on how to carry out the survival and rescue procedures, the pain in my back began to intensify. I decided against the use of painkillers in order to obviate masking any symptoms which might hinder the doctor's diagnosis. I also wanted to be aware of every movement to ensure that my back remained straight.

At 12:25 I heard the rescue Puma for the first time and attempted to raise the Puma on my Pelba radio, but received no response. I therefore reselected the VHF beacon so that the Puma could home in on my Pelba beacon. It transpired that the Puma pilot could hear my call but, whenever he answered, he could only hear the beacon carrier wave.

After the Puma had landed behind me the doctor attended to my injuries, gave me an injection for pain and set up a drip. Shortly thereafter I was flown to Military Hospital for treatment.

LESSONS LEARNED

MY DECISION TO EJECT

Shortly before my accident, Maj. N. Meikie's article on "The Ejection Decision" was discussed during a flying safety meeting at 3 Squadron, prior to its appearance in the *Nyala* (an aviation safety magazine). This article had a marked effect on my thinking regarding when to eject and when to attempt to salvage the aircraft. In fact it had a direct bearing on my survival and being able to write this article. On the day of that meeting I had already established in my mind when I would decide to eject and, as it turned out, that decision had to be made only a few weeks later when I had seconds within which to act.

If any pilot is not familiar with the content of Maj. Meikie's article, I strongly recommend that they acquaint themselves with it, and that they take heed of his suggestions.

FALSE SENSE OF SECURITY

From the moment when I realized that I was going to hit the mountain, my brain refused to accept the fact that this was really happening. My immediate thoughts were that this was a nightmare and that I should not be unduly concerned about the situation. I think that the sudden transition from feeling completely safe to being totally out of control was too much of a shock for my mind to accept. This is possibly a built-in safety "circuit breaker" in the brain which prevents one from having to assimilate the full impact of such a shock which in itself could kill you.

I think the instantaneous decision to eject prior to hitting the mountain may have resulted from that small measure of concern which helped me to overcome my false sense of security. Added to this, I could hear myself screaming, hear the roar of rushing air, and could sense the fire on the exposed parts of my face. All these factors contributed to overcoming this sense of *unreality*.

The point that I am trying to make is that aircrew should be fully aware of this phenomenon and, should a similar situation be experienced in the future (God forbid), at least this article may serve to remind such victims of this feeling.

TEMPORAL DISTORTION

I experienced an incredible feeling that time had slowed down. One's brain has to process so much information in such a short period (far more than in normal situations) that it actually feels as though time has become protracted. One feels that there is still plenty of time to get out of the aircraft, when in actual fact it may already be too late!

RATE OF DESCENT IN PARACHUTE

We are all aware that the parachute canopy installed in the Mirage ejection seat is smaller than normal and that this increases the rate of descent. I was fully aware of this fact, but the rate of descent was still far in excess of my expectations, and I suffered a fractured leg from the impact upon landing.

BACK INJURIES ON LANDING

Several of my colleagues who have experienced ejection from aircraft have suffered back injuries: either from the force of the ejection, or from the impact on landing.

When I landed my first reaction was to check myself for injury and free myself from the parachute. Although I could feel no pain in my back, I forced myself to restrict my movements and to lie still until I was rescued. The lesson learnt is that you should move only if you have to.

SURVIVAL/FIRST AID

We are taught that it is always advisable to drink as much water as possible to diminish the state of shock which is likely to follow from such an experience. When the doctor arrived I told him that I had drunk the 400 ml dextrose. His advice to me was to be very cautious about administering or taking dextrose, since internal or external injures may necessitate an emergency operation on site.

Painkillers are also provided in the emergency first-aid kit. Unless it is absolutely necessary, rather endure the pain until medical assistance arrives. This enables the doctor to have full jurisdiction regarding the best treatment for you.

Test your 50" pencil flares and day/night flares regularly. As it turned out, my 50" flares failed to work when I needed them most, simply because I failed to test them regularly.

When I heard the rescue helicopter, I attempted to raise its pilot on my Pelba. Because I received no reply from him, I reselected "Beacon," then he could home in on me. It transpired that he had no homing facility and that he could only hear my transmissions. It would have been better had I sent him blind transmissions and talked him toward my position. Finally, if my experience serves to endorse Maj. Meikle's article, may it also possibly assist in improving flying safety in general. Incidentally, it is quite ironic that Maj. Meikie was my first flying instructor back in 1978/79. We have come a long way.

45

LT. COL. JOHN PAUL STAPP—1947

In the spring of 1946, just months after the end of World War II, a B-17 bomber nosed skyward on an urgent mission. Stripped down to a bare airframe, and naked of guns and bombsights, the B-17 had heavily modified engines that allowed it to do something unprecedented: fly into the stratosphere. It cruised for hours at altitudes of nearly forty-five thousand feet, its flight crew shivering in the sub-zero cold, while in the rear fuselage a lone man conducted a risky set of experiments. Captain John Paul Stapp, a medical doctor and member of the AAF Aero Med Lab, was studying the effects of high altitude flight. And he was using himself as the guinea pig.

The questions Stapp was attempting to answer were absolutely critical to the future of aviation. Could men actually survive for any length of time in extremely high altitudes? Could they fully function, physically and rationally? And how could they keep themselves from freezing, severely dehydrating, or becoming incapacitated by the bends—the deadly formation of bubbles in the bloodstream? These were riddles Stapp was duty bound to solve, and he did, one by one. The riddle of the bends, however, proved an extremely tough nut to crack. But after nearly sixty-five hours in the air, Capt. Stapp found an answer. If a pilot breathed pure oxygen for thirty minutes prior to takeoff symptoms could be avoided entirely. That was an enormous breakthrough. As far as man was concerned, the sky now truly was the limit. The discovery pushed

Capt. Stapp to the forefront of the Aero Med Lab, a facility he had joined only months before. Once he'd planned to become a pediatrician, but now he had decided to dedicate his life to research. The Lab's mandate, to study medical and safety issues in aviation, was a perfect match for his talents. During WWII it had produced a steady stream of innovations including advanced breathing systems, parachutes, even pressure suits for fighter pilots. And it had emerged as the premiere facility in the world for the study of human factors and the new science of biomechanics.

As a reward for his diligent work on the high altitude problem, Capt. John Stapp was assigned to supervise the Lab's most important research project: human deceleration. This was, simply put, the study of the human body's ability to withstand G forces. (A "G" is the force of gravity acting on a body on Earth at sea level.) According to most sources, 18 G's was the most a human could receive and expect to survive. As a result, all military airplane cockpits were built to withstand an 18-G impact.

Yet during the war a great deal of contradictory evidence had emerged about this figure. There were some well-documented cases where Navy pilots had crashed into the islands of aircraft carriers or even other aircraft at very high speed. Statistics and physics said they should have been killed.

Yet they had walked away. More troubling were a whole host of low magnitude yet fatal crash landings—the Lab routinely reviewed accident reports—in which pilots' seats broke loose or their harnesses failed. Many within the Lab suspected that these pilots had probably survived the initial impact, only to be killed by the structural failure of the cockpit and its affiliated components.

In April 1947, Capt. Stapp traveled out to Los Angeles to view the "human decelerator" being built at Muroc (later Edwards Air Force Base). That remote base was about as far as you could get from Wright Field, but a key component was already in place there: a two-thousand-foot-long rocket sled track. Built during WWII for tests of Nazi V-1 "buzz bombs," it would form the core of the decelerator. At one end Northrop engineers installed forty-five foot-long sets of hydraulic brakes, capable of slowing a rocket sled from 150 miles per hour to half of that speed in one precious fifth of a second. When it did, G forces would be produced equivalent to those experienced in an airplane crash.

The sled that would ride down this track would be called the "Gee Whiz." Built out of welded tubes, it was designed to withstand 100 G's of force with a 50 percent safety factor. The 'Whiz was 15 feet long, 6.5 feet wide, weighed about 1,500 pounds, and sat on a series of magnesium slippers. Atop the chassis was a lightweight metal cab (later removed to facilitate photography) that enclosed a rugged, specially built seat and a bed for prone position tests (also later removed). To the rear were a telemetry antenna mast and a rack capable of holding four rocket bottles. The bottles, the same type used to boost heavy aircraft off short runways, would be capable of generating five thousand pounds of thrust apiece. By varying the number of bottles, and the brake pressure, a wide variety of G forces could be applied to the sled and its occupant.

That occupant, by the way, was intended to be a 185-pound dummy named Oscar Eightball. The staff at the Aero Med Lab had designated, in fact, that all the tests would be run with dummies; no human runs were contemplated. If 18 G's of force was lethal, after all, then even lower G runs weren't worth the risk.

But the Aero Med Lab had reckoned without Stapp, who proved from day one that he was a bit of a maverick. When he first introduced himself to George Nichols, Northrop's project manager, Stapp noticed Oscar Eightball right away. "He walked over and patted that," remembers Nichols, "and then he said, 'We're not going to use these. You can throw this away. I'm going to be the test subject.'"

Nichols was flabbergasted and immediately called his boss, Jack Northrop. Believing the Aero Med Lab must be behind the change in plans, Northrop promptly endorsed human testing. But he also admonished Nichols to "keep track of the fact that our equipment has to withstand the force that you're developing." Oscar Eightball could survive any miscue. With a person riding the sled, the consequences of a failure would be catastrophic. Before human tests could begin, therefore, all the bugs would have to be worked out.

In this regard Stapp was nothing if not methodical. He was, after all, a scientist. So, Oscar would make the first rides on the Gee Whiz. It proved a wise strategy: On the first run, April 30, 1947, the hydraulic brakes and backup restraint system failed, and the 'Whiz slid off the track and into the desert. It wasn't badly damaged, but the brakes were another story. A series of steel teeth intended to trip cams had instead broken clean off on impact. When the teeth were beefed up, George Nichols recalls, the cams broke off instead. It was the type of thing that happened all summer long.

At one point, to learn more about what they might be up against, Oscar Eightball was sent down the track at 150 mph wearing only a light safety belt. At the end of the run the brakes locked up, instantly producing 30 G's. The belt neatly parted and Oscar, in meek obedience to Newton's Second Law of Motion, sallied forth. He went right through an inch-thick wooden windscreen as if it were paper, left his rubber face behind, and finally came to a halt 710 feet downrange. Clearly, some damnable forces of physics were at work.

In December 1947, after eight months and thirty-five test runs, John Stapp felt his team had obtained enough experience to attempt a manned run. (Perhaps he had also gained some inspiration from Chuck Yeager, who, two months earlier, broke the sound barrier in the skies above the sled track. "The real barrier wasn't in the sky," Yeager would later say, "but in our knowledge and experience.") Ever the cautious scientist, on the first ride Stapp used only one rocket, and he faced backward to minimize the acceleration effects and G-load. It was no sweat. The 'Whiz barely reached 90 mph, and the deceleration was only about 10 G's. The next day, Stapp added two more rockets and the sled reached 200 mph. Afterward, it was clear that the captain had hardly been affected by the ride. In fact if he appeared giddy, it was from anticipation, not fear. The secrets of human deceleration seemed well within his reach.

Within a few weeks' time, Stapp began to vary the number of rockets used on the sled, and tested various braking configurations. The idea was to not only increase the G forces involved, but vary the

"rate of onset"—the time it took for forces to build to a maximum—
and their duration. By August 1948, Stapp had completed sixteen
runs, surviving not just 18 G's but a bone-jarring, jaw-dropping 35.
And he felt he was still far from any kind of limit.

But while his first run had involved "no unpleasant sensa-
tions," the later runs were torturous. Even at low G's the straps of
Stapp's harness dug painfully into his shoulders. At higher ranges
of acceleration and deceleration, they cracked his ribs. Over the
course of the tests at Edwards, he suffered a number of concussions,
lost a few dental fillings, and dinged his collarbone. On a couple of
other occasions, he broke his wrist. Being a physician and a bit of
a stoic, he set one fracture on his way back to his office.

Out of all the things Stapp was subjected to, the most disturbing (concussions aside) was blurry vision, which he began experi-
encing while facing backward at speeds above 18 G's. The cause
was intuitively obvious. Blood was rapidly leaving his eyeballs and
pooling toward the back of his head in response to gravity, resulting in a "white out." During later tests, when he faced forward and
the blood was pushed up against his retinas, Stapp would experience "red outs" caused by broken capillaries and hemorrhaging.
Clearly, when it came to G forces the most vulnerable part of human anatomy were the eyes.

Beaten, bruised, and battered though he was by the tests, Stapp
initially refused to allow anyone else to ride the 'Whiz. He had his
reasons. He feared that if some people, especially test pilots, were
allowed on the sled their hot-doggedness might produce a disaster.
Volunteers might make some runs—eventually at least seven did—
but whenever a new profile was developed, Stapp was his own one
and only choice as test subject. There was one obvious benefit at
least: Dr. Stapp could write extremely accurate physiological, not
to mention psychological, reports concerning the effects of the experiments on his subject, Capt. Stapp.

When after many months the results of all Stapp's work were
presented to the Aero Med Lab brass, they were horrified. Surprisingly, the words "court-martial" were never mentioned, perhaps
because Stapp had shown such courage. His initiative, however,

was another matter entirely. To rein him in, Stapp was promoted to the rank of major, reminded of the 18-G limit of human survivability, and told to discontinue tests above that level. And he was told in no uncertain terms that human tests had to end. Chimpanzees, his superiors advised, would be acceptable substitutes.

Now-Major Stapp retreated back to Edwards with scarcely an argument. He wasn't worried; he sensed that, after the Lab reviewed his data, they would cave. They did. And soon, Stapp's data was having an impact. The rocket sled had clearly proven the inadequacy of certain types of aircraft restraint systems, and these shortcomings were addressed immediately. Stapp had also clearly shown that passengers in rear-facing seats could survive much higher G-loads than forward-facing passengers. The military rapidly seized on this concept, and ordered seats on all new transport aircraft reversed.

The most significant development, of course, lay in the debunking of the 18-G limit. When it was finally acknowledged by the Air Force, it had serious implications. If a pilot or passenger could survive a 30 G–plus deceleration, then his seat, harness, and cockpit ought to be augmented so they could survive it as well. The next series of rocket sled tests, which would feature a new heavyweight harness—permitting the first forward-facing human runs—represented an attempt to produce truly definitive data about that subject. Beginning in June 1949, the Northrop team put the Gee Whiz through various profiles, sometimes with Stapp, sometimes with volunteers, and sometimes with chimpanzees.

Two years later, in June 1951, Stapp made his last run on the Whiz, absorbing more than 35 G's of deceleration in the forward position. By then he'd also survived a 46-G run with a rate of onset of 500 G's per second, and a 38-G run with an onset of nearly 1,300. That was about as much punishment as the sled could produce with four rockets blazing and with the brakes at their maximum setting. In total, seventy-four manned runs had been made on the sled. More than eighty additional runs had taken place with the chimps. The tests established a standard strength requirement for aircraft seats (32 G's) that was rapidly adopted. And Stapp developed and tested a new regulation pilot's harness, passenger restraints, and invented a "side saddle" harness for paratroopers.

YET while the Gee Whiz had allowed Stapp to answer most if not all of the crash deceleration questions, new ones had emerged. In 1951, no one had yet ejected from an aircraft at supersonic speed and lived to tell about it. Very little was, in fact, known about the effects of windblast and deceleration acting on a pilot ejecting at those speeds. Yet it was obvious that many pilots, whether they wanted to or not, were going to be attempting those kinds of escapes in the near future. Could they survive? And what could be done to help them survive?

Answering questions such as those were beyond the limits of the Gee Whiz, and while Stapp did some tests in a special open-cockpit F-89, it was clear that another rocket sled would have to be developed in the search for answers. So beginning in 1953, Stapp relocated to the Aeromedical Field Laboratory at Holloman Air Force Base in New Mexico. Here there was a 3,550-foot sled track, originally built to test the Snark missile. It terminated in a segment that could be dammed and filled with water. By equipping a sled with water scoops, and varying the water depth precisely, various braking speeds and durations could be produced.

Northrop was put to work constructing a new sled, the Sonic Wind No. 1. Slightly longer and wider than the Gee Whiz, Sonic Wind could carry up to twelve rockets that could produce well over fifty thousand pounds of thrust. Additionally, it had a sophisticated two-stage design. After the rocket bottles burned out, the "propulsion sled" would be jettisoned, allowing the "subject sled" to continue onward without the extra weight. Engineers calculated that the Wind could travel at upward of 750 supersonic miles per hour, and withstand an astonishing 150 G's.

In November 1953 the Sonic Wind was tested with Sierra Sam, a second-generation crash test dummy. A few months later in January 1954 the first live subject run was made with a chimpanzee. Everything seemed to work well. On March 19, Lt. Colonel Stapp (he had been promoted again) made his first trip down the track.

"I assure you," he said to a reporter as he boarded the sled, "I'm not looking forward to this." Burning six rockets, the Sonic Wind reached a speed of 421 mph in five seconds, and was still traveling at 313 mph when it hit the water brake. In the span of 200 feet, the Wind slowed from that speed to 153 mph, producing up to 22 G's of force. For a brief instant Stapp's body weighed more than 3,700 pounds. More impressively, for 0.6 seconds, Stapp endured 15 G's of punishment. That was a duration nearly twice as long as any ever produced at Edwards. "I feel fine," the lt. colonel said after the run. "This sled is going to be a wonderful test instrument. I'm ready to do it again this afternoon."

The next human run, however, didn't occur for nearly five months owing to the complexity of the task. Stapp hoped to explore the effects of abrupt windblast. To do this, a pair of doors was added to the sled's windscreen. Tripped by a cam placed far down the track, they opened at high speed, hitting Stapp with a torrent of air estimated to be moving at 736 feet per second at 5.4 psi. Then he was decelerated 12 G's. The effects were described as negligible, and Stapp characterized it as the "easiest" sled run he'd ever done. This despite the fact that grains of airborne sand had impacted his face, creating bloody blisters and bruising.

November and the beginning of December were spent preparing for what turned out to be John Stapp's twenty-ninth and, as it turned out, final sled ride. This time he would attempt to push the envelope all the way to the post office. The sled would travel into the transonic speed zone, Mach 0.9. The heavy door mechanism would be removed, and Stapp would face the wind protected only by a helmet and visor. And when the sled stopped, and it would in a mere 1.4 seconds, Stapp would be subjected to more G's than anyone had ever willingly endured. It made George Nichols extremely apprehensive just thinking about it. Stapp wasn't just out to prove that people could survive a high speed ejection; he was seemingly trying to find the actual limit of human survivability to G force. "To me there was no real justification for being killed from the deceleration," says Nichols. "I didn't want to see it. He was just too good a friend to see get hurt."

Air Force pilot Joe Kittinger, who had been participating in another groundbreaking set of Stapp experiments—flying zero-G profiles to study the effects of weightlessness—remembers being asked to fly a photo chase plane for the run. "Stapp said, 'Captain we have a project coming up here in a couple weeks. It's a sled run and we're going to get up to 614 miles per hour,'" remembers Kittinger. "But he didn't say it was a human sled run. And he did not tell me it was him." It wasn't until a day before the test that an astonished Kittinger finally learned the truth. "I was flabbergasted he was going to be going that fast," Kittinger says. "It was a point of departure—a new biological limit he was going to be establishing on that run." If he lived, it would be as significant a human achievement as breaking the four minute mile.

AT X-minus ten on December 10, 1954, George Nichols helped fit a rubber bite block, equipped with an accelerometer, into John Stapp's mouth. Then with a final pat for good luck, he headed down to the far end of the track. As X-minus two approached, the last two Northrop crew members left the sled and hustled into a nearby blockhouse. Sitting alone atop the Sonic Wind, Stapp looked like a pathetic figure. A siren wailed eerily, adding to the tension, and two red flares lofted skyward. Overhead, pilot Joe Kittinger, approaching in a T-33, pushed his throttle wide open in anticipation of the launch. With five seconds to go Stapp yanked a lanyard activating the sled's movie cameras, and hunkered down for the inevitable shock.

The Sonic Wind's nine rockets detonated with a terrific roar, spewing thirty-five-foot long trails of fire and hurtling Stapp down the track. "He was going like a bullet," Kittinger remembers. "He went by me like I was standing still, and I was going 350 mph." Just seconds into the run the sled had reached its peak velocity of 632 mph—actually faster than a bullet—subjecting Stapp to 20 G's of force and battering him with wind pressures near two tons. "I thought," continues Kittinger, "that sled is going so damn fast the first bounce is going to be Albuquerque. I mean, there was no way on God's earth that sled could stop at the end of the track. No way." But then, just as the sound of the rockets' initial firing reached the ears of far-off observers, the Wind hit the water brake. The rear of the sled, its rockets expended, tore away. The front section continued downrange for several hundred feet, hardly slowing at all until it hit the second water brake.

Then, a torrent of spray a hundred feet across exploded out the back of the Sonic Wind. It stopped like it had hit a concrete wall. To Kittinger, flying above and behind, it appeared absolutely devastating. "He stopped in a fraction of a second," Kittinger says, the shock of the moment echoing in his voice. "It was absolutely inconceivable that anybody could go that fast and then just stop, and survive."

Down below, George Nichols and the ground crew raced to the scene, followed by an ambulance. An agitated Nichols vaulted onto the sled, and much to his relief, saw that Stapp was alive. He even managed what looked like a smile, despite being in great pain. Once again, he'd beat the odds. He'd live to see another day.

But could he see? George Nichols wasn't sure, and what he vividly remembers from that day, fifty years later, were John Stapp's eyes. He had suffered a complete red out. "When I got up to the sled I saw his eyes . . . Just horrible," recalls Nichols, his voice cracking with emotion. "His eyes . . . were completely filled with blood." When the Sonic Wind had hit the water brake, it had produced 46.2 G's of force. And for an astonishing 1.1 seconds, Stapp'd endured 25 G's. It was the equivalent of a Mach 1.6 ejection at forty thousand feet, a jolt in excess of that experienced by a driver who crashes into a redbrick wall at over 120 miles per hour. Only it had lasted perhaps nine times longer. And it had burst nearly every capillary in Stapp's eyeballs.

As George Nichols and some flight surgeons helped Stapp into a waiting stretcher, Stapp worried aloud that he'd pushed his luck too far. "This time," he remarked, "I get the white cane and the Seeing Eye dog." But when surgeons at the hospital examined him, they discovered that Stapp's retinas had not detached. And within minutes, he could make out some "blue specks" and a short time later he could discern one of the surgeons' fingers. By the next day, his vision had returned more or less to normal.

But John Stapp's life would never be the same. Dubbed "The Fastest Man on Earth" and "The Bravest Man in the Air Force" by the media, his celebrity rose to dazzling heights. Stapp graced the pages of *Collier's* and *Life* magazines, was the subject of a Hollywood "B" movie, and was featured in an episode of *This is Your Life!* If the attention was a bit much for the soft-spoken lt. colonel, it nevertheless provided him with an opportunity he had longed for—to promote the cause of automobile safety.

For even in the earliest days of the Gee Whiz tests, Stapp had realized that his research was just as applicable to cars as it was to airplanes. And perhaps, in the general scheme of things, automobile safety was even more important. At every opportunity, in every interview, and at every appearance therefore, Stapp urged Detroit to examine his crash data, and to design their cars with safety in mind. He lobbied hard for the installation of seat belts—at that time not even an option on American cars—and improvements such as soft dashboards, collapsing steering wheels, and shock-absorbing bumpers. "I'm leading a crusade for the prevention of needless deaths," he told *Time* magazine (he made the cover in 1955). It was a cause that would continue the rest of his life.

Meantime, Stapp announced plans to make a Mach 1.0 and, beyond that, a 1000 mph run on the 'Wind. But it was not meant to be. At Mach 0.9, the safety factor had become too tenuous for the brass to contemplate another go and, as fate would have it, their fears turned out to be justified. In June 1956, while performing an 80-G test, the Sonic Wind left the track and was severely damaged. So if Stapp had traveled as fast as a bullet, he'd also managed to dodge one. Human tests were suspended, and although he would participate in subsequent tests on an air-powered sled known as the "Daisy Track," his days as a rocket man were over.

It didn't really matter. Stapp had already proven what he'd set out to prove: that a pilot, if adequately protected, could survive a high-speed, high-altitude ejection. And he had determined to a great extent a limit, if not *the* limit, of human physiology. The rest could be left to the chimpanzees, dummies and, in more modern times, computer simulators. "It was a proper decision to make," says Joe Kittinger about the end of rocket sled tests. "(Stapp) had already defined the limit. Now the engineers could go back and design the escape system so that they could keep the man within that envelope." And they would. Equipped with Stapp's data, engineers would produce a new generation of aircraft which could fly higher, faster, and were safer than any ever built.

They would also build much safer automobiles. Using his powers of persuasion, Stapp convinced the Air Force to build an automobile test facility, and conducted the first-ever crash tests with dummies. He also brought together auto manufacturers, researchers, and politicians for The Stapp Automobile Safety Conference, a groundbreaking symposium which continues to this day. And, when in 1966 President Lyndon Johnson signed a law requiring seat belts in all new cars, Stapp was by his side. So when you put your seat belt on, just remember that you do so in part because of the "Fastest Man on Earth."

Stapp's work in aeronautics and automobiles continued right up until his death in 1999 at age eighty-nine. During his career, he'd received numerous awards and honors, including the Presidential Medal of Technology and the Legion of Merit. But for Stapp, the biggest reward was likely the knowledge that the work he had done helped save so many lives, not just in aviation, but on highways in the United States and around the world. And in that sense, his legacy not only continues, but grows with each passing day.

46

AIR COMMODORE PETER TAYLOR
AFC–1972

At about midday on May 4, 1972, I ejected from Harrier GR1 XV794 in northern Germany. I was not hurt and, on the face of it, that could have been the whole story. Except that it wasn't. There was a bit more to it than that.

CASTING my mind back to the early 1970s, the Harrier had only recently been introduced into the RAF. In 1971, the Wildenrath Wing in RAF Germany had been formed with 3, 4, and 20 Squadrons and I was posted to 4 Squadron as a flight commander. The early Harrier was a tremendous aeroplane, albeit a bit of a handful. I think most of us had great respect for her and simply couldn't get airborne often enough. However, a combination of a novel aircraft, demanding operational flying, and a general lack of experience resulted in occasional accidents and incidents. We had our share at Wildenrath, and the station commander, Gp. Capt. George Black, would "encourage" us to the effect that while we could and should press on operationally, we should do so with care!

On the morning of May 4, I was tasked to lead a four-ship attack mission on several targets in the Flensburg area of Northern Germany. The formation was also to be attacked by two other Squadron Harriers which were acting as enemy defensive fighters armed with simulated air-to-air missiles and guns. The planning and briefing for this type of sortie was lengthy and very thorough.

I remember filling at least two blackboards with administrative and operational detail.

At the appointed hour, six aircraft were allocated to us and the four attack pilots and their two defensive counterparts gathered for the briefing. This lasted about an hour. However, as the briefing progressed, I kept getting messages that first one aircraft, then another, then another had all become unserviceable. In the end, there was just one available: mine! There was no alternative but to go on the sortie by myself, converting the profile to a solo attack/recce mission. So much for planning!

At about midday, I got airborne in XV794, turned south, and headed for my first target, flying at 420 knots and 250 feet AGL. All went well until I was preparing to attack my second target. I had just looked into the cockpit to rearrange my maps, when looking up I saw a formation of three large (they have got much larger over the years!) birds flying straight at me. Instinctively, I pushed forward. I missed two of the birds, but the third went straight into the intake.

There followed an almighty bang, followed by some rather worrying mechanical noises from the normally robust Pegasus 100 engine. Clearly, it did not like what was going on. I noticed that the RPM was just below idle, the JPT in the middle of its range, height 200 feet and speed about 400 knots, although rapidly declining.

Generally, I was in open country, which was fairly flat with a few houses in my path. I opened and shut the throttle, but nothing much seemed to happen. I broadcast a quick Mayday but since I was quite low, I had no great expectation that anyone would hear me. Since I had made up my mind that the engine had suffered what sounded like catastrophic damage, I turned my mind to what to do next. (In reality, I said to myself: "I'd better jump out quite soon or I'm going in with the aeroplane!") Then, exactly as you read it in books and newspapers, I saw that I was still close to houses, and steered the aircraft away from them toward open ground as best I could. Time was now getting short, and as I reached open ground, I saw a small hill ahead with trees at the summit. I pointed the aircraft at the hill, took one last look at the height and speed (100 feet and 200 knots respectively), trimmed the aircraft straight and level, tightened my straps, and pulled the handle.

I recall everything working perfectly in my Martin-Baker Mk. 9 seat. I was quickly in my parachute and heading for a field full of cows. Also in the field were some quite large concrete blocks, and remembering a parachuting technique I had learned some seventeen years previously, I steered myself away from the blocks, and executed a hard, but perfectly serviceable, side-right landing.

The whole event had taken less than sixty seconds.

To my astonishment, I saw the aircraft continuing to fly beautifully in a slight climb away from me to the north. I cannot tell you the feelings I had as I watched what now seemed to be a perfectly serviceable aircraft leaving the scene of my ejection. Indeed, the aircraft eventually flew into cloud at about seven thousand feet and disappeared from sight.

Except for the cows, I was now completely alone in a field in Northern Germany with no means of communication, a used parachute, the remains of an ejection seat, and no method of transport. I had also forgotten in the heat of the moment that on ejection, a radio signal was initiated on the emergency broadcast frequency, so that the emergency services were becoming aware that there was an aircraft in distress.

I gathered myself together and began to walk across fields until I could find a road. After about twenty minutes, I found a road, absolutely deserted, and eventually came upon a farm. My German wasn't too good at the best of times, and my attempts to explain to the farmer's wife what had happened to me took some time. Eventually, and mainly through a combination of sign language and the sight of my parachute, I managed to explain my predicament and persuade her to let me use her telephone to contact the Squadron at Skrydstrup. The resulting conversation with 4 Sqdn. Ops, about an hour after my ejection, was surreal.

The phone was answered by Flying Officer Andy Bloxam. The conversation went something like this:

"Four Sqn. Ops, Fg. Off. Bloxam speaking."

"Hello Andy, Pete Taylor here."

"Oh! OK, aren't you still airborne? Anyway, I'll get Roger Austin."

That was it. No questions, no "How are you?", "What's happened to the aircraft?", or "Where are you?" Andy just put the phone down and took about five minutes to find Roger.

After that, things moved fast. Roger Austin established what had happened and the rescue process was put into action. Apparently XV794 had climbed to over twenty thousand feet and continued to broadcast on the emergency frequency. Because the aircraft was close to a Warsaw Pact border, a German F-104 was sent to intercept and was, I understand, mildly surprised to find a Harrier flying very nicely, but with no one on board. Shortly after that, the aircraft ran out of fuel and glided into Southern Denmark, where it crashed in an open field, narrowly missing a farmhouse. The Harrier had stayed airborne for thirty-eight minutes after my ejection. Apparently, the reason for XV794's thirty-eight minute solo trip was that the bird which I hit had spread itself quite thinly across the engine's compressor. The flames and gases from the Martin-Baker ejection seat dislodged the bird as I left the aircraft. The engine heaved a sigh of relief, drew a deep breath, and started working normally again. As it happens, I had trimmed the aircraft rather well and XV794 flew until she ran out of fuel! For my part, having given Roger an idea of where I was, the German Air Force sent an S-65 helicopter to pick me up. However, as I was apparently difficult to find, I had to use my SARBE beacon and flares to direct the S-65 to me. As far as I know, I was at that time the only person to have used my SARBE beacon on land, and the company very kindly presented me with a silver pot.

At Skrydstrup I met up with the rest of the squadron, was given a brief, but thorough, examination by a lady doctor, and went back to the Officers' Mess. Life was never dull at Wildenrath in those days. I have a SARBE silver mug, membership of the Caterpillar and Martin-Baker clubs, an ejection seat handle, and my log book to prove it all.

47

CAPT. SCOTT "SPIKE" THOMAS—1991

October 1985, my All-American season with the Air Force Academy Falcons. I'm on the thirty-yard line in Notre Dame Stadium. The house is packed. I'm on the receiving end of a beautiful spiraling punt. The crowd is deafening. I hear nothing but silence. Eleven angry Fighting Irish are converging upon me. I'm defenseless and at the mercy of my teammates. I'm calm. I focus on the ball and make the catch. It's still silent. I look ahead and see the picture I anticipated. #18, #24, #48—AJ, Dwan, and Pat dueling the Irishmen, creating a small opening to squeeze through. Go! Hit the hole! Break for daylight!

In the story that follows, many critical concepts, methods, and a positive "corporate" culture from generations of military fighter aviation training result in a successful rescue of a downed pilot. Without the strict adherence to those concepts, this story could have resulted in disaster. Here is my story.

February 17, 1991. Operation Desert Storm. One month into the operation and operations were going better than anyone had expected. United States airpower was decimating the Iraqi Military. I was #3 of four F-16s, call sign Benji 51, tasked to fly reconnaissance on the Euphrates River. I had the good fortune and distinct honor of having Lt. Eric "Neck" Dodson as my wingman. Neck was my best friend in the squadron and this was our first combat mission together. We were to launch as a four-ship, rendezvous with a tanker for aerial refueling, split into two-ships and prowl the Euphrates River. The Iraqis were replacing the blown-up concrete bridges spanning the river with pontoon bridges. Our job was to locate and destroy those bridges, disrupting their ability to move personnel and supplies toward the Kuwaiti theater of operations.

The briefing was routine, but detailed, as are all fighter briefings. Our greatest concern that day was the weather. The weather over Iraq during this period was the worst in a decade, and had affected most of our missions to this point. Takeoff was normal, and we pressed out over the Persian Gulf northbound to the tanker rendezvous point. The ceiling gradually sloped lower as we proceeded, eventually forcing us down to a thousand feet above the water just to stay out of the clouds. Our flight lead climbed us through the weather in close formation toward our gas station in the air. The milkbowl effect set in quickly—no ground, no blue sky, and no visible horizon with which to orient ourselves. My sense of speed and motion was reduced to believing what my instruments displayed.

Once established on the wing of the tanker, waiting my turn to refuel, I experienced the worst case of the leans I had ever encountered. I perceived the tanker (a KC-10, a military version of the DC-10) to be on its side in ninety degrees of bank, turning into me. Of course I knew this was ridiculous—they wouldn't use more than thirty degrees of bank—but my eyes and inner ears told me differently. One eye on the instruments, one on the tanker, I was actually in straight and level flight! It took five minutes to convince my body and brain to match what my eyes saw. Full of gas, we separated from the tanker and split into two flights of two, Benji 51 and Benji 53. Still in the clouds, we pushed north toward the border. Climbing through twenty-eight thousand feet, I, in accordance with my responsibilities as flight lead, decided that if we found clear air prior to the border, we would proceed. If we did not break out of the weather, we would abort the mission and try it again another day. There were very few missions worth hanging it out for at this point in the war.

Through thirty thousand feet, *poof!*—clear and beautiful on top. We eventually crested the backside of the weather and were met with unrestricted visual access of the target area. On to the Euphrates River—searching, marking, selecting, and bombing targets. We encountered no hostile fire, just some spurious radar warnings here and there. It was strange to be destroying things in the cradle of civilization. After several passes, we were out of bombs and ready to return to base. Mission accomplished! Well, part of it anyway.

Climbing through 32,000 feet, airspeed 320 knots, 100 miles north of the Saudi Arabia/Iraq border, we were planning to level off above the weather and head directly back to base without hitting the airborne tanker for refueling. This is where things went downhill, both figuratively and literally.

You see, as the pilot of a single-engine fighter, any strange noise—a pop or bang—gets your attention in a hurry. I still remember it as "the noise." The metallic *thunk* was paralyzing. I can only describe it as similar to the noise of your car's transmission falling out from beneath and hitting the freeway pavement. The sound was distinct and the accompanying deceleration grabbed my attention immediately, driving my eyes to my engine instruments. I immediately turned south, making a straight line for the Saudi border. As I completed the emergency procedure for an engine malfunction from memory, Neck was flying in tactical formation one mile to my right. While I directed him to close in on me, I further assessed the situation. I had hoped to recognize something familiar and apply additional approved and checklist-directed solutions from simulator training. To my surprise, the engine readings were still in the "green" (normal range). The engine was still turning and burning, but it just wouldn't put out thrust.

Over the next ten minutes, I made several critical decisions, but I don't remember thinking about them prior to making them. The decisions and actions stored in the recesses of my brain and reinforced through continuous training just seemed to spill from my brain to my hands.

CAST OF PLAYERS

BENJI 53—Capt. Scott "Spike" Thomas
BENJI 54—Lt. Eric "Neck" Dodson
BULLDOG—Airborne Warning and Control System (AWACS)
BENJI 51—Original Flight Lead

BENJI 53: "Benji 4, 3."
BENJI 54: "Go ahead."
BENJI 53: "Dude, I've got an engine problem. I'm turning south. . . .
      Bulldog, Benji 53."
BULLDOG: "Benji 53, Bulldog. Go ahead."
BENJI 53: "Bulldog, Benji 53 has an emergency. I'm currently 100 north
      of Customs heading south, 32,000. . . . Neck, rejoin. I'm punching off
      my tanks."
BENJI 54: "Copy."
BENJI 53: "Neck, I want to get to the nearest border, then maybe
      KKMC." (King Khalid Military City)
BENJI 54: "I've got Hafr Al-Batin closer. Just stay on this heading."

Neck closed in to inspect my jet for damage as I jettisoned my external fuel tanks, reducing my weight and drag. I established a glide and started planning. I was thankful for the training that ingrained in my mind "flexibility is the key to airpower." I needed it on February 17, 1991. The engine was producing *some* thrust, just not enough to maintain altitude. *No sweat.* I set a course for Hafr Al-Batin, a small piece of concrete in Northern Saudi. I was going to nurse this baby home and dead-stick it in. That option was only available for a short time.

As I flew lower and slower, pieces of metal (compressor and turbine blades) and fuel were spitting out of the tailpipe. I had turned into a $20-million glider. *No sweat.* I changed the plan. I'll coax it across the border and eject in friendly territory. I honestly gave thought about Neck getting to see a real-life ejection-seat ride. Just briefly.

Throughout this jaunt, Neck took control of the external communication. He coordinated with the AWACS controller without any direction from me. I never had to tell him what I needed. He knew.

BENJI 51: "Benji 3, 1 Victor."

BENJI 54: "Go ahead."

BENJI 51: "Roger . . . ah, you headin' for Hafr Al-Batin?"

BENJI 54: "Ah, negative. Right now we are going straight towards the border, the closest border. I've got the nearest divert for you, Hafr Al-Batin one-eight-zero for one-three-four, is that what you've got?"

BENJI 53: "Yeah, I got it. I'm not gonna make it."

BENJI 54: "Why not?"

BENJI 53: "I won't make it there. I'm, ah, looking to get across and get out."

BENJI 54: "Is there something wrong still?"

BENJI 53: "This is all I can get, man. . . . Neck, I'm gonna go a little bit—I'm going less than max range. I guess I should go max endurance."

BENJI 51: "What's your FTIT (engine temperature) and, ah, RPM say?"

BENJI 53: "Okay, my FTIT is 870, RPM is 94. I'm just not gettin' any thrust. Oil pressure's at 40."

Neck soon matched my aircraft configuration, punching his tanks off, sending them tumbling earthward.

BENJI 54: "Okay, lemme come back and look at you again, okay?"

BENJI 53: "Cool."

BENJI 54: "Dude, I'm gonna punch my tanks off so I can stay with you, all right?"

BENJI 53: "Cool."

BENJI 54: "Ah, what's your gas reading?"

BENJI 53: "46."

I know what you're thinking. You thought fighter pilots always spoke in standardized terms, with tactical jargon, and we do—just not always. From day one in the F-16, I learned communication discipline. We strive for Clear, Concise, and Correct (C3) Comm. This situation called for a different level of "correct" comm. We all have friends and colleagues that we relate to and communicate with on a different level. For Neck and me, this was personal. The first rule of flying and talking is: You have to sound cool. If you sound like a dork, you lose credibility instantly. We all wish we sounded like James Earl Jones but for those of us who don't, we do our best. Throughout this stressful situation, we still communicated effectively. We were clear, concise, and even correct. Though not correct by tactical standards, the messages and information we shared were correct to us.

I knew I wasn't alone. Neck had my back. So did a flight of F-15s, call sign Exxon. They followed behind us, covering our six o'clock. The familiar sound of their radar triggering my radar warning receiver was comforting.

BULLDOG: "And five-three, you have some friendlies north four."

BENJI 54: "You are leakin' tons of fluid and it looks like gas—that's why I am wondering what your gas is."

BENJI 53: "Okay."

BENJI 54: "It's all comin' out right where the hook meets the engine."

BENJI 53: "Copy. Okay, Bulldog, how far do I have to go . . . to the border?"

BULLDOG: "Border is sixty miles."

BENJI 53: "I might make it, Neck."

BENJI 54: "Yeah, you will, Homer, man, don't worry." (Neck often called me Homer, invoking cartoon character Homer Simpson.)

BULLDOG: "And Benji, ah, your friendlies are tally with you."

BENJI 53: "Copy."

BENJI 54: "Is this all the airspeed you can get?"

BENJI 53: "That's it, man. I can dump the nose, but I really don't want to. I wanna keep this wind goin' for me."

I continued milking every mile out of my crippled jet. As time went by, she wasn't responding to my nursing. She needed a surgeon—and I wasn't wearing scrubs. It was obvious that I wasn't going to make it to the border. Neck knew it too. We never spoke of it directly, but we both knew. I resigned myself to the fact that I was jumping out of this bird on the wrong side of the line. We still managed to maintain some levity and humor until the end.

BULLDOG: "Five-three, ah, confirm you're a single-ship?"
BENJI 53: "Negative. I've got a wingman here."
BULLDOG: "Rog."
BENJI 54: "Ya know, Spikey, if you need some more lift, you might want to throw your flaps down."
BULLDOG: "Five-three, border is, ah, fifty-five miles."
BENJI 53: "Copy. Think I'll hang out for a little while, Neck."
BENJI 54: "Okay."
BENJI 53: "Say distance to border, Bulldog."
BULLDOG: "Border fifty-four."

Another communication objective we live by is that information passed should be Situational Awareness (SA) building. Unnecessary or incomplete comm tends to be SA dumping, meaning it reduces or degrades one's mental picture of the current environment. Inexperience is also a factor, as well as responding with what the inquiring mind wants to hear. A perfect example is our young AWACS controller. Ultimately, he did a nice job; however, some of his transmissions were less than effective. A request for Search and Rescue (SAR) was clear. The response was incorrect. Neck calmly requested the controller to coordinate for helicopter support to effect my rescue. AWACS confirmed that the choppers were airborne (not true) well before I ejected.

BENJI 54: "Understand you've got choppers in the air?"
BULLDOG: "Benji, you want choppers?"
BENJI 54: "That's affirm. You guys better scramble them now!"
BULLDOG: "Rog."

BENJI 54: "Vector 'em to where we're gonna be. . . . How you doin',
Homer?"

BENJI 53: "Hangin' in, man."

BENJI 54: "Cool. I'm with you all the way."

How many coworkers will stay by your side as you're going
down in flames? Words can't express the calm and confidence that
fell over me when he made that call to me.

BENJI 53: "I'm gonna try the flaps (interrupted)."

BULLDOG: "Benji, border fifty."

Neck inquired about known threats in our path.

BENJI 54: "Copy fifty. Bulldog, Benji."

BULLDOG: "Benji, go ahead."

BENJI 54: "Copy. Understand that ah, this border area is pretty clear
with threats?"

BULLDOG: "That's affirm, I'll check for ya."

BENJI 54: "Check, please. . . . Flaps help a little bit, Homie."

BENJI 53: "Cool. My AOA (angle of attack) is down a little bit."

BULLDOG: "And five-three, we're checkin' for ya."

BENJI 53: "Okay."

Our original flight lead, Benji 51, monitored our comm. He stayed out
of our business until he needed information, or could provide help.

BENJI 51: "Benji 4, 1."

BENJI 54: "Go."

BENJI 51: "Anything we can do to help?"

BENJI 54: "Say again?"

BENJI 51: "Anything I can do to help?"

BENJI 54: "Ah, you might wanna get on a tanker, get some gas, and be
able to, ah, help with SAR."

BENJI 51: "Okay."

BULLDOG: "Five-three, border forty-four."

BENJI 54: "Eight staff, left ten." (threat)

BULLDOG: "Benji five-three, if you could, squawk emergency, please."

BENJI 54: "Do you got that, Spike, or do you want me to do it?"

BENJI 53: "Yeah, I got it. I dunno if that's such a good idea, is it?"

BENJI 54: "I dunno. Bulldog, Benji, is that a good idea right where we're at?"

BULLDOG: "That's what I was instructed . . . ah, I'd say no, I've got a good contact with you."

BENJI 54: "Okay, good, keep that contact. Do you got choppers in the air?"

BULLDOG: "Affirm, they are on their way."

BENJI 54: "Copy that."

In the heat of the battle, AWACS asked us to squawk emergency (code 7700 on the IFF transponder—the same as in civil aviation), which would have highlighted us to every Iraqi watching. Unnecessary. My confidence level in AWACS was sinking. I could tell he was nervous and it seemed like someone was looking over his shoulder, providing poor input to his decision tree. We call it pushing the rope. It's impossible.

Lower and slower I went, trying to stay out of the clouds and remaining aloft as long as I could. Every minute airborne meant a minute less on the ground. I was buying time for the Search and Rescue (SAR) forces to push north. Neck and I kept track of our distance to the border, and I had a good gauge on my location, which was a plus. However, all of my efforts eventually gave way to the inevitable—this jet was going back to the taxpayers.

For a while, it got too quiet, so I had to break the silence.

BENJI 53: "Bummer, dude."

BENJI 54: "What's goin' on, man?"

BENJI 53: "Just bummer."

I prepared the cockpit by clearing out everything strapped to my legs and near the seat. Water bottles got stuffed in my pockets, helmet bag, maps and checklists set aside. I tightened my harness straps and cinched down my helmet, ready to take the ride of a lifetime. I was ready. I had no choice.

BENJI 54: "Okay, now you've got fire comin' out of your engine. Looks like it's falling."

BENJI 53: "What's falling?"

BENJI 54: "Well, it looks like you've got sparks and s*** comin' out of your engine now."

BENJI 53: "Okay . . . Bulldog . . ."

BULLDOG: "Go ahead."

BENJI 53: "Okay, I'm having a more serious problem now, okay?"

BULLDOG: "Rog."

Tick, tick, tick. Time passed slowly.

BENJI 54: "Understand, choppers are in the air?"

BULLDOG: "That's affirm. Border forty."

BENJI 53: "Neck, you tell me if you see any fire."

BENJI 54: "Okay, it's red sparks poppin' out right now."

BENJI 53: "Okay, just tell me if you see a fire."

BENJI 54: "Okay. Stay with it, dude."

My jet shuddered and smoke began to enter the cockpit. The training took over.

BENJI 54: "Okay, you're—"

BENJI 53: "I-I'm gettin' out!"

BENJI 54: "Okay, you're on fire."

I instinctively moved my feet to the rudder pedals, back of my head to the headrest, elbows in, reached for the handle and pulled. *BOOM!*

BENJI 54: "Okay, Bulldog, we've got him out, we've got him out! He's out of the jet. . . . Bulldog, we have a good chute. Bulldog, Benji, do you copy?"

BULLDOG: "I copy. Marked."

I know I closed my eyes. All I saw was red as the ejection seat rocket motor exploded to life. Other pilots who have taken an ACES II ejection seat ride have experienced time compression and felt the seat riding up the rails into the wind. Not me. I felt no time between the initial blast and flying through the air on my back. The free-stream wind caught the lip of my helmet, threatening to rip it off. My oxygen mask compressed to my face like a Bo Jackson stiff-arm. Luckily, I was only doing 150 knots. Neck saw the show from his wingside seat. He said I looked like a rag doll, arms flailing and all. I say I was just waving.

Still breathing. That's good. Checklist! Canopy! Visor! Mask! Seat Kit! LPU! 4-Line Release!

Automatic.

Whoa! What a sight! From between my legs flies a flaming unmanned convertible Viper. It's nothing like in the movies—no sound track playing in the background. In fact it's eerily silent. No wind noise because I'm moving the same speed and at the mercy of the wind. The jet vanished into the clouds trailing flames the length of the jet. I looked down and saw so much detail. The ejection seat, trailing its drogue chute, was plummeting to the ground. Behind it, the canopy tumbled out of control. *I hope no one is on the ground to greet the uninvited American.*

The ride from twelve thousand feet seemed to take an eternity. Snow was falling and swirling in the clouds. My harness was digging into my crotch. I cautiously moved the straps around to make more of a seat. I felt like I might fall out of the straps while adjusting them; an irrational thought, I know, but the brain works in strange ways. I emerged from the clouds at around three thousand feet above the ground. The surface resembled the moon—very rocky and surprisingly hilly. I struggled to maneuver the parachute with the steering cords, finding that I could only turn right. I figured it would behoove me to be good at right turns, so I practiced them. Scouting the area, I noticed a grouping of black spots in the dirt. Old campfires? *Hopefully very old.*

Approaching the ground, I again reverted to my ingrained life support and parachute training. Eyes on the horizon. Eyes on the horizon. Of course, my curiosity got the best of me. The rocks below looked pretty big. *This landing is going to leave a mark.* I looked away. *Big rocks, big rocks.* Looking down again. *Big rocks. No, small rocks! Eyes on the horizon. Oh great, survive this to break a leg.* Knees together, three-point roll. I hit the ground! A totally uneventful landing. *I'll take it.*

As I sat up in the dusty rocks, my mouth was as dry as the

scorched earth surrounding me. Checking myself for injury, I noticed blood on my neck and chest. I only then noticed the gash under my chin—most likely caused by my harness or chinstrap during the ejection sequence. It was the least of my worries at this point. I attempted to gather my chute, but the risers had become intertwined in the rocks. I decided to conserve energy, assess my surroundings, and drink some water. I performed our established communication procedures, and radioed to Neck that I was okay on UHF 243.0, the emergency frequency. Needing a more discrete frequency, I audibled Neck to our secondary emergency frequency: UHF 282.8.

Silence. We crave it sometimes. In my world it was so silent it was loud. I heard tones and ringing in my ears. I was in a lonely place—for a while, anyway. Out of the clouds came Neck, hauling ass below the weather to help me out. He scouted the area, exposing himself to the threat of antiaircraft artillery and surface-to-air missiles. He didn't have to do it. He just did.

I was surrounded by excellence.

He accurately marked my position using latitude and longitude from the inertial navigation system.

We determined it would be best for me to stay put. The immediate area was clear for the time being. No need to beat feet for safer surroundings. I eventually gathered my parachute and inventoried my supplies. I had a full survival kit with plenty of water, a smaller kit known as a Hit and Run kit, which contained only essentials, and my survival vest. The vest held a 9mm pistol with extra clips, signaling devices (flares, mirror, and a strobe), the survival radio, and a compass. Assessing the threat, my highest threat wasn't the enemy; it was what we call environmentals. The weather we overflew to enter Iraq was moving my way. I had to remain dry. Hypothermia . . . I sure didn't consider the possibility when I took off and the temperature was 85 degrees. I was positioned in a depression where someone would have to be within five hundred yards to see me. I had nowhere to go though, nowhere to hide . . . Except—in the middle of the desert I had a seemingly useless item that was potentially lifesaving. We often flew over the Persian Gulf, and were equipped with one-man life rafts integral to our survival kit. I flipped the raft over, and propped it against a tumbleweed. It served as a great lean-to. The spray shields hung down, acting as a sort of curtain. I was able to get all of my gear inside, minus a portion of the parachute. I became a black dot in a sea of wasteland—the proverbial needle in a haystack.

Assuming the choppers were on the way, I prepared for my pickup. What do I need? *Take the Hit and Run kit, and my helmet, so I can fly again. That should do.* On the horizon to the west, I watched the thunderstorm brewing. I knew I was close to Kuwait and a north/south running road was a few miles west of me. Anticipating a quick pickup, I stuffed a handful of rocks into my G-suit pocket. I had to get souvenirs after going through all this.

Under my raft, I leaned back against my survival kits, propped my helmet under my knees, and waited in my combat recliner. I used this time to check out my survival vest. This was the first time I seriously thought about confronting the enemy and being captured. Most of the decisions I made up to this point were easy because they were solutions prescribed by repetition and training. The subsequent choices were on me. I ensured my 9mm pistol was loaded and considered my options if confronted. The last thing I wanted was to be on a flatbed truck getting hauled away by the enemy. *If two show up, I'll fight—kill them, then trek south. If three or more show up armed, I'll do whatever it takes to stay alive.* Was that weak? Should I fight? On my soil, Yes. On theirs, No. Many of my brothers in arms had already shown up on CNN, beaten, but alive. I would take my chances. I wouldn't let them defeat my will.

Here came the rain—big drops. I love a great thunderstorm, just not this one. I struggled to hold the raft down. As the cold gusts of wind tried to pry it away, lightning struck nearby and I felt the hair on my arms rise up from the static electricity. I slowly put my radio aside. I was holding the only metal lightning rod within miles. I was laughing inside for a moment. The storm was as strong as it was quick. I achieved victory! I was completely dry. The skies cleared as night fell, revealing more stars than I knew existed—a hauntingly beautiful sight.

I strictly followed the emergency radio procedures. Listen at preset times, otherwise sit tight and wait. The Iraqis had the ability to home in on radio transmissions and locate the source. I hadn't transmitted since talking to Neck, who had handed me off to another flight for cover. I was glad it was dark. Due to the risk and recent problems with resistance during daylight rescue attempts, no one was coming until darkness fell. I was comforted by the faint sound of jet noise—the sound of freedom—high above me.

I was surrounded by excellence.

One hour gone. I expected a ride by now. Are *they coming? The storm must have delayed them. I hope it slowed up everyone else too. They can't find me.* Silence. Prayer. My wife. My baby daughter. My wedding ring. I always wear it. We are supposed to take them off, for safety reasons mostly. An even more important factor was security in the case of capture. The enemy would play on your fears and fabricate lies about the safety of your family if they knew you were married. I took off my ring and stored it in my pocket. At the first sign of trouble, I would swallow it. I'd do whatever it took to retrieve it as nature took its course. It was that important to me.

More waiting. Nothing over the radio. Silence—and a lesson in responsibility. In the darkness, I dropped my compass. I also misplaced my strobe light. *Nice job, Spike.* I dropped these critical objects, but never lost them. Each item contained in my survival vest was attached to its respective pocket by a thin lanyard. I simply pulled the lanyard and presto!—there was my gear. Simplicity at its finest. Someone, most likely an airman who earned twelve thousand dollars a year, was responsible for tying off our survival gear with simple knots and string. That single person took his responsibility seriously. His or her devotion to duty, no matter how mundane or tedious, was crucial to my survival.

I was surrounded by excellence. "Excellence in all we do." It matters.

Time passed slowly. My day had started early. I was comfortable and tired. I did the "jerk"—that spasm you sometimes experience when you fall asleep. Not good. I stuck my head out of the raft for some cool air. Waiting for my ride home was a lot like waiting for someone to pick you up and drive you somewhere. Clock watching, confusion, impatience. Then when your ride shows, the past disappears and you get in and go, focusing on the task at hand. My ride was the same. It was a sound I had heard before—on the TV show *MASH*. The helicopters were unmistakable, the rotor blades cutting through the dusty night air south of my position.

It was like music. I grabbed my Hit and Run kit, helmet, and radio. The Blackhawks (helicopters) were maybe two hundred yards away heading northeast.

"Benji 53 is up! I'm on your left! Turn left!"

Why aren't they talking to me?

"You passed me up! You passed me!"

They disappeared.
The strobe!
I activated my strobe.

"My strobe is on! Come back left!"

I never heard a response. *What a great radio—if I needed a door-stop.* Silence . . .

Then the music reappeared. Like the rising sun over a knoll, a helicopter filled the sky. The tips of the rotor blades were lit up like a ring of fire as the sand billowed upward. The first Blackhawk flew directly over me, too close to turn and land. I had moved away from my raft so as not to get hit by it if it blew around.

"I'm holding the strobe! I'm holding the strobe!"

Crouching on one knee, I saw the second chopper appear. Following some world-class maneuvering, it set down twenty yards away. I shielded myself from the pelting sand, still holding the strobe. No one came to get me for what seemed like several minutes. I was trained to stay put until the pararescue crew approached me, but that green light pointing my way from the cockpit was too inviting. *They must not want to get out.* As I emerged from my crouching position, a figure appeared from opposite the chopper and grabbed me by the arms. This man with arms the size of my legs spun me around to face him. I knew the Cyclops-like figure was friendly. His single eye was a night-vision device. The first word out of his mouth was, "Sir."

I was surrounded by excellence.

"Sir, are you okay?"
"Yes, I'm Benji 53, let's get the hell out of here!"

With his guidance, I ran to the chopper. *Break for daylight! I've been here before . . .*

The soldier directed me to sit on the floor, where I was flanked by my escort and another "Snake Eater" (Army Special Forces) who jumped in via the left-hand door. He had sprinted to my raft first. When he came up empty, the second soldier emerged to circle around and recover me. After jumping back in, he couldn't get the door closed. Just go. The medic immediately tended to me, offering water and food, examining my injury, and making me comfortable. Two mini-gunners were positioned mid-cabin, left and right with two pilots at the controls. Seven warriors in each Blackhawk. Fourteen men sent to rescue one. I'm still humbled.

As we lifted off, I was unaware of any threat in the immediate area. I cheered my rescuers, thanking them, and celebrating, when the professional next to me simply reached over and placed his hand on my chest. Without a word, I knew what he meant. *Spike, sit down, shut up, and color.* I quickly realized that even though I felt finished, they weren't. We departed southwest bound in a hurry. From the north, a SAM launch! Flares dispensing, the pilot maneuvered defensively, watching the missile hit the desert floor. The angels who lifted me from earth sped south a mere 20 feet off the ground at 180 knots in complete darkness. The cold breeze from the open door made me feel more alive than I had ever felt in my life.

I was surrounded by excellence.

No one on that helicopter so much as blinked until we reached the border. As we climbed up to altitude, I knew we were home free. I finally got to thank the crew as we proceeded to King Khalid Military City in northern Saudi. I had flown missions out of KKMC just ten days earlier, and knew that some squadron pilots would be there. To my surprise, my wingman, Neck, emerged from the crowd to meet me. I could have kissed him. Neck had diverted to KKMC after burning every last drop of his available fuel overhead my position in Iraq. There couldn't have been a better reunion.

It turns out that Neck was able to listen to the entire rescue at the Special Forces Command Post. The Special Forces had teamed up with an Army Aviation Unit from Savannah, Georgia, and trained for the SAR. The whole world anticipated huge U.S. aircraft losses to Iraqi air defenses. Based on those estimates, we, as a military, feared we wouldn't have the number of SAR crews required. So through their commitment and some raw chance, the boys from Fort Campbell, Kentucky, received the orders to go find me that night.

Through debriefing at the Special Forces command center, I discovered information previously unknown to me. Two separate groups were hunting me, one from the south, and the other from the north. The rescue crew estimated I had an hour before they ran across me. Upon receiving the "all clear" from the SAR forces, my brothers above—the invisible jet noise—rolled in and eliminated the unlucky soldiers looking to track me down. The helicopters hadn't launched as was reported by AWACS. In fact, after landing at KKMC, Neck saw the rescue helicopters on the ground. They had been delayed by the weather and an aircraft malfunction requiring maintenance prior to launching. The crew in the Blackhawk was calling me on their way in to the rescue zone. Neither of us heard the other. Following the debriefing, I was fed some fine United States Army cuisine, stitched up, and released to the Air Force side of the base. I was able to call my wife. She initially thought

I was joking around. I was glad *I* was the one passing the news to her. It was a good thing I kept my helmet. I got to fly combat missions again one week later.

I set out to make my story entertaining in writing. Secondarily, I wanted to reveal some of the keys to why I'm able to write this success story. After every mission we fly, we debrief the flight to come up with Lessons Learned. Lessons Learned are statements regarding mission execution that can be shared with the entire squadron or used individually. They reveal our errors and provide solutions to correct those errors, or simply reinforce the techniques and procedures that make us successful. They are pieces of the unsolved jigsaw puzzle. Each piece provides us with a clearer picture and pushes us toward excellence in our mission execution.

I'm thankful for the scores of quality individuals who have supported me professionally, personally, and emotionally, making it possible for me to survive and be around to share my experiences. I take pride in the way we do business as fighter pilots, and deeply believe in the principles we operate upon. Success is contagious, and the tools I will offer you are my attempt to spread the fever of excellence. Your application of the concepts I touch on has little to do with the mission objective of my writing. If I bring you into our world of tactical aviation and get you to think outside of *your* cockpit, my mission is accomplished.

Surround yourself with excellence. It worked for me.

48

LT. JON VANBRAGT—2005

Carrier qualifying before my first nugget cruise was supposed to be a good time: Go out to the boat (always an adventure), get more traps, and finally feel a little more like a fleet aviator and a little less like an FRS student. However, the situation I found myself in during my night CQ turned out to be a whole lot less than a pleasurable experience.

The fun began in the bolter, wave-off pattern. After one discontinued approach and a trip around the pattern, I was ready to get on deck. Bull's-eye and needles were both "on and on" at three-quarters of a mile, when my WSO (weapons systems officer) made the ball call. Just like paddles had briefed me, I kept the ball on the happy side of the lens, proactively flying it to the best of my ability. My reward was a 3-wire, and I went to mil power. That's when life got a little more complicated.

On the rollout, I felt the familiar tug of the hook catching the cross-deck pendant, as the arresting-gear motors dissipated my jet's energy. Approaching the edge of the angle, I felt a jerk and then another. Even with my very limited experience around the boat—this was my tenth night trap—I knew something was wrong. I watched in horror as the edge of the angle passed beneath the nose of my aircraft.

I screamed, "Eject!"

I grabbed the handle with my right hand, but, fortunately, my WSO had beaten me to the punch; then there was a fireball.

Next thing I remember was a riser hitting the side of my helmet. I was disoriented and thought I was upside down. It made no sense to me to see an inflated parachute in what I believed was the space below me. Just as I realized I was right side up, I hit the water. Because of the attitude of the jet during ejection, I had received only a single swing in the chute—almost the worst-case scenario taught at water survival.

More chaos ensued as my horse collar auto-inflated. I found myself floating in the water, being dragged by my chute. I reached up as the SEAWARS (seawater activated release system) auto ejected one of the two risers, but I then noticed what I assessed to be a bigger problem: The aircraft carrier was headed right for me.

I paddled in vain, trying to get away from the carrier as it lumbered toward me. I looked up just in time to watch the angle pass me for the second time that night. The carrier surprisingly was quiet as it pushed through the water a mere ten feet away. I heard none of the familiar noises of the flight deck, just the splashing of waves. As I approached the aft end of the ship, I started to get sucked into the wake. I ended up almost directly behind the carrier. The stage now was set for my third surprise of the night.

My left Koch fitting, which I had completely forgotten about, still was connected to my harness. Unfortunately, my SEAWARS had not activated on that fitting, and I was about to find out firsthand just how strong the pull of a parachute could be. As mine got caught in the wake of the carrier, I was tugged underwater with a force I couldn't resist. Frantically, I pawed at the Koch fitting, trying to overcome the force pulling me below. I was able to free myself and float to the surface after having been pulled about ten feet underwater. When I reached the surface, I realized one of my options from the IROK (inspect/inflate, release raft, options/oxygen, and Koch fittings) procedure just had saved my life. I had not yet removed my mask, and oxygen from the emergency bottle in my seat pan still was being pumped to me while I was underwater.

As I sat in the wake of the ship, wondering what just had happened to put me in the ocean, I started to look around for the SAR assets. To my left, I viewed one of the saddest sights of my life: The tails from my FA-18F still were protruding from the ocean.

"Well," I thought, "better try to get rescued."

The first thing I did was to try to free my raft from my seat pan. After unsuccessfully fumbling with the box, I decided to remove it; I again was unsuccessful. I couldn't free the fittings wedged between my body and personal flotation.

Giving up on the raft, I began to scour my survival vest for the items I thought were important for my current situation. I reached into my left pocket and felt what seemed like my strobe light. I couldn't see a thing in the dark, and, with my gloves on, I was fumbling even more. I pulled out the object and got exactly what I didn't need just then: my water bottle. After a few curse words, I let the bottle go and went back into my left pocket.

Next, I pulled out my flashlight. Twisting the top, it flickered to life. Light, oh yeah! I flashed that light at everything I could see. I flashed it at the helos, the plane guard, the carrier, and even my helmet to get the SAR crew's attention. I finally concluded the light alone was not enough, and I decided to go for the other pocket.

Reaching into my right pocket, I felt around some more and found something I knew would come in handy: the day/night flare. During my search in the right pocket, though, I dropped my light and again was without illumination. Pulling out the nearest end of the flare, I held it away from me and popped the actuator. I was greeted with a large spark, which made me very happy—until a huge cloud of smoke emerged. I had popped the wrong end! Once again, after mumbling a few expletives, I turned the flare around and actuated the night end, waving it at the nearest SAR helicopter.

As the flare burned out, I went back into my left pocket to try to find the pencil flares. Instead, I got my arm wrapped in the cord that secured the light to my vest. I noticed the light still was on in the water below me and pulled up the cord to retrieve my light. As the helo began to circle over me, I flashed my helmet light again to help them see me.

The SAR helo dropped off a rescue swimmer, who very calmly

came over to me, asked me if I was all right, and began to clear any lines that may have been wrapped around me. I was very impressed with his patience and thoroughness, as I probably was much more anxious than he to get aboard his helo. Once sure I was clear, he attached my D-ring to the helo hoist, and I was on board the SH-60 before I knew it. My WSO already had been picked up by the helo crew and had no injuries from his ejection.

I learned many things that evening. The ejection, while intense and overwhelming, was just the very beginning of the survival process. I'm thankful I wore my dry suit in the cold water. I'm fortunate I had not removed my mask immediately on water entry and that I had gotten the second Koch fitting off while in the ship's wake.

I also did many things poorly that evening. I should have concentrated on removing that second Koch fitting immediately after water entry. While the SEAWARS is designed to operate automatically, I should have been ready to free myself from my chute. When I was in the wake, I should have taken a few deep breaths, relaxed, and removed my gloves. The added dexterity greatly would have helped me in locating and actuating my survival gear. If my hands had gotten cold, I could have put the gloves back on. I should have been more familiar with the location of my survival gear. Five minutes more in the PR shop to refamiliarize myself with the location of survival items in my vest could have saved me precious moments of fumbling while in the water.

It's easy to say you know where your gear is, and it won't be a problem to find a certain item, but, with the disorientation and shock of ejection, I found even the simplest of tasks was very difficult. Just because you can find the gear when you're suiting up does not mean it will be readily available while you float in the water on a dark night.

Finally, I never should have have put my wallet and my iPod in my helmet bag. It's bad enough to eject, but losing those items added insult to injury.

ANALYST COMMENTS

Blue Threat number one: Our aircrew may not be able to execute post-ejection procedures completely and in the correct order. Once you pull the handle, the mishap is unpreventable, but your life can still be lost. How can we go about preparing for an ejection that comes when least expected? Worse yet, the ejection might occur at very low altitude and place us in the water uncomfortably close to a very big, fast-moving gray piece of steel. The best we can do, outside of our recurring aviation-physiology course, is to revisit the procedures on a regular basis. Rote memorization is our friend. Think about the possibility of pulling the ejection handle every time you walk to your jet. Rehearse what happens next (IROK). Make those procedures so familiar and automatic that you can execute them even in the midst of extreme stress.

Blue Threat number two: Aircrew inability to locate and retrieve gear inside the survival vest, especially under water. Not knowing where your signaling devices are located can delay your rescue and possibly result in a failed rescue. Even if you know where those items are located around your abdomen, they can be very difficult to retrieve. We've all taken the aviation-physiology courses every four years. We've been briefed on the locations of our gear. Be able to get at those items blindfolded. A great way to combat this threat is to task the flight-equipment personnel with creating a diagram, manikin, or some sort of visual aid in the flight equipment room that constantly reminds aircrew of gear locations. Move it around and highlight particular items so it never becomes stale.

—Maj. Mark Budde, USMC, FA-18 analyst, Naval Safety Center

49

LT. GEOFF VICKERS—2002

My squadron and air wing were detached to NAS Fallon, Nevada, for strike training. Most of us attended lectures all day, but I was tasked with giving the battle-group-air-warfare commander an orientation flight in the F-14D. As skipper of the cruiser in charge of the battle groups air defenses, he had been spending time with the air wing to better understand how we conduct our missions. He had observed a number of the strike events through the tactical air combat training system (TACTS) replays, and he had flown with the E-2C and EA-6B squadrons. He was proud that the Prowler guys hadn't been able to make him sick.

My job was to demonstrate the Tomcat's performance and tactical capabilities. Though this flight was my first without a qualified radar intercept officer (RIO) in the backseat, I had flown with a number of aviators who had very little Tomcat experience.

The captain arrived at the squadron a half hour before the brief to receive his cockpit orientation lecture and ejection-seat checkout. Once in the ready room, we briefed the flight with our wingman. I covered the administrative and tactical procedures in accordance with our squadron's standard operating procedures (SOP).

I told the captain that after the G-awareness maneuver, we would do a quick inverted check to verify cockpit security. Looking back, I should have recognized his anxiety when he mocked me and said, "Just a quick inverted check?" then laughed. I didn't realize hanging upside down with nothing but glass and eleven thousand feet of air separating you from the desert floor might not be the most comfortable situation in the world for a surface-warfare officer.

I continued the brief and told the captain we would do a performance demo and a couple of intercepts, followed by tanking from an S-3. I told him if, at any point, he felt uncomfortable, we would stop whatever we were doing; roll wings level, and take it easy. I was determined to avoid the temptation to intentionally make him sick and uncomfortable.

The start, taxi, and takeoff were normal. We joined with our lead and did the standard clean-and-dry checks. We pressed into the working area and assumed a defensive combat-spread formation in preparation for the G-warm. I told him what was happening, and he seemed to remember the sequence of events from the brief. After we completed the checks, I asked him, "Are you ready for the inverted check? Do you have everything stowed?"

"All set," was the last thing I heard him say.

I checked the airspeed and confirmed it was above the 300 knots recommended to do the check, and I rolled the aircraft inverted. I decided not to really put on a lot of negative G and unloaded to about .3 to .5 negative G's—just enough to make anything float that wasn't stowed properly. If he was uncomfortable in such a benign maneuver, it would be better to find out then, rather than when we were racing toward the earth during a radar-missile defense.

As I started to push on the stick, I heard a loud pop, followed by a roar. The cockpit filled with smoke, and we suddenly lost cabin pressure. I first thought a catastrophic environmental control system (ECS) had failed. I said to myself, "This is new. I've never even heard of something like this happening."

Time compression turned the next few seconds into an eternity. I knew the first thing I had to do was to roll the jet upright and assess the situation. About three seconds after the first indication of a problem, I had the jet upright and knew exactly what had happened.

I transmitted, "Lion 52. Emergency—my RIO just ejected."

I was yelling into the mic, thinking I would have to make all the calls in the blind. I never would have thought I easily could communicate with all the noise of flying at 320 knots without a canopy.

As I turned the jet to try and get a visual of my wayward passenger, Desert Control asked, "Understand your wingman ejected?"

"Negative, my RIO ejected. I'm still flying the plane."

"OK. Understand your RIO ejected. You're flying the plane, and you're OK?"

I almost said I was far from OK, but I just told them I was all right, except I was flying a convertible. I was relieved to see a good parachute below me, and I passed this info to Desert Control. Very quickly after the emergency call, an FA-18 pilot from the Naval Strike and Air-Warfare Center, who also was in the area, announced he would take over as the on-scene commander of the search-and-rescue (SAR) effort.

I told my wingman to pass the location of the captain because I could not change any of my displays. Once my wingman started to pass the location, I started dumping gas and put the needle on the nose back to NAS Fallon.

One of our air-wing SH-60s was in the area and responded, along with the station's UH-1N. The captain was recovered almost immediately and transported to the local hospital for treatment and evaluation.

The only F-14D boldface procedures for a canopy problem include placing the canopy handle in "boost close" position and then moving the command eject lever to "pilot." Obviously, the canopy already was gone, so that lever action didn't apply, and, if the command-eject lever wasn't already in "pilot," as briefed, I also would have been ejected.

I slowed the aircraft and lowered my seat because that's what I remembered from the rest of the steps in the checklist. However, after sitting at eye level with my multifunction display for about thirty seconds, I thought it would be more prudent to see outside, so I raised my seat. Slowing the aircraft had little effect on the windblast, but, as long as I leaned forward, the wind hit only my shoulders. Because it was very cold at altitude, I decided to return quickly to base, but I needed to watch my airspeed since the ejection had occurred.

The PCL says to fly less than 200 knots and 15,000 feet and to complete a controllability check for the loss of the canopy, but I never pulled out my PCL to reference it. I figured with the way my day was going, I'd probably just drop my PCL down an intake and complicate my problems. In retrospect, I should have requested my wingman break out his checklist and talk me through the steps. Though this practice of having a wingman assist is common in single-seat communities, Tomcat crews tend to forget this coordination technique is a viable option.

I did consider the controllability check, and I directed my wingman to check for damage to the vertical stabilizers—she found none. The faster I got on deck, the faster I would get warm.

I slowed to approach speed in 10-knot increments at about 3,000 feet AGL and had no problems handling the jet. As I approached the field, I was surprised at how quiet it got. The noise was only slightly louder than the normal ECS roar in the Tomcat. I'll admit I felt silly saying the landing checklist over the ICS when no one else was in the cockpit, but I didn't want to risk breaking my standard habit patterns.

The landing was uneventful, and, when I pulled back into the line, I was surprised to find how many people had come out to see the spectacle. The magnitude of the situation finally set in when my skipper gave me a hug after I got out of the jet.

The captain and I were very fortunate: All of the ejection and aviation life support systems (ALSS) equipment functioned as expected. Our PR1 had taken the time to properly fit the captain, using components from three different sets of flight gear. This action caused a problem after the mishap—getting everyone's gear replaced—but it renewed my faith in our escape systems. A forty-eight-year-old man ejected from the jet when it was inverted, at negative .5 G's, at 320 knots, and the only injuries he had were two minor cuts to his face.

After talking to the captain at the O'Club later that night, I realized I better could have briefed elements of the flight. Though I covered all of the details, I didn't fully consider his perspective. He said he didn't know where to put his hands. Consequently, he just left them in loosely clenched fists on his lap, about two inches away from the ejection handle. It never occurred to me that someone would not know what to do with his hands. Obviously, I fly with the stick and throttle in my hands 95 percent of the flight, but I failed to consider his situation.

The Mishap Board surmised that, during the inverted maneuver, he must have flinched when he slightly rose out of the seat and pulled the ejection handle. Now, before any brief, I try to place myself in the other person's shoes (even if they are black shoes) and imagine what the flight will be like for him. Whether it is the person who never has flown a tactical aircraft before or just the nugget pilot who never has flown with NVGs, remembering what it was like when I was unfamiliar with the environment will prevent this type of mishap from recurring.

50

LT. JASON WALKER—2004

The day almost was over. I already had my four day passes of two touch-and-goes and two traps, and I now was in the pinkie event for night carrier qualification (CQ). After one bolter and one trap, I launched a last time with a fuel state of 500 pounds above hold-down. After a bolter on my next pass, and with 3,600 pounds of gas remaining, approach control said my signal was bingo-divert to NAS North Island (NASNI)—a profile that required 2,900 pounds of fuel.

I immediately cleaned up and turned to put NASNI on the nose—initial bearing 026 degrees. I accelerated to 450 knots and initiated a climb, which soon put me on top of the typical scud layer that lingers off the San Diego coast. I continued my ascent to forty thousand feet and spoke on the primary radio with my squadron representative. Meanwhile, Beaver, the area controlling agency, began to query me on my auxiliary radio for information. As I worked to communicate my situation on both radios, I realized I had held too great of a nose-up attitude. This attitude caused my aircraft to decelerate below the bingo climb airspeed/Mach and consequently required me to level off at nineteen thousand feet to regain airspeed.

After resuming my climb, I declared an emergency, squawked 7700, and notified Beaver I was an emergency aircraft. Passing twenty-five thousand feet, I double-checked the F-18's Flight Performance Advisory System (FPAS) page, which showed me on deck at NASNI with 1,900 pounds of fuel. I decided to level off at twenty-nine thousand feet, thinking I could make up fuel in the descent. Beaver requested several times I say the altitude I planned to exit the area, and, wanting to satisfy them, I said I would leave at twenty-five thousand feet. The controller said that altitude would be fine and asked me to change my squawk. I assumed this request came so Beaver no longer would have to give me priority handling over the commercial traffic entering San Diego. I foolishly consented to let my priority change.

As Beaver pushed me to So Cal approach control, I ran through the ship-to-shore checklist in my cockpit. Runway 36/18 was out of service at NASNI, so So Cal immediately gave me a vector for a PAR approach to runway 29. I continued a gentle descent, hoping to conserve fuel, but I soon realized I was setting up for an extremely steep approach if I quickly didn't lose some altitude.

With my speed brake deployed and pushing the minute-to-live rule, I made it down to my assigned altitude. I lined up for the approach just as So Cal switched me to the NASNI final controller. His initial calls said I was "well right of course," which was confusing, because I could see the runway straight ahead, aligned perfectly off my nose.

My controller began to pass instructions about noise-abatement procedures, and I suddenly recalled the divert lecture our squadron had received on NASNI: The final-approach corridor was offset from runway 29 by eight degrees to the left. Looking out, I saw the famous Hotel Del Coronado dead ahead, along with a number of other apartment buildings along the Coronado coastline; I decided to make a quick jog to the left to avoid them. Once past the buildings, I returned to runway centerline and received the call that I was "well above glide slope." This information was disheartening, to say the least, considering I had not heard any previous glide-slope calls from my controller. With the runway in sight, I immediately pushed over and set the velocity vector four degrees down on the landing environment, establishing a thousand to twelve-hundred-feet-per-minute rate of descent. Although I had sight of the landing area and the instrument-approach markings at the end of the runway, I could not see the Fresnel lens, which I knew had to be there somewhere.

While on short final, I double-checked my velocity vector was set on the captain's bars, roughly five hundred to a thousand feet down the runway. However, once I saw the familiar airfield markings, I unconsciously became complacent and gave up looking for the ball. Continuing with my steep approach, I never did achieve a three-degree glide slope and subsequently touched down with an eight hundred to nine hundred-feet-per-minute rate of descent. I landed, pulled the throttles to idle, and programmed in aft stick as the jet decelerated through 100 knots. I also checked my brakes and felt what I thought was a solid lurch of the jet when I applied pressure to the pedals.

Approach told me to switch to tower; I momentarily looked down to scan for their frequency on the approach plate. I quickly decided against searching for the frequency. Feeling like I had lost track of time, I looked back up and immediately got the sensation I was going way too fast. I began to slowly apply brake pressure. Upon reaching about half the pedal depression, I realized something was not right. I released the brakes and tried again, but still nothing happened. As panic began to creep in, I stood on the brakes, and got the same result. My throttles were at idle, my speed brake was out, and my antiskid switch was on. My mind raced to determine why I wasn't stopping.

Seeing the red runway-end lights fast approaching, and with no distance-remaining markers in front of me, I threw down the hook. As soon as I dropped it, the wire came into view. I was hoping and praying the hook would get down in time, but a voice in my head was saying "no chance."

After making sure my nose wheel steering was engaged, I briefly considered taking a high-speed turnoff but quickly realized I was going way too fast. I was roughly 600 to 700 feet from the end of the runway and still traveling at 60 to 70 knots when I reached for the emergency-brake handle. I couldn't find it. Seeing the runway-end lights racing up at me, I screamed into my mask as my left hand continued to fumble for the brake handle. As I passed through the runway 29 overrun, my taxi light illuminated a cliff and the dark void of water just beyond. I had not even thought of the ejection handle until this point, but, as the water got closer, I quickly grabbed it with both hands.

I pulled the handle and heard a zip as the charges fired through the seat. I then saw the flash of the canopy blowing off, while my cockpit filled with smoke. I remember seeing a large fireball erupt around me as the main rockets in the seat fired, pushing me down with a significant rush of G's and launching me up into the black abyss of the night. I quickly was pulled out of my seat, and I looked up to find a good chute. Grabbing the risers, I got about one and one-half swings before hitting the water and submerging.

When I finally reached the surface, I managed to remove my mask and heard the flotation devices on my harness inflating. I began to back away from the parachute when I realized my leg restraints and kneeboard, amazingly, still were attached but were hung up on the parachute lines. I cleared myself of the lines, only to discover my left Koch fitting still was attached. The parachute was being dragged by the current and was sinking, taking me along with it. The inflated LPU was restricting my access to the Koch fitting. I eventually released it, freeing myself from the tangled mass. I was in the water for about five minutes before crewmen in a Coast Guard zodiac rescued me.

After a thorough investigation, the aviation mishap board determined I lost my normal antiskid braking because of a transducer circuit failure. The transducer is located in the aft portion of the brake hub and has a wire protruding from it that is adjacent to the aft wheel tie-down point. Because of its proximity to the tie down, the transducer on my aircraft had become damaged during flight-deck operations.

As background, the antiskid transducer's purpose is to monitor the antiskid system and completely shut it off should the antiskid fail or the brakes lock up. With the switch on, all braking is lost should a transducer failure occur. The easy fix is to simply turn off the antiskid switch, which will provide full braking without antiskid. This failure is quite common during shipboard ops, with more than nineteen confirmed cases of this failure in the FA-18. The failure can be recognized by a cockpit antiskid caution and an MSP code of 907 or 908 (left/right antiskid, transducer-circuit failure). The night of my mishap, the Deployable Flight Accident Recording System (DFIRS) noted an antiskid caution illuminating about one second after touchdown, but I do not remember seeing or hearing that caution.

In retrospect, I should have taken a different course of action the instant I realized the brakes were not working. There were several actions to choose from. First, I could have gone around and come back for an arrested landing. The Hornet can get airborne with as little as a thousand feet of runway remaining, and I certainly had that much concrete in front of me when I realized my brakes were gone. Second, once I did decide to keep the jet on the runway, my priorities should have been to select emergency brakes, not check my throttles and put out the speed brake. Finally, I let myself get distracted; I was wondering why I was having this braking problem instead of reacting to the emergency. Once I knew I had the runway made, I allowed myself to become complacent. I no longer was ready to handle, with split-second precision, any problem or emergency that might arise.

The administrative portion of flight is where most mishaps occur. We must continue to aviate, navigate, and communicate until the aircraft is stopped. While NATOPS (Naval Air Training and Operating Procedures Standardization) is our guiding publication and must be followed to the letter, it "is not a substitute for sound judgment." Many situations can arise that NATOPS explicitly will not cover; so, we must rely on experience—ours and that of others. The information that comes out of SIRs, hazreps and publications, such as this one, are there to help you deal with compound emergencies or situations others have faced. Study them, break them down, and talk about them within your ready room.

Aviators gain invaluable experience by traveling to unfamiliar fields. Cross-countries, out-and-ins, and detachments are essential to becoming a better, more experienced pilot. Studying your divert fields also is essential to preflight planning. Destination information, including runway lengths, arresting gear location, obstacles, procedures, emergency-safe and minimum-safe altitudes, and field lighting is information you must be armed with before walking to your aircraft.

Preflight planning also includes knowing your aircraft's performance characteristics. An FA-18, at landing weight and with two good engines in max afterburner (AB), still can take off from a stop in less than 1,500 feet. On average, E-28 gear is 1,500 feet from the end of the runway. The obvious take-away here is if you are trying to take the long-field gear and miss the wire, do not be afraid to take it around. Know your line speeds and maintain a good inside-outside scan of your instrument and the distance-remaining markers while on landing rollout. A line speed of double the distance-remaining board is a good rule of thumb for the Hornet (for example, no greater than 80 knots at the four board and 60 knots at the three board).

Never let anyone talk you into doing something that is against your best judgment, no matter how persistent or distracting they may be. Take charge and use the good headwork that you have developed as a naval aviator. If you are told to bingo, fly the profile, no matter how much excess gas you have.

51

WILLIAM WEAVER—1966

Over the course of a thirty-year career with Lockheed, most of which was spent as a test pilot, I had the opportunity and good fortune to fly some of the most advanced and exciting aircraft of their times. These included all models of the F-104, the first operational Mach 2 fighter aircraft, and the Blackbird family of Mach 3+ airplanes (A-12, YF-12 and SR-71). I had a great many memorable experiences and, although there is a well-known saying that flying is hours of boredom punctuated by moments of stark terror, I don't recall too many periods of boredom on these programs.

By far, the most memorable experience occurred on January 25, 1966 on an SR-71 test flight out of Edwards Air Force Base. Jim Zwayer, a Lockheed Flight Test Reconnaissance and Navigation systems specialist, and I were scheduled to conduct a flight to evaluate these systems and also to investigate procedures to improve high-Mach cruise performance by reducing trim drag. This involved flying with the center of gravity (CG) further aft than normal, which also reduces longitudinal stability.

We took off from Edwards at 11:20 A.M. and completed the first leg of the mission without incident. After refueling from a KC-135 tanker, we climbed back up to cruising speed and initial cruise-climb altitude (Mach 3.2 and 78,000 feet) proceeding eastbound on the test plan route. Several minutes after start of cruise, a malfunction of the right inlet automatic control system was experienced and manual control was required to correct the condition.

During supersonic flight, the engine inlet control functions to decelerate airflow in the inlet so that it is at subsonic speed at the face of the engine. This is accomplished by aft translation of the inlet center body spike and modulation of inlet forward bypass doors. These are normally scheduled automatically, as a function of Mach number, to position the normal shock wave (where the airflow becomes subsonic) at a location in the inlet which will provide optimum performance. If the proper inlet scheduling is not maintained, inlet disturbances can occur which result in the shock wave being expelled forward of the inlet. This phenomenon is called an inlet "unstart" and results in an instantaneous loss of thrust on that engine, accompanied by loud, explosive banging noises and violent yawing of the aircraft.

It was once described as like being in a train wreck. Unstarts were not uncommon at that time but with a properly functioning system, the shock wave could be recaptured and normal operation resumed.

Shortly after entering a programmed turn to the right in a 35-degree bank, an unstart occurred on the right side. The aircraft immediately rolled farther right and started to pitch up. With the control stick as far left and forward as it would go and no response from the airplane I knew we were in for a wild ride. I tried to tell Jim what was happening and to stay with what was left of the airplane until we reached lower speed and altitude because I didn't think the chances of surviving an ejection under those conditions (Mach 3.18 and 78,800 feet) were very good.

However, the G forces built up so rapidly that the words came out garbled and unintelligible, as revealed when the cockpit voice recorder was recovered. It wouldn't have made a difference anyway because the cumulative effects of malfunctions combined with reduced stability, higher angle of attack in the turn, speed, altitude, etc., resulted in forces being imposed on the aircraft that exceeded the restoring authority of the flight controls and Stability Augmentation System. Although everything seemed to be happening in slow motion, I was later informed that the time from onset of the event until catastrophic departure from controlled flight was a matter of two to three seconds.

As I was trying to communicate with Jim, I blacked out from the extremely high G forces and, from that point on, was just along for the ride. My next recollection was thinking that I was having a bad dream and hoping that I would wake up and get out of this mess. As I began to regain consciousness, I realized that this was not a dream and that it had really happened. That was disturbing because I was convinced that I could not have survived what had happened, so I thought I must be dead. Then I remember thinking that, since I didn't feel bad—kind of a detached, euphoric feeling—being dead wasn't so bad after all. I became fully conscious and realized I was not dead and had somehow become separated from the airplane. I had no idea how this could have happened because I did not intentionally activate the ejection system. I could feel myself falling and could hear the rushing of air and what sounded like straps flapping in the wind, but could not see anything because my pressure suit faceplate had frozen over and I was looking out through a layer of ice. The pressure suit was inflated so I knew that the emergency oxygen supply in the seat kit attached to my parachute harness was functioning. This was of critical importance because it not only supplies oxygen for breathing but also for pressurization of the suit which prevents the blood from boiling at those extreme altitudes.

I didn't appreciate it at the time, but with the suit pressurized as it was, I was also provided with physical protection against the intense buffeting and G forces I had been subjected to—kind of like being in your own escape capsule.

My next thoughts were about stability and my body tumbling at that altitude. If the body starts tumbling at high altitude where there is insufficient air density to resist these motions, centrifugal forces sufficient to cause physical injury can develop. For that reason, our parachute system included a small diameter stabilizing chute designed to deploy automatically shortly after ejection and seat separation. Since I had not intentionally activated the ejection system and assumed all these automatic functions were dependent on initiation of a proper ejection sequence, I was concerned that the stabilizing chute may not have deployed.

However, I was able to determine that I was falling vertically with no tumbling motion, so the little chute had deployed and was doing its job. My next concern was about the main parachute, which is designed to open automatically at fifteen thousand feet. Again, I wasn't sure the automatic opening function was going to operate. I still couldn't see through the iced-up faceplate so was unable to determine my altitude and didn't know how long I had been blacked out or how far I had fallen. I tried to feel for the manual opening D-ring on the front of my chute harness but, with the suit inflated and my hands numb from the cold, couldn't locate it. Finally, I decided I'd better open the faceplate and try to estimate my height above the ground and find the D-ring. Just as I reached up to open the faceplate, I felt a sudden deceleration indicating main chute deployment. It was a reassuring feeling indeed!

At this point, I raised the faceplate and found that the up-latch was broken so, if I wanted to see, I had to keep the frozen faceplate raised with one hand. It was a clear, winter day with unlimited visibility. One of the first things I saw was Jim's parachute, which appeared to be about a quarter of a mile away. I didn't think either one of us was going to survive, and to see that Jim had also made it was an incredible lift. I could also see some burning wreckage on the ground a few miles from where we would be landing. The terrain did not look at all inviting—it appeared to be desolate, high plateau country with patches of snow on the ground and no signs of habitation. I tried to turn the parachute so I could see in other directions but, with one hand occupied keeping the faceplate raised and both hands numb from the cold, I was unable to manipulate the risers to do so.

The incident occurred during a turn over an area near the New Mexico, Colorado, Oklahoma, and Texas borders and, with a turning radius of about 100 miles at that speed and altitude, I wasn't even sure what state we were going to land in. It was about 3:00 P.M. and I was certain we were going to have to spend the night there. I tried to remember what survival items were in the seat kit and think of some of the things I had been taught in survival training. When I descended to about three hundred feet above the ground, I pulled the seat kit release handle, which releases the kit on a lanyard so that you don't have to land on it. As I was looking down to observe this process, I was startled to see a fairly large animal directly beneath my descent path. Evidently, he was also startled because he literally took off in a cloud of dust. I learned later that this must have been an antelope, which are quite common in that area.

This was my first parachute landing and it was pretty smooth— fairly soft ground and no rocks, cacti or antelopes to contend with on touch down. My chute was billowing in the wind and, as I was trying to collapse the chute with one hand while holding up the still frozen faceplate with the other, I thought I heard a voice saying, "Can I help you?" I figured I must be hallucinating until I looked up and saw a guy in a cowboy hat walking toward me with a helicopter sitting behind him. If I had been at Edwards Air Force Base and told them that I was going to bail out over the lake bed at a particular time, they couldn't have gotten to me that fast.

I later learned that this gentleman, Albert Mitchell Jr., owned a huge cattle ranch in Northeast New Mexico and I had landed about a mile and a half from his ranch house and the hangar where he kept his Hughes two-place helicopter. I told him I was having a little trouble collapsing the chute so he went over, collapsed the canopy, and put some rocks on it. He told me he had seen us coming down and radioed the highway patrol, the Air Force and the nearest hospital. As I was starting to get out of my parachute harness I noticed the cause of the flapping strap noises I had heard on the way down. My seat belt and shoulder harness were still draped around me, attached and latched. The seat belt had been shredded on each side where the straps go through knurled adjustment rollers and the shoulder harness shredded in a similar manner where each side joins in the back. The ejection seat had never left the airplane—only the occupant with his seat belt and shoulder harness still fastened.

After helping me with the chute, Mr. Mitchell said he'd go over and check on Jim. He got into his helicopter and returned about ten minutes later with the devastating news that Jim was dead. When I saw his chute on the way down, I was thrilled to think that Jim had survived, but apparently he had been killed instantly as a result of a broken neck suffered during the breakup of the airplane. Mr. Mitchell said his ranch foreman was on his way to watch over the body until the authorities arrived. I asked him to take me over to see Jim and, after verifying that there was nothing more that could be done, agreed to have him fly me to the Tucumcari hospital, which was about sixty miles to the south.

I have vivid memories of that flight, as well. I didn't know much about helicopters but I knew a lot about red lines and the airspeed was at or above the red line all the way to Tucumcari, with the little helicopter vibrating and shaking a lot more than I thought it should be. I tried to assure him that I was feeling okay and no need to rush, but he said the hospital staff had been notified, and insisted we get there as soon as possible. I couldn't help but think how ironic it would be to have survived the previous disaster only to be done in by the helicopter that had come to my rescue. However, we made it to the hospital safely, as well as quickly, and I was able to contact Lockheed Flight Test at Edwards.

After having been notified about the loss of radio and radar contact with our airplane, they were aware that the aircraft had been lost and, knowing the flight conditions at the time, they assumed that no one had survived. I explained what had happened and was able to describe the conditions leading to the breakup of the airplane in fairly accurate detail. The flight profile was duplicated on the SR-71 Flight Simulator at Beale Air Force Base the next day, with identical results. Steps were immediately taken to prevent a recurrence of such an incident. Testing with CG aft of the normal limits was discontinued and trim drag issues were subsequently resolved through aerodynamic means. The inlet control system was continuously improved and, with later development of the Digital Automatic Flight and Inlet Control System (DAFICS), inlet unstarts became rare.

Investigation of the accident revealed that the nose section of the aircraft had broken off aft of the rear cockpit and came down about ten miles from the main part of the wreckage, although various parts were scattered over an area approximately fifteen miles long and ten miles wide. The extremely high air loads and G forces, both positive and negative, had literally ripped us out of the airplane. There are no explanations, other than unbelievably good luck, why I survived with only minor injuries. In addition to escaping from the airplane relatively unscathed, I found out some other bullets had been dodged. After landing, it was noted that one of the two oxygen supply lines to my pressure suit had come loose and the other one was barely hanging on.

If that one had become detached at altitude, it would have been all over and I wouldn't have been able to fully realize the protective capabilities of the pressure suit. I knew it was critical from a breathing and pressurization standpoint, but didn't realize the sort of physical protection an inflated pressure suit could provide. That the suit could withstand forces sufficient to break the airplane, shred the heavy nylon seat belts, and leave me with only a few bruises and a minor whiplash is impressive—I truly appreciated my own little escape capsule.

Two weeks after the accident, I made my next flight in an SR. This was the first flight of a brand-new bird out of Lockheed's Assembly and Test facility at Palmdale. The flight test engineer in the backseat may have been a little apprehensive about my state of mind and confidence, particularly since it was my first flight since the accident. As we roared down the runway and lifted off, I heard this anxious voice on the intercom saying, "Bill! Bill! Are you there?"

I said, "Yeah, George, what's the matter?"

He said, "Thank God. I thought you might have left."

The rear cockpit of the SR-71 has no forward visibility—only a small window on each side. For this reason, there is a big red light on the master warning panel in the rear cockpit that says PILOT EJECTED and it had illuminated just as we rotated for takeoff. Fortunately, for both of us, the cause was a misadjusted microswitch and not my departure.

52

LT. ROBERT WUCKER—1991

In 1987, shortly after I checked in as a student radar intercept officer (RIO) to VF-124 "Gunfighters," the F-14 Tomcat training squadron at NAS Miramar, I was in a student briefing when the instructor had us look around the room and take notice of our fellow trainees. He calmly advised us that the longer we were assigned to a fighter squadron, the greater the odds were that one day we would have to eject from a jet and that there was a fair percentage who would not survive such an event. Being young and immortal at the time, his Rasputin-like prognostication didn't have much impact on me.

On July 16, 1991, about fifty miles off the coast of San Diego, I, along with my pilot, "Tex" Whatley, learned that no matter how good we fighter guys thought we were, there were circumstances that were going to test our immortality.

Our squadron, the VF-51 "Screaming Eagles," was preparing to bring the USS *Kitty Hawk* (CV-63) from the east coast to her new home port in San Diego, CA. The zero-dark-early brief for our refresher carrier qual mission aboard the USS *Ranger* (CV-61) went smoothly and most importantly, the weather forecast was for CAVU conditions: clear and visibility unlimited. Tex and I manned up Eagle 104 and launched in plenty of time to make our overhead time for the *Ranger*, which was fresh off of her very successful (and mishap-free) Desert Storm cruise.

All was proceeding well and as we taxied to the catapult after our third trap on that sunny morning, we were in that "can't believe we get paid to do this" mood. We launched off the bow and turned downwind for trap #4. Tex was hitting the numbers as he had been all morning and as we approached three-quarters of a mile behind the ship, I "called the ball," confirming our glide slope for the ship's landing signals officer. Tex put the jet down on the deck and the sudden force of deceleration threw me forward into the seat restraints, making it readily apparent that we had successfully caught a wire. A split second later, though, the deceleration forces eased in a very uncomfortable way and in my peripheral vision, I saw the control tower passing by us in much too quick a manner. I realized something was wrong as we were not slowing quickly enough. The effect of time compression hit me as everything began to happen in slow motion. My first thought was that we were going to have to eject, followed by the thought that I really didn't want to do that. Scenes from safety films passed through my mind: aircrew ejecting from a jet only to have it fly off without them, aircrew ejecting only to have the aircraft stop on the deck, and aircrew waiting too long to eject as the jet tumbled awkwardly off a carrier deck.

As we headed down the angle deck, I knew we didn't have enough airspeed to fly and decided that I would pull the handle if/ when we went off the deck. Sure enough, the Tomcat didn't stop so I grabbed the lower ejection handle and pulled. The first thing that struck me was the white flash and the sound—which I compare to the sound I imagine hearing if you were in an oil drum and someone hit it with a sledgehammer. Almost simultaneously, the force of the rockets in the ejection seat hit me. I remember tumbling a bit in the air and seeing the orange, green, and white parachute canopy deploying out behind me. When all settled and I was hanging in the straps, I looked up and saw a full chute over me. I then looked to my side and saw I was right out in front of the mighty *Ranger*, which was not a good place to be. I did not want to land on a nonskid deck—or worse yet, get sucked into one of the many turning jet engines on it.

I grabbed for the four-line release and did what I could to get out of the way of the carrier, and once clear (probably due to a favorable wind gust more than anything else) my next thought of doom was of getting pulled under by the ship's draft. I waited until my feet hit the water before releasing the chute off my back via the Koch fittings. As I went underwater, I realized that in my preoccupation to avoid getting run over or sucked under by the carrier, I had skipped steps 1 and 2 of the IROK procedure (my apologies to my water survival class instructors) in that I had not inflated (I) my flotation vest, nor had I released (R) my raft. Luckily, the bladders of my vest were activated by the sea water and had already begun filling with air before I could pull the beaded handles.

When my head cleared sea-level, I was greeted by the awesome yet frightening sight of an aircraft carrier cruising by me about 50 feet away at 25 or so knots. Still being concerned with getting pulled under by the ship's screws, I made sure I was clear of the parachute and began an enthusiastic backstroke figuring if I was going down, I was going down fighting. I saw some people waving down at me from the deck which made me feel better. When the ship cleared me, I saw the broken nose cone and then the rest of Eagle 104 floating in the water before she headed down to Davy Jones's locker. It was a sickening sight but it provided reassurance that ejecting had been the proper choice.

I yelled for Tex and was comforted when he responded that he was okay. We speculated what had gone wrong, guessing either the cable or the hook had broken. I saw the rescue helo heading our way and elected not to deploy my raft in the water, which was a minor mistake. Because of the adrenaline rush, I felt warm but in fact I was getting mildly hypothermic due to the chilly ocean water. I was quickly plucked up out of the sea, though, by the rescue crew and after Tex was picked up, we were flown back aboard the ship.

We were met on deck by a medical crew and assured them that we could walk and didn't require stretchers. I saw the arresting cable sprawled loosely on the deck, which provided the answer as to what had gone wrong as well as further reassurance that a $40-million fighter jet wasn't in the ocean due to aircrew/aircraft fault.

Our commanding officer, "Sobs" Sobieck, then met us and asked who had pulled the handle and advised Tex that he owed me a beer after getting the answer (Tex has made good on that many times since). Sobs later told us (with a wry smile on his face) that his first thought after seeing an F-14 go in the water was that he hoped it belonged to our sister squadron.

After being checked out in the ship's sick bay, Tex and I were heloed back to NAS Miramar. Sobs caught up to us there and told us that the admiral had viewed the videotape of our mishap and since it was clear that we had done all we could, cleared us to fly as soon as Tex and I were up for it. That was a big break, since aircrew involved in a mishap are normally grounded until a determination can be made as to what happened. Tex and I agreed we were ready to go again whenever and despite some aches and mild bruises, were flying back out to the ship the next day. We didn't get called down for any traps that day but while we were in a holding pattern overhead the ship, we watched intently as every landing aircraft came to a complete stop.

When we eventually did get our first, post-ejection trap (delayed due to another mishap as an A-6 Intruder had its hook break while trapping aboard the *Ranger* two days after our mishap), we snagged a 4-wire, which made for a long, nerve-wracking rollout on the deck before we stopped completely. I never did get comfortable with 4-wire traps again.

The positive outcome was that the experience made me even more confident in regards to flying. Despite a rare, catastrophic failure of the arresting gear at a critical time, no one was injured. It was a true testament to the professionalism of those involved in U.S. Navy Carrier Aviation. My eternal thanks goes out to many, but especially to the VF-51 Maintenance Department—particularly the AMEs who maintained the ejection seats (who I often told that if one thing works right on the jet, it better be the ejection seat!), and the PRs who rigged the parachutes and maintained our personal survival equipment; the Martin-Baker Company, who designed and made the ejection seats that have saved many lives; the crew of HS-14 Chargers who pulled us out of the ocean; the survival instructors who prepared us for the worst; and the crew of the USS *Ranger.*

July 16 is a memorable date for me but not only because of the mishap in 1991, but more importantly, it was nine years later to the day that my daughter, Kendall, was born.

53

GEN. CHUCK YEAGER—1963

Lockheed's Starfighter, the F-104, was the first Mach 2 fighter aircraft, and the first to break the sound barrier in a climb. I had flight-tested it for the Air Force back in 1954. The airplane had a bad pitch-up problem. Flying it at a thirty-degree angle of attack, its short, thin wings blanketed its T-shaped tail, causing the nose to suddenly rise dramatically. The next thing a pilot knew he was in a flat spin toward the earth, pushing the throttle forward as far as it would go, high engine RPMs being the only way to recover a 104 out of a flat spin.

The special rocket-powered 104s we had at the space school had the same pitch-up problem. Lockheed delivered three of them to us in 1963 for use in high-altitude, zero-G training. Before our students began flying them, I decided to establish some operating parameters to learn at what altitude the aerodynamic pitch-up forces would be greater than the amount of thrust in the hydrogen peroxide rockets installed on the nose. We had two 250-pound thrusters to train for maneuvering in zero-G conditions. We thought we would encounter pitch-up somewhere around ninety-five thousand feet. And while I was at it, I wanted to establish an altitude record in the rocket version of the 104. I flew it on the morning of December 12, 1963, and had the airplane up to 108,000 feet. It had gone beautifully, and I was scheduled for a second flight in the afternoon. Mom was visiting us, and Glennis drove her over to base operations. We had a quick lunch; I was still wearing my bulky pressure suit because once you get sweaty and take it off, you can't get it back on. Then they took off, and so did I.

I climbed to thirty-five thousand feet, about one hundred miles from Edwards at the foot end of the San Joaquin Valley near Fraser Peak, and headed for Rogers Dry Lake at thirty-seven thousand feet in afterburner. I was traveling at better than Mach 2 when I fired the six-thousand-pound-thrust rocket in my tail that burned a mixture of hydrogen peroxide and jet fuel. By then, I was climbing at a steep seventy-degree angle, whistling through sixty thousand feet, and the afterburner flamed out, oxygen-starved in the thin atmosphere. That was expected. Later, I planned to go into a shallow dive to allow the engine blades to windmill in the rush of air, working up the necessary revolutions enabling re-ignition in the lower air, at about forty thousand feet. So I shut down the engine and let the rocket carry me over the top. I had to watch my tailpipe temperature, because at my steep climbing angle it would overtemp even though I was on idle.

I went over the top at 104,000 feet, and as the airplane completed its long arc, it fell over. But as the angle of attack reached twenty-eight degrees, the nose pitched up. That had happened in the morning flight as well. I used the small rocket thrusters on the nose to push it down. I had no problem then. This time, the damned thrusters had no effect. I kept those peroxide ports open, using all my peroxide trying to get that nose down, but I couldn't. My nose was stuck high, and the damned airplane finally fell off flat and went into a spin.

I was spinning down like a record on a turntable, and because I couldn't get into a shallow dive and drive air through the engine turbine, my rpms were falling off drastically. I had no hydraulic pressure because that operated off the engine, which had wound down to the point where it stopped and locked at about forty thousand feet. I was feeling kind of hopeless about this ride. The data recorder would later indicate that the airplane made fourteen flat spins from 104,000 until impact on the desert floor. I stayed with it through thirteen of those spins before I punched out. I hated losing an expensive airplane, but I couldn't think of anything else to do.

I went ahead and punched out. My pressure suit was inflated and a rocket charge underneath blew me and my seat straight up at 90 mph. An automatic device unhooked my seat belt and released the parachute ring from the seat. A seat-butt kicker, another small charge, kicked me out and straight down. I began falling, picking up speed, tumbling headfirst toward earth, and I saw that damned seat tumbling with me, somehow becoming entangled in my chute lines. There was still residual fire in the back of that seat from the rocket charge and my shroud lines began smoldering. Christ, I saw that clearly. The chute popped, jarring me, and I sweated that those lines hadn't burnt through. I had a quick sense of relief, though, because the popping chute dislodged the seat. Then the seat smashed into my face. I got clobbered by the tube end of the rocket, glowing red hot.

It just knocked the shit out of me. It hit me so hard that I really didn't know what happened. Busted the faceplate out of my helmet; I saw stars. Suddenly there was a roar. Burning stuff on that seat ignited the rubber seal around my helmet and in the pure oxygen environment, it erupted like a blow torch. My head was engulfed in flames and smoke. I couldn't breathe. I couldn't see out of my left eye where the seat had bashed me. I was choking to death on smoke, gasping to draw a breath. I stuck my hand inside the open faceplate and tried to scoop in air to breathe. My gloved hand caught on fire. I thought, "What a way to go!" I was still hooked to an emergency oxygen bottle, feeding oxygen to the flames. By instinct, I pushed up the visor on what was left of my helmet. That automatically shut off the oxygen. By then, I was very close to the ground and there was still residual flame, smoke, and soot pouring out of my helmet. I hit the ground hard.

I could hear Andy buzzing me and managed to wave at him on his second go-round. I finally got up and took off my parachute harness, pulling apart the scorched shroud lines with my bare hands. Then I pushed the release locks on the neck ring connected to my pressure suit helmet, rotated it, and took off my helmet. Until then, I don't think anyone had ever taken off a pressure suit helmet without help. It is literally impossible to get all those latches unlocked by yourself; I don't know how in hell I did it. I recall glancing at my helmet with my good right eye, and it really looked like war, I was bloody and burned and smashed.

I was dazed, standing alone on the desert, my helmet crooked in one arm, my hand hurting so bad that I thought I would pass out. My face didn't hurt at all. I saw a young guy running toward me; I had come down only a mile or so from highway 6 that goes to Bishop out of Mojave, and he watched me land in my chute, then parked his pickup and came to offer his help. He looked at me, then turned away. My face was charred meat. I asked him if he had a knife. He took out a small penknife, unfolded the blade, and handed it to me. I said to him, "I've gotta do something about my hand. I can't stand it anymore." I used his knife to cut off the rubber-lined glove, and part of two burned fingers came off with it. The guy got sick.

Then the chopper came for me. I remember the medics running up. I asked them, "Can you do something for my hand? It's just killing me." They gave me a shot of morphine through my pressure suit. They couldn't get the suit off because it had to be unzipped all the way down, and then I'd have to get my head out through the metal ring, but my face was in such sorry condition that they didn't dare. At the hospital, they brought in local firemen with bolt cutters to try to cut that ring off my neck. It just wouldn't do the job. Finally, I said, "Look in the right pocket of my pressure suit and get that survival saw out of there." It was a little ring saw that I always carried with me, even on backpacks, and they zapped through that ring in less than a minute.

I began dozing off from the morphine, only half-aware that Glennis was there, but Doc Stan Bear, the flight surgeon, kept shaking me awake. He was probing into the blood caked over my left eye, where there was a deep gash. The blood was glazed like glass from the heat of the fire, and Doc kept poking through it asking me if I could see anything. I said, no. I heard him mutter, "Christ, I guess he lost it." But suddenly I saw a ray of light through a small hole. I told Doc and he smiled. "That dried blood saved your sight, buddy," he said. Then he let me pass out.

They had me on an IV, and I was so groggy the next day that when General Branch came by and I tried to tell him what happened, I fell asleep in the middle of a sentence. Glennis, Andy, Bob Hoover, and test pilot Tony LeVier came to visit, but I was hardly aware. They were keeping me on painkillers.

So, it was several days before I realized how bad things really were. My face was swollen to the size of a pumpkin, badly charred from being blowtorched. Ol' Stan Bear came in and sat down. He said, "Well, Chuck, I've got good news and bad news. The good news is that your lungs have not been permanently damaged from inhaling flame and smoke, and your eye looks normal. The bad news is I'm gonna have to hurt you like you've never hurt before in your life to keep you from being permanently disfigured. And I'm gonna have to do it every four days."

I stayed in the hospital a month, and every four days, Doc started from the middle of my face and neck, scraping away the accumulated scab. It was a new technique developed to avoid horrible crisscross scars as the skin grew beneath the scabs. And it worked beautifully. I have only a few scars on my neck, but my face healed perfectly smooth. The pain, though, was worse than any I have ever known. I remember Jackie insisting that I recuperate at her ranch after I was discharged from the hospital. She said, "I was once a nurse and if something comes up, I'll know how to handle it." Doc Bear flew down there, too, to do scraping, and told her, "Jackie, you might want to leave. This is pretty rough." And she huffed, hell, no; she was a nurse, and all that. Man, she lasted twenty seconds and had to leave the room. How I wish I could've gone with her. In the end, though, I came out no worse than losing the tips of two fingers, and I'd call that getting away cheap.

CONCLUSION

The quest for pilot safety and protection will never end. Multitudes of future flight safety systems are being contemplated, designed, and tested, including parachutes that float an entire aircraft to safety, as well as systems for airline passengers and spacecraft.

To date, there are more than seven thousand pilots whose lives have been saved by ejection seats, and to these intrepid survivors the Martin-Baker Company awards each a distinctive tie, to celebrate another life saved. They are then officially members of the Caterpillar Club, having floated to safety under silk canopies. This group meets regularly to honor the bright British engineers whose work allowed them to live through some of the most perilous conditions known to man: surviving high-speed ejections.

CREDITS/PERMISSIONS

1. 1st Lt. John Bailey—1957: from "How I Became a Member of the Caterpillar Club," John Bailey, August 2, 2001 (Revised October 24, 2004).
2. Lt. Gary L. Bain (1)—1969: Courtesy of Gary Bain.
3. Lt. Gary L. Bain (2)—1969: Courtesy of Gary Bain.
4. Lt. Gary L. Bain (3)—1977: Courtesy of Gary Bain.
5. Capt. Michael R. Brunnschweiler—2001: from "This Was Supposed to Be a Good Deal!" Capt. Michael Brunnschweiler, *Approach* magazine, October 2001.
6. Lt. Col. John W. Capito—1985: Courtesy of *Approach* magazine/ U.S. Navy.
7. Gen. James H. Doolittle—1929: Excerpt from *I Could Never Be So Lucky Again*, General James H. Doolittle and Carroll V. Glines, copyright © 1991, The John P. Doolittle Family Trust.
8. LCdr. Kevin L. Duggan—1997: from "How I Survived a Midair," by LCdr. Kevin L. Duggan, *Approach* magazine, May 2001.
9. LCdr. Steven R. Eastburg/Lt. Sean Brennan—1989: Excerpt from *Flying the Edge*, George C. Wilson and LCdr. Steve Eastburg, Naval Institute Press.
10. Donald D. Engen—1949: Excerpt from *Wings and Warriors: My Life as a Naval Aviator*, Donald D. Engen, Smithsonian Institution Press, 1997.
11. Finkelman—1959.
12. Cdr. Wynn F. Foster—1966: from "Will to Survive," Commander Wynn F. Foster, *Approach* magazine, December 1966.

13. Lt. Jack L. Fruin—1949: from "The First Ejection Seat," Peter Mersky, *Approach* magazine, November–December 2005.
14. Lt. Keith Gallagher—1991: from "Lieutenant Keith Gallagher's Account of the Incident," *Approach* magazine, November 1991.
15. Lt. Keith Gallagher/Lt. Mark Baden—1991: from "Lieutenant Mark Baden's (Pilot) Account of the Incident," *Approach* magazine, November 1991.
16. RADM Paul T. Gillcrist—1966: Excerpt from "The Survival Instinct," RADM Paul T. Gillcrist, USN (Ret.), *Feet Wet: Reflections of a Carrier Pilot,* Pocket Books, copyright © 1990 Paul T. Gillchrist. All rights reserved. Used with permission of the author.
17. Wesley Gish—1956: from "F7 Useless," Wesley Gish, *Flight Journal,* April 2009.
18. Maj. James Hall—1965: from "Project 90, A Study in 0-0 Ejection," copyright © 1965 Monogram Systems. All rights reserved. Used by permission.
19. Capt. Ralph Harrison—1980: from "Canadian Armed Forces/F-104 Starfighter pilot," Ralph Harrison. Courtesy The Ejection Site. Used by permission.
20. Capt. Joseph M. Harter—1963: from "Bailout! Bailout!" Captain Joseph M. Harter, *SAC Combat Crew Magazine*, July 1963.
21. Capt. Richard Hauck—1973: from "Is It Worth the Risk?" (revised) Rick Hauck, *Air & Space* magazine, July 2003.
22. Lt. Neil P. Jennings—1995: from Neil P. Jennings, LT USN, Courtesy Neil P. Jennings. Used by permission.
23. Lt. Matthew P. Klemish—1994: Courtesy of *Approach* magazine, 1994.
24. Lt. Neil P. Jennings: Klemish/Hultgreen Incident—1994: Courtesy of Neil P. Jennings.
25. Col. Randy Lovelace—1943: from "The Lovelace Medical Center," Jake W. Spidle, Jr., University of New Mexico Press, 1987.
26. Maj. Raoul Lufberry—1918: Excerpt from *The Shoulders of Giants,* Phil Scott, Addison-Wesley Publishing, 1995.
27. RADM John Lynch—1937: Courtesy of Steve Gozzo on behalf of RADM John Lynch. Used by permission.
28. Lt. Linda Maloney—1991: Courtesy of Linda Heid-Maloney. Used by permission.
29. Cdr. Neil May—1985: from "Too Bad to Be True," Commander Neil May, *Approach* magazine, October 2000.
30. Gen. Merrill Anthony McPeak—1967: from Tony McPeak story, courtesy of Merrill A. McPeak.

31. LCdr. John A. Morrison—2000: from "Checking to See If Survival Training Works," LCdr. John A. Morrison, *Approach* magazine, 2000.

32. Commandant John R. "Dick" Muehlberg—1944: Excerpt from "Two Takeoffs, One Landing," Dick Muehlberg, in *Test Flying at Old Wright Field*, copyright © 1993 Ken Chilstrom (author), Penn Leary (editor), published with permission of the Wright Patterson AFB Educational Fund.

33. Flt. Lt. S. A. E. "Ted" Newton—1953: from "Early Meteor Ejection," Flight Lieutenant S. A. E. "Ted" Newton, reprinted from www.ejectionsite.com.

34. Cdr. Russ Pearson—1969: from "Underwater Ejection," Commander Russ Pearson, USN (Ret). Reprinted with permission of *The Hook* magazine.

35. Célestine-Adolphe Pégoud—1913: Excerpt from *The Shoulders of Giants,* Phil Scott, Addison-Wesley Publishing, 1995.

36. Flt. Lt. Craig Penrice—1985: from "High Speed Ejection from a Lightning F6 XS921," Flight Lieutenant Craig Penrice, copyright © Craig Penrice. Used by permission.

37. Flt. Lt. Craig Penrice—2003: "Ejection from Hunter G-BVVC on 1st June 2003," Flight Lieutenant Craig Penrice, copyright © Craig Penrice, August, 9, 2004. Used by permission.

38. S. M. "Pete" Purvis—1973: from "The Day I Shot Myself Down," (revised) Pete Purvis, from *Wings of Gold* magazine, Fall 2002, courtesy of Pete Purvis. Used by permission.

39. Lt. George B. Quisenberry—1950: Excerpt from "First and Last Flight: FL-23," George B. Quisenberry, in *Test Flying at Old Wright Field,* Ken Chilstrom and Penn Leary, Westchester House Publishers, 1993. Published with permission of the Wright Patterson AFB Educational Fund.

40. Lt. Richard "Dick" Rutan: Strobe 01 Incident—1968: from "The Psychology of Combat," Dick Rutan, from *Misty 40,* courtesy of Dick Rutan, www.dickrutan.com. Used by permission.

41. Lt. Richard "Dick" Rutan—1970: Courtesy of Dick Rutan, www.dickrutan.com. Used by permission.

42. LCdr. E. D. "Sandy" Sandberg—1960: from "Up and Down—A Unique Experience," LCdr. E. D. (Sandy) Sandberg, *Approach* magazine, April 2001.

43. Jack L. "Suitcase" Simpson—1955: from "Starfighter Down: Ejection from a YF-104 Starfighter," (revised) Jack L. "Suitcase" Simpson, from *Flight Journal*, February 1998. Used by permission of the author.

44. Capt. John Sinclair—1987: from *"No Time to Think,"* Captain John Sinclair.

45. Lt. Col. John Paul Stapp—1947: from *"The Fastest Man on Earth,"* Nick T. Sparks, *Wings and Airpower* magazine. Used by permission.

46. Air Commodore Peter Taylor AFC—1972: from "Ejection from a Harrier," Air Commodore Peter Taylor AFC, in *Today's Pilot,* Key Publishing Ltd.

47. Capt. Scott "Spike" Thomas—1991: Courtesy of Scott Thomas.

48. Lt. Jon Vanbragt—2005: from "Not So Fast," Lieutenant Jon Vanbragt, *Approach* magazine, March–April 2004. "Analyst Comments," Major Mark Budde, USMC, FA-18 analyst, Naval Safety Center, *Approach* magazine, September–October 2006.

49. Lt. Geoff Vickers—2002: from "I've Lost My RIO," Lieutenant Geoff Vickers, *Approach* magazine, March–April 2004.

50. Lt. Jason Walker—2004: from "Late-Night Swim," Lieutenant Jason Walker, *Approach* magazine, January–February 2007.

51. William Weaver—1966: Courtesy William Weaver. Used by permission.

52. Lt. Robert Wucker—1991: Courtesy of *Approach* magazine/U.S. Navy.

53. Gen. Chuck Yeager—1963: Excerpt from *Yeager: An Autobiography,* General Chuck Yeager with Leo Janos, Bantam Books, 1986, copyright ©1985, Yeager, Inc. Used by permission.